HOW BANKS, BROKERAGES,
AND THE WEALTHY
STEAL BILLIONS
FROM CANADIANS

THIEVES
OF
BAY STREET

BRUCE LIVESEY

RANDOM HOUSE CANADA

PUBLISHED BY RANDOM HOUSE CANADA

www.randomhouse.ca

Random House Canada and colophon are registered trademarks.

Library and Archives Canada Cataloguing in Publication

Livesey, Bruce
Thieves of Bay Street : how banks, brokerages and the wealthy
steal billions from Canadians / Bruce Livesey.

Issued also in an electronic format.

ISBN 978-0-307-35963-6

1. Banks and banking—Corrupt practices—Canada. I. Title.

HG2704.L59 2012   332.10971   C2011-904095-6

Cover and text design by CS Richardson

Image credits: Guy Vanderelst/ Getty Images

Printed and bound in the United States of America

10 9 8 7 6 5 4 3 2 1

For Gabrielle,
the love of my life, who has made
all of this possible.

— CONTENTS —

"The rich are different: they are more ruthless."
—economist Sam Khater

"Fuck my victims."
—Bernie Madoff, Ponzi swindler

"MY GOD, THAT'S DISGUSTING," said Alice Campbell, wiping away a tear. "That just blows me away, it really does. There's no justification, there's no justification for that. The greed—it's unbelievable."

"You think that's what it is—greed?" asked Gillian Findlay.

"Yes, I believe that. It's total greed. That's all it is," replied Campbell.

It was November 2009 and Findlay, a veteran television reporter with the Canadian Broadcasting Corporation (CBC), was interviewing Campbell at her one-storey home in the bedroom community of Georgetown, Ontario. A sixty-year-old grandmother and former plant worker at Nortel Networks Corp., Campbell was immobilized due to botched back surgery she had undergone in 1987 and was in desperately poor health when Findlay and I visited that fall. She had diabetes and a weak heart, and needed oxygen from a portable tank. The ventilator and a kaleidoscope of pills for her various ailments were costing her $800 a month.

Nortel had gone bankrupt the previous winter and Campbell was one of the 400 former Nortel employees in Canada whose long-term disability income—which in her case amounted to $1,100 a month—was going to disappear as a result. Adding to her woes was management's removal of $103 million from the company's health and welfare fund, which meant her pension would be woefully inadequate. Campbell and her retired husband faced a daunting future: even with the disability income, they were barely scraping by.

But insult was about to be added to the former plant worker's injury. As a producer with the CBC's Investigative Unit, I'd been leaked an internal document which revealed that seventy-two executives and managers still employed by Nortel had quietly awarded themselves US$7.5 million in bonuses, and that was on top of US$45 million in bonuses promised to the company's managers earlier that year. Nortel had gone bust, losing tens of billions of investors' dollars and laying off most of its staff, and now the bosses appeared to be rewarding their own failure. When we showed Campbell the document, she was understandably outraged: her once-proud employer had gone to the dogs, in her view, and left people like her to the wolves.

With annual revenues of $9 billion and shares selling at $120, by the mid-1990s Nortel had become Canada's pre-eminent high-tech multinational, praised as a paragon of innovation and a surefire investment, and few forward-thinking Canadian investors didn't hold Nortel stock. The corporation was the talk of the town on Toronto's Bay Street, Vancouver's Howe Street, in the financial districts of

Montreal and Calgary, and at Tim Hortons outlets across the country. Later in the decade, however, Nortel's senior management began messing with the books, giving investors a fraudulent picture of the company's financial health. While this manipulation of numbers fattened executives' bonuses and stock option plans, it would eventually engulf the company in scandal and send it into a fatal tailspin. By 2007, the Ontario Securities Commission (OSC), the U.S. Securities and Exchange Commission (SEC) and the RCMP had charged eight of Nortel's former top executives, including one CEO and a chief financial officer, for fraud and the company was forced to pay nearly $3 billion to settle investors' lawsuits. It would not recover.

The demise of Nortel was but one more outbreak in a widespread epidemic of executives enriching themselves at the expense of investors and employees. In case after case, companies had cooked their books, falsified quarterly reports and inflated share prices; then, after the firms went bust, bankruptcy receivers moved in and sold off the pieces, usually to foreign bidders who, in turn, moved key research and development and management jobs offshore. The worst of this corporate culture caused the 2007–2009 credit crisis and the near-total meltdown of the global financial system, a debacle initiated by bankers and traders and hedge fund managers who peddled bogus investment products to unsuspecting investors. Banks and brokerages in the United States and across Europe collapsed or required government bailouts, and by 2012 the value of total writedowns and losses resulting from the global crash had surpassed $4 trillion.

The credit crisis exposed the moral turpitude of a financial industry more than happy to sell products that would destroy its own business and ruin its customers along the way. If it wasn't short sellers driving up oil prices by as much as $60 a barrel in 2008 (as they would again in 2011), exacerbating the post-crash recession and causing food shortages in some parts of the world, it was revelations about the world's most powerful investment bank, Goldman Sachs Group Inc., that "great vampire squid wrapped around the face of humanity relentlessly jamming its blood funnel into anything that smells like money," as *Rolling Stone* described it. Goldman grew adept at selling securities to investors based on pools of mortgage debt. They would then conspire with hedge funds who shorted those very same pools: that is, Goldman was betting that its own lousy product would collapse so they and the hedge funds could cash in on their investors' losses.

While this house of cards was tumbling down in the United States, Canada's $6.3 trillion financial sector (which is the total value of our capital markets) seemed to be weathering the storm. The nation's chartered banks and brokerage houses had remained solvent and some important people noticed. As Andrew Coyne remarked in *Maclean's* magazine in 2009, "One of the odder turns in the financial crisis has been the emergence of what can only be described as a worldwide cult of the Canadian banks."

The *Financial Times* called Canada's banks "the envy of the world," and no less than U.S. president Barack Obama, former Federal Reserve chairman Paul Volcker and *Newsweek* editor Fareek Zakaria piled on the praise. Even Nobel Prize–winning economist Paul Krugman, under the headline GOOD AND BORING, added to the hype in his *New York Times* column: "We need to learn from those countries that evidently did it right. And leading that list is our neighbor to the north. Right now, Canada is a very important role model."

Had Canada truly got right what its southern neighbour had allowed to go so catastrophically wrong? I've been reporting business stories since the late 1980s and have interviewed countless CEOs, and despite the time I've spent in that world, the banking and brokerage industry has always remained an arcane and mysterious landscape for me. This view changed after I began researching the credit crisis for the CBC and was able to inch back the curtain on this little-understood industry and reveal a much darker reality beneath. The hype about Canada's financial business, it appeared, was just that.

For one thing, the federal government *had* bailed out Canada's banks. In October 2008, Prime Minister Stephen Harper's Conservative government created a program to move tens of billions of dollars in assets off the banks' balance sheets in order to free them up to continue lending. For another thing, overwhelming evidence revealed that Canada was actually a premier haven for investment fraud, a country where white-collar criminals faced little fear of being caught or seriously punished for their crimes. Over the quarter century leading up to 2012, fewer than twenty Canadian white-collar criminals had actually gone to jail. Yet the damage caused by these crooks and others like them was reflected in the nearly $15 billion worth of losses due to securities fraud that plaintiffs were pursuing in lawsuits during 2010 alone.

Court actions like theirs were proliferating. In 2008, with the credit crisis unravelling and rampant corporate malfeasance coming to light north of the border, investors filed a record nine new securities class action lawsuits in Canada—a 125 percent increase over the previous year. Over the two decades leading up to the crisis, the number of investment fraud stories had indeed been piling up—from Bre-X to Conrad Black, Nortel, YBM Magnex, Portus, Norshield, Livent, asset-backed commercial paper (ABCP), income trusts, and rogue brokers including Ian Thow and Harry Migirdic, just to name a few—and investors were taking notice. Above all else, they were astonished by the lack of action on the part of market regulators and law enforcement agencies, the very institutions they expected to control and punish those who had swindled them. And therein lies another story, one particular to Canada.

VIRTUALLY ALL CANADIANS are affected by investment fraud, because we are all investors. Every pension plan, RRSP, mutual fund, insurance contract, mortgage, car loan, commercial lease, bank loan and dollar worth of credit card debt ends up in the financial markets as a direct investment or as debt that's turned into an investment product. For this reason, when the credit crisis struck, it produced a widespread domino effect that has continued knocking down victims over the ensuing years and touched nearly all of us in some way.

If Alice Campbell's situation opened my eyes to how corporations can remorselessly gorge themselves at their investors' and employees' expense, even after being proven guilty of criminal wrongdoing, a more personal story shows how the financial industry not only harbours fraud but has changed into a system that encourages it—or, in cases you'll read about later, even requires it. As I look back at what I've learned about this business, I see that, like the experiences of so many Canadian families, those of my own serve as a microcosm of how investment fraud became so widespread.

In the 1980s, just as they were about to retire, my parents sank their savings into the Principal Group, an Edmonton-based investment company. They did so on the recommendation of their accountant, who happened to be the father of a good friend of mine. In 1987, Principal collapsed amidst charges of fraud and $457 million of investors' money, including my parents' savings, vanished. Provincial governments across Canada had to step in and bail out Principal's investors. My parents, who fortunately got most of their retirement money back, had trusted my friend's father, who in turn had trusted Principal's owners, who had convinced regulators that they were running a legitimate company, which they were not. This is a pattern I've seen repeated time and time again while researching this book.

Years later, in 2007, I took the advice of a Bank of Montreal (BMO) investment adviser and parked my CBC pension monies in an RRSP made up of mutual funds. There were two things I didn't know when I did this: one, banks skim sizable fees even from simple investment products like mutual funds, and I would be looking forward to a substantially more comfortable retirement if I had left the cash in the pension plan; two, the credit crisis's first tidal wave was about to crash over the markets. Of course, my investments tanked. Then, throughout 2008, my retired and ailing mother (my father passed away in 1992) failed to recognize that her portfolio had plummeted by $130,000 as a result of the global financial crisis. This was money she could ill afford to lose as we, her children, contemplated moving her into assisted living.

As I was both witnessing the all-encompassing power of the financial industry and feeling its impact on my own life, I also understood something fundamental about the way Bay Street had come to operate. The financial industry has drifted far from its original purpose, which had been—and which most of us presume remains—to raise money to help companies grow and to enrich investors willing to risk money in those businesses. Instead, it has morphed into a wealth destroyer, a parasitic reaper of money from the middle and working classes, transferring it to the very people who run the financial industry and Canada's wealthiest citizens. In 2011, our richest 1 percent made 14 percent of the nation's total income (that figure approached 24 percent in the United States), a share that has doubled since the

1970s. One-third of all income gains across Canada since 1997 have gone to that lucky group. For the very rich (those who average $1.5 million per annum), their share of national income has more than doubled in that time to 5.5 percent. In 2010, bonuses paid by the Big Six banks reached $8.9 billion, the highest ever before jumping to $9.5 billion in 2011. Meanwhile, the top federal marginal income tax rates dropped from 43 percent in 1981 to 29 percent in 2010.

But this reaping of riches has come at a terrible cost. In Canada, while the rich got richer, middle-class incomes stagnated. The median family income in 1980 was $58,000. By 2006 it had actually fallen to $57,700 as expressed in 2005 dollars when inflation is taken into consideration. Unable to make ends meet, Canadians have increasingly tapped into the easy credit the financial industry offers. In fact, Canadian household debt has soared at a rate of 9 percent a year. A study released by the Vanier Institute of the Family, an Ottawa-based independent research organization, said that Canadian households had an average debt load of $100,000 in 2011, or 150 percent of income, meaning that for every $1,000 in income people earned, they owed $1,500. (The Certified General Accountants Association of Canada, using a slightly different yardstick, said that if household debt was spread evenly across all Canadians, a family in 2011 with two children was carrying about $176,000 in debt, which included mortgages.) The bulk of this $1.5 trillion in consumer debt is owed to the financial industry.

This pauperization of the middle and working classes is the main reason the credit crisis occurred in the first place, and why the subsequent recession has lingered. Saddled with debt and earning less income than in the past, consumers no longer have the disposable income to buy goods and services or, in too many cases, to pay down their mortgages. This latter shortfall triggered the collapse of the U.S. subprime mortgage market in 2007, which in turn led to the entire financial industry's deep tumble into the abyss. As Nouriel Roubini, the New York University economist known as "Dr. Doom" (because he predicted the credit crisis), told *The Wall Street Journal* in 2011, capitalism risks destroying itself because "you cannot keep on shifting income from labour to capital without having an excess capacity and a lack of aggregate demand. That's what has happened. We thought that markets worked. They're not working. . . . Every firm wants to survive and thrive, thus slashing labour costs even more. But my labour costs are someone else's income and consumption. That's why it's a self-destructive process."

Moreover, bankers and brokers once raised money to bankroll manufacturers, but as Canada has deindustrialized, this role has declined enormously. Leading up to the crash, manufacturing as a vital sector was on the wane, with hundreds of thousands of often well-paying jobs lost. Employment had been growing instead in the "financial services industry," part of the paper economy of virtual wealth. It's as if Canada was (and still is) getting out of the value-added business and returning to its colonial status as drawers of water and hewers of wood—and, of course, extractors of minerals and hydrocarbons. Overlaying all of this was a financial sector that was becoming "too big to fail." And that financial sector was making money less by investing in manufacturing and more by playing on the markets, often with synthetically created products that had no real economic purpose.

The accumulation of wealth by a small percentage of the population and the imaginary quality of our financial sector are not specific to Canadians, but worsening the situation here is the fact that neither of these trends have been mitigated by regulators or government oversight. With the exception of Bosnia-Herzegovina, Canada is the only

nation of the more than one hundred countries that make up the
International Organization of Securities Commissions (IOSCO) that
does not have a national securities regulator. In place of such a cru-
cial body sit thirteen largely ineffectual provincial and territorial
securities commissions. Whether it's for want of a strong regulatory
arm or a more general unwillingness to police a financial industry
run amok, the federal government habitually allows financiers to
walk away with dollars that rightfully belong in public coffers. Former
RCMP fraud inspector Bill Majcher told me about an investigation
he once participated in that uncovered a massive tax scam engineered by the financial industry through "dividend swaps"—basically
a way to avoid paying non-resident taxes on dividends that cross the
border. The practice was found to be commonplace on Bay Street,
he said, but the federal government had no interest in doing anything
to stop it. Says Majcher: "The Canadian government is being ripped
off by billions of dollars." Strangely enough, it doesn't seem to care.

Diane Urquhart, who spent two decades working on Bay Street as
a financial analyst for the big brokerage houses, estimates Canadians
lose roughly $20 billion a year because of investment fraud and
related scams. One survey says that more than one million Canadians
have lost money at some point in their lives to this type of crime.

Which invites the question: why has Canada become a sanctuary
for this behaviour? The answer might stem from the nature of the
Canadian establishment. Modelled on the Family Compact—that
sclerotic group of officials who dominated the legislative bodies, top
bureaucratic positions and judiciary of Upper Canada as an incestuous pseudo-aristocracy up until the 1840s—today's establishment
coalesces in clubby fiefdoms in Halifax, Montreal, Toronto, Winnipeg,
Calgary and Vancouver, where they live and work together, protecting
each other's interests. "Canada is dominated by business oligopolies

and the consumer is fucked!" one former high-ranking (and very wealthy) banker told me on condition of anonymity. And yet the consequences of financial fraud suffered by Canadian consumers are huge. International investors are leery of putting their money into countries where there is poor regulation of capital markets and little punishment for those who commit securities fraud; why would they risk their money in such nations? Thus, rampant fraud in our capital markets means less investment in Canada's economy and stunted growth overall. For victims, especially senior citizens, it also might mean the loss of a lifetime's worth of hard-earned savings.

As I began researching fraud on Bay Street and in the rest of Canada's financial industry, I was constantly amazed by how many financiers would steal from clients, widows, friends and even their own families, without remorse. I saw how banks and investment houses manipulate the system so that once they control your money, it's almost impossible to get it back—even if you're blatantly robbed. American Ponzi schemer Bernie Madoff's remark to a cellmate— "Fuck my victims"—could serve as an epithet to be carved on the porticoes of Canada's financial institutions.

AND WHAT BECAME OF ALICE CAMPBELL? She didn't live to see the final pillaging of Nortel, during which the company's rich technological heritage was sold off piecemeal to foreign companies. Alice passed away in April 2010, and undoubtedly hastening her decline was the stress of knowing she was about to lose her disability income. In that conversation with Gillian Findlay, she summed up the feelings of everyone affected by investment fraud: "They don't care about the little man. They want to have the whole world to themselves. They are taking our share and it's not right."

"Good and Boring," as Paul Krugman declared? I don't think so. "Hear no evil, speak no evil," is more like it. This book sets out to reveal why Canada has become a popular place for investment fraud and thievery, and what the consequences are—and not just for the Alice Campbells of this country, those small investors who can lose a lifetime of savings with one wrong turn. It will examine how bankers and brokers and the very wealthy rob from investors and companies, and how our vaunted financial institutions peddle dangerous investment products and contributed to the U.S. subprime mortgage crisis, the reverberations of which are threatening entire national economies. It's about the ways that credit rating agencies, underwriters, analysts and lawyers enable fraud, and how regulators and law enforcement sit on the sidelines and do little to stop the fiascos from unfolding. If, like so many of us, you've bought the line that Canada's financial industry is safe and sound and worthy of your respect, prepare to be robbed of something yourself: your faith.

ONE

MAKING OUT LIKE BANDITS

FROM HIS CORNER OFFICE on the forty-first floor of the Three First National Plaza in downtown Chicago, Eric Sussman gazes out over the cobalt-blue waters of Lake Michigan. Now a high-earning partner with one of the city's corporate law firms, Kaye Scholer LLP, Sussman has arrived, and done so at the relatively tender age of forty.

Since 2008, he has represented white-collar criminals accused of fraud. However, he garnered his current position largely as a result of his stint as one of the "The Kids," a group of four precocious and fearless prosecutors who worked for the United States Attorney General's office. He helped prosecute the president of the largest food storage company in the Midwest as well as the Chicago Police Department's former chief of detectives for operating a multi-million-dollar jewellery theft ring. I was visiting him in the spring of 2010 to discuss the biggest case of his first career: the conviction of media mogul Conrad Black.

During a four-month trial in 2007, Sussman and his fellow wunderkinds nailed Black for defrauding millions (though on appeal only hundreds of thousands) from Hollinger International Ltd., the Chicago-based media company Black once controlled, an event closely followed by Canada's national newspaper, *The Globe and Mail*, whose front page from the day Black was convicted hangs prominently beside Sussman's desk. For his crimes Black was initially sentenced to six and a half years in prison. I had come to Chicago to better understand why American authorities pursued the media mogul when Canadian authorities made no real effort, especially given that his crimes were mostly engineered from Canada *and* with the help of his Canadian executives and holding companies.

With the wiry physique of a marathoner, a high forehead and wavy brown hair, and dressed in a rosé-coloured shirt, black slacks and polished shoes, Sussman was reserved, slightly aloof. "I don't think the case would have been brought to trial in Canada even at this point in time," he mused sarcastically, "this point in time" being three years after Black was found guilty in an American court. When I later spoke to one of Sussman's fellow prosecutors, Jeffrey Cramer, he was blunter still: "We knew the Canadians wouldn't do it."

Lulled by the gentle treatment meted out by regulators in Toronto, Black had been broadsided by the buzz saw of America's "Second City." Chicago is a rough-and-tumble metropolis, the gateway to the Midwest and more interested in pork-belly futures than derivatives. It also takes law and order seriously. While I was there, Illinois' governor, Rod Blagojevich, was being prosecuted for corruption and I couldn't help but feel that despite Sussman's current comforts, he was probably happiest in his role as prosecutorial sheriff sticking up for the little guy.

I pressed Sussman for more observations about the Canadian justice system and its apparent lack of interest in pursuing white-collar crime. Visibly agitated and with his voice rising, he brought up the famous incident when Black was videotaped lugging home thirteen boxes full of private files from Hollinger's downtown Toronto offices. It was late on the Friday afternoon of the Victoria Day long weekend, May 20, 2005, when nobody was around, and the day after the U.S. Securities and Exchange Commission (SEC) told Black's lawyers they would be seeking the documents as part of their investigation. More importantly, an Ontario Superior Court judge had ordered nothing could be taken away without the approval of a court-appointed inspector from the accounting firm of Ernst & Young. Nonetheless, at one juncture, Black pointed at the back-door surveillance camera, clearly aware he was being filmed.

"In the United States, if a judge ordered you not to touch any documents and you flagrantly violated that court order, and it's on videotape that you flagrantly violated that order, and the judge, in fact, has to order you to return the documents—if that happened in the United States, you would be in jail," Sussman said, his eyes snapping angrily. "Or, at the very least, you'd be up on very serious allegations. In Canada, not only did nothing happen to Black, the Canadian judge basically blocked as long as he could our ability to get those documents to prosecute our case.

"What is going on up there?" Sussman demanded. "How can any court system gain the respect of citizens or litigants if they allow that sort of thing to go on? And there are no repercussions! Black clearly violated the Canadian court order. He gets convicted of it in the United States and no one up there seems to care."

———

A FEW WEEKS AFTER I met Sussman, Conrad Black was unexpect-edly released from his Florida prison cell. In June 2010, the U.S. Supreme Court narrowed one of the doctrines upon which he'd been convicted, ruling the "honest services" statute is restricted to mean no executive of a publicly traded company could enrich himself at the expense of shareholders by accepting a bribe or a kickback, neither of which Black was accused of accepting. Freed into the waiting arms of his wife, Barbara Amiel, Black claimed vindication, painting himself as a victim of an overly aggressive American judicial system.

That summer, Black was once again wrapped in our media's hot embrace: Canada's favourite robber baron, an object of enduring fascination given his once-extravagant lifestyle, arch vocabulary, and contempt for minority shareholders and the common man alike. A fascination that persists despite his open disdain for the country of his birth: in a fit of pique, Black disposed of his Canadian citizenship in 2001 to sit in Britain's House of Lords, and once called Canada an "uncompetitive, slothful, self-righteous, spiteful and envious nanny-state." The irony, of course, is that despite Black's open love affair with seemingly all things American, and his view of Canada as a nation of welfare-loving mediocrities, it was the U.S. justice system that threw him in jail (and returned him there in September 2011 after two charges he was originally convicted on were upheld on appeal and Black was forced to serve another thirteen months behind bars). In contrast, Canadian police and securities regulators refused to lay a finger on him—something he was used to. "Throughout his life Conrad so admired the United States—there was no country he was more desperate to be successful in," John Fraser, one of his boy-hood chums, told *Men's Vogue* magazine in 2007. "But he was terri-bly naive to think he could behave the same way in the U.S. as he did in Canada." As one former Hollinger director told me, "Conrad sinned far more in Canada than he did in the U.S." The difference was that he was never pursued in Canada for his misdemeanours.

Black's coddling at the hands of Canada's securities regulators and courts speaks volumes about how our justice system favours the well off. When I spoke to journalist Peter C. Newman, Canada's foremost chronicler of the Canadian establishment (including a 1982 biography of a young Conrad Black), and asked him why he thought Canadian authorities hadn't laid a hand on Black, he sighed and replied: "I think there is a club and the club decided they were not going to do anything [about Black]. They did nothing. There are lines of friendship and debts and counter-debts."

All of which points to Canada's rich and super-rich being treated with kid gloves even when they do outrageous things with other people's money.

Take Frank Stronach, the permanently tanned, Austrian-born founder of Magna International Inc. While Stronach built himself an auto parts conglomerate from scratch, he also helped himself to extraordinary levels of compensation, even as he gave up day-to-day management of the company to his daughter and minions. In 2010, for example, he pocketed nearly $60 million in salary. Between 2002 and 2007, he received US$168 million—or nearly US$34 million a year. And yet Stronach controlled the company by owning only 0.6 percent of its 113 million shares. Magna has a dual-class share structure, and Stronach's 720,000 Class B shares each carried 300 votes, while the remaining 112 million Class A shares got one vote each.

In 2010, Stronach said he was willing to walk away from Magna for good if shareholders paid him an enormous premium for his controlling stake. He was basically putting a gun to their collective heads. He demanded and received $300 million, and was given nine million Class A shares, plus a five-year consulting contract that paid him between 2 and 3 percent of the corporations' pre-tax profits. Finally, Stronach got a 27 percent controlling stake in Magna's electric car business. The total price tag for all this came to a mind-boggling $1 billion, representing a 1,800 percent premium on the value of his shares.

Magna's board, which includes former Ontario premier Mike Harris (infamous for his cutbacks to the province's welfare and other social programs when he was in government), also rewarded themselves handsomely. Harris was paid nearly $750,000 for his part-time job in 2010 as a director, while the board okayed a pay package for Magna's six top executives that amounted to US$128 million.

The Ontario Securities Commission (OSC) was unhappy with the Stronach deal, which paid a minority shareholder vast sums of money, and said they would hold a hearing into the matter. Yet in 2011 the commission let the deal pass anyway, after giving Magna investors only limited standing at the hearing, which lasted a mere day and a half.

THE FACT THAT Stronach and Black were not flayed by Canadian authorities comes as no big shock. After all, none of the so-called masters of the universe who ruled Wall Street and whose actions caused the 2007–2009 financial global meltdown and subsequent recession have been held to account either. American regulators have been turning a blind eye to rampant venality in the U.S. financial industry for decades.

While the credit crisis put a spotlight on what was happening on Wall Street and in other centres of finance, revealing how the financial system was designed to enrich the very few at the top of the socio-economic pyramid at the expense of the rest of us, not much has been done to correct the imbalance. The world had 1,210 billionaires in 2010, with a total net worth of US$4.5 trillion—up from 476 and US$1.4 trillion in 2002—and as wealth has accumulated at the very top, most of this money has been funnelled into the hands of bankers and brokers and traders to play with. Between 2000 and 2007, the amount of cash wrapped up in fixed income securities—government bonds, for example—that was sloshing around global markets doubled from $36 trillion to $70 trillion. Such accumulation of capital translates into economic and political power and, essentially, explains why banks and brokerages teetering on the brink of insolvency due to their reckless behaviour were bailed out by governments with few strings attached. Most gallingly perhaps, by 2011 executive salaries and corporate profits rebounded to record levels while unemployment in most Western countries remained stubbornly high. A Conference Board of Canada survey found that directors' compensation jumped 33 percent between 2008 and 2010. And in the U.S., CEO pay leapt on average from 27 to 40 percent. American hedge fund manager John Paulson alone made US$5 billion in compensation in 2010—the largest one-year haul in investing history. Meanwhile, American unemployment that year peaked officially at 9.8 percent. Observers also recognized an unofficial unemployment rate—a measure that includes not only those actively searching for work, but also those who'd given up or who were underemployed in part-time work. That number had hit 16.6 percent.

Despite reports to the contrary, the concentration of wealth and power in Canada is even tighter, making the elites less likely to be held accountable. In a decentralized nation of city-states sprawling across a huge, sparsely populated land mass, the corporate, financial, legal and regulatory establishments form close-knit, even insular subsections of the population. Captains of industry, corporate lawyers, bankers and the mandarins who regulate capital markets live cheek by jowl in leafy neighbourhoods such as Halifax's south end, Montreal's Westmount, Rockliffe Park in Ottawa, Forest Hill and Rosedale and the Bridle Path in Toronto, Tuxedo in Winnipeg, Calgary's Upper Mount Royal and West Vancouver. They are bound together as corporate oligopolies and by a handful of dynastic families that dominate the economy. The Bronfmans created Brookfield Asset Management Inc., a real estate and energy empire with over $150 billion in assets; the Thomsons oversee Woodbridge Company Ltd., a private holding company that controls Thomson Reuters and assets including *The Globe and Mail*; and the Rogers family owns Rogers Communications Inc., a conglomerate rooted in the television, telephone, magazine, sports and Internet industries. Canada, in short, is run by very few people.

And their wealth is concentrated in the financial industry, arguably the most influential sector in the country. Employing over 750,000 people and generating over 6 percent of national GDP—by comparison, the mining, oil and gas sectors combined represent less than 5 percent—it generates annual revenues totalling $78 billion. And yet, says Stephen Jarislowsky, a Montreal-based billionaire investor often referred to as Canada's Warren Buffett: "All the financial business tries to do is separate the investor from his money . . . In the meantime the poor investor is like a sheep being shorn in all directions." Furthermore, when thievery in our capital markets occurs, it's often invisible. Our business class is barely regulated and therefore able to game the system and help themselves to the hard-earned cash of ordinary people, even as they're busy driving companies into the ground.

———

CONRAD BLACK STANDS OUT in this regard. While infamous for his lavish lifestyle and right-wing views, his real gift was playing fast and loose with other people's money. And due to his pedigree, he was given tremendous leeway. As *Globe and Mail* business reporter Jacquie McNish, co-author of a 2004 book on Black's downfall called *Wrong Way*, once remarked, throughout his career Black was "enabled by shareholders, by the media, by regulators."

Black was born into the bosom of the Canadian establishment. His father was president of Canadian Breweries Ltd., an international brewing conglomerate, and a director of Argus Corp., the powerful conglomerate that dominated the Canadian business landscape during the postwar era. After his father died in 1976, Black manoeuvred his way into taking control of Ravelston Corp. Ltd., a management company that controlled Argus. With this foundation, he built the third-largest newspaper corporation in the world, controlling at its peak 528 papers with US$2 billion in annual revenues by the end of the 1990s. The personal wealth of the Blacks—he married right-wing columnist and socialite Barbara Amiel in 1992—included a sprawling, 21,000-square-foot British Colonial–style residence in Palm Beach, a Park Avenue condo, a mansion on Toronto's Bridle Path, two private jets, a Rolls-Royce Silver Wraith, maids, chefs, chauffeurs, footmen, housemen, guards and seventeen butlers.

Black's corporate holdings, meanwhile, were managed under a most Byzantine structure. Through Ravelston, he and right-hand man David Radler owned nearly 80 percent of Hollinger Inc. (HLG), a Canadian company trading on the Toronto Stock Exchange (TSX). In turn, HLG owned 30 percent of Hollinger International Inc., a Chicago-based publicly traded company that Black formed in 1994 to run his American newspapers and magazines. This structure, along with a two-tier share system that gave their shares ten times the voting power of shares held by the public, allowed Black and Radler to control the U.S. company through their Canadian companies, Ravelston and HLG, without actually entirely owning it. Profits and management fees generated by Hollinger International flowed north.

This arrangement also permitted them to gain access to American investors, a critical requirement as, after a series of unflattering Canadian headlines in the 1980s, "nobody would be a shareholder with him in Canada," in the words of a former senior banker at the Canadian Imperial Bank of Commerce (CIBC) who spoke to me on condition of anonymity. It appears there was a "Black factor"—a term coined by Bay Street analysts to explain the deflated value typically applied to Black's company's shares. This deflation would seem to be rooted in his disregard for minority shareholders, a point of view illustrated by an email Black wrote in 2002: "We have said for some time that [Hollinger International] served no purpose as a listed company other than the relatively cheap use of other people's capital." (When asked by *Vanity Fair* magazine in 2011 whether he would ever again be involved with a publicly traded company, Black said no. "The regulators, the minority shareholders, all that crap. Oh, I can't stand it.")

Black's business methods fell under scrutiny by American shareholders after he began downsizing his empire in 2000. While Hollinger International was a large company, it was also highly leveraged, sitting on US$1.8 billion of debt. In 2001, it lost US$337 million and the banks were pressuring Black to cut his losses and pay down debt. Soon he began selling off assets, dumping newspapers and magazines.

As Black unloaded these properties, some of Hollinger International's institutional investors noticed peculiar things in the paperwork. Eugene Fox, managing partner of Cardinal Capital Management LLC, a Connecticut-based investment firm that held Hollinger International shares, saw references to non-compete payments in the company's proxy statements, which are documents submitted to the SEC that include rates of executive compensation. A non-compete payment is a fee paid by the purchaser of an asset to the seller in return for a guarantee that the seller won't compete in the same market. "We started to ask questions about what was happening," remembers Fox, and he began to map out the contracts of all sales agreements. In April 2001, Fox telephoned Herbert Denton, whose New York–based investment firm, Providence Capital, also owned Hollinger International stock, and told him to "take a deeper look at Hollinger." Denton put an analyst on the matter, and when his report came back, Denton told Fox that he thought Black was "taking $60 million a year out of the company."

Denton then contacted Christopher H. Browne of Tweedy, Browne Co. in New York, which owned 18 percent of Hollinger International's stock and is one of the most successful investment firms on Wall Street. In October 2001, Browne wrote to Hollinger International's directors, demanding to know exactly how they determined Black's compensation. Between 1995 and 2000, his letter pointed out, Hollinger International had paid more than US$150 million in management fees to Ravelston. The amounts topped US$40 million in 2000 alone. That Black and his executives were removing these huge sums from a company that was actually shrinking in size reveals how distorted executive compensation had become. As Hollinger International began posting huge deficits, losing US$337 million in 2001 and another US$231 million the following year, Black and five senior Hollinger International officers were compensated with about US$110 million for this two-year period.

In June 2003, because of the fuss made by the American shareholders, Hollinger International's board established a special committee to examine what Black and his top people had been doing
with the U.S. company's money over the previous decade. Made up
of three board members, the committee hired Richard C. Breeden,
the former head of the SEC under President George H.W. Bush, to
spearhead the investigation, alongside the prominent corporate law
firm O'Melveny & Myers LLP. Over the next few months, the committee interviewed over sixty witnesses and reviewed nearly 750,000
pages of documents. It uncovered US$32.2 million in previously
undisclosed payments to Black, Radler and the other Hollinger
International executives that hadn't been authorized by or even
known to the board, a discovery that cost Black his position as CEO
and chairman and sent Radler and the other executives packing. In
August 2004, the special committee submitted a voluminous 513-
page report to the SEC and Illinois courts detailing what the committee found Black and his top associates had been up to. Famously,
the report claims that the men not only looted the company but
created a "corporate kleptocracy."

While it's since been damned by Black and his supporters and was
the focus of a libel lawsuit, the Breeden report shows that as Hollinger
International's fortunes waned and its stock underperformed, the
company's top executives stuffed their pockets with as much money
as they humanly could. Most dramatically, investigators discovered
that Black and Radler and their associates had taken out more than
US$400 million in "management fees" over a seven-year period.
This was on top of the already generous salaries they collected from
Hollinger International. While not illegal, as they'd been approved
by the American company's board and audit committee—with the
board being made up of a clutch of Black's hand-picked cronies who

failed miserably at governing the company—the management fees were nonetheless excessive. "The fact that the security guard is asleep does not mean you can rob the bank," explains Eric Sussman. "Black knew the directors were not paying attention."

Clearly, investors were not getting any of this money. Between 1995 and 2003, Hollinger International's stock price rose 15 percent—from $6.74 to $7.76 per share—while the S&P 500 index rose 69 percent and the Dow Jones 92 percent. Someone who invested $1,000 in Hollinger International in 1995 would have made a $150 profit eight years later, compared to $690 for someone who invested in the S&P 500, and over $900 for an investor in the Dow Jones. "This was truly awful performance for the stock," the Breeden report said, making the case that instead of profits flowing to shareholders they were lining the pockets of senior executives. Indeed, the Hollinger International committee found that Black's two Canadian companies, Ravelston and HLG, were the primary recipients of the management fees.

The special committee also found that Black and Radler either hid, obscured or downplayed the amount of compensation paid to top executives, thereby misleading the board and the audit committee (and were equally obfuscatory in public filings). It determined that Hollinger International's five most highly compensated officers (all Ravelston shareholders) received US$234 million in compensation from 1999 to 2001, while Hollinger's proxy documents submitted to the SEC for this period disclosed only a total of US$9.4 million (or about 4 percent of the total).

To establish benchmark comparisons among similar media companies, the committee hired a compensation firm, Frederic W. Cook & Co., which found that total compensation paid to the top five executives of *The New York Times* and *The Washington Post* during the 1997–2003 period was 4.3 percent and 1.7 percent respectively of net profits; at Hollinger International, it was a staggering 95 per-cent (Black claims it was more like 17 percent). Black and his col-leagues had paid themselves at a rate *twenty times* greater than their peers at *The New York Times* and over *fifty-five times* higher than those at *The Washington Post* as a proportion of net profits. At the same time, Hollinger International had performed poorly com-pared with the other media companies analyzed—not surprising given that Black and Radler used its shareholders' money to cover some of their extravagant expenses. Black had even arranged for his wife to receive US$1.1 million a year in compensation as a Hollinger vice-president—a "job" that paid her to do virtually nothing at all, according to the committee.

None of this, however, became the focus of the criminal case Sussman and his colleagues in the Attorney General's office aimed at Black and three of Hollinger's senior officers (Radler pled guilty to fraud and in return for a lesser sentence agreed to testify against Black). In 2005, when American prosecutors charged Black and the other executives with stealing from Hollinger, it was over smaller sums of non-compete payments (amounting to US$80 million) they said belonged to investors (Black was ultimately convicted for theft of a much smaller sum).

BLACK LIVED HIS LIFE in the spotlight, courting controversy and attention, and spouting off loopy denunciations of his enemies. So when his sins as CEO emerged, they drew scrutiny. But Black is no anomaly; many other Canadian executives help themselves to the booty at the expense of shareholders without attracting much heat or attention. Among the much-heralded Canadian banks, there is no more flagrant example than that of the executives who run the Canadian Imperial Bank of Commerce (CIBC).

The second-largest Canadian bank in terms of revenues during the early 1990s, CIBC had fallen to number five by the 2000s, largely due to executive mismanagement. A laundry list of the bank's fiascos from that period seems unprecedented. It was embroiled in the Enron fraud (which cost it US$2.4 billion in settlements), Global Crossing (the fourth-largest bankruptcy in U.S. history when it occurred in 2002, costing the bank US$16.5 million in payouts), mutual fund manipulations (US$125 million in fines) and asset-backed commercial paper (another $60 million in settlements and fines); hundreds of clients' confidential information was faxed to a scrapyard in West Virginia for a period of three years; and the entire value of the bank was bet on U.S. subprime mortgage debt ($9 billion in pre-tax losses). On top of all of this, it has been beset by lawsuits from its own employees and shareholders. In short, wherever there's been a catastrophe in the financial industry in recent years, it's a safe bet that CIBC was somehow in the middle of it (the other banks have their fair share of cock-ups, but CIBC tops the list in that respect). And the bank's disasters hurt shareholders.

In 2009, Candace L. Preston, a partner with Financial Markets Analysis LCC, a New Jersey–based securities analysis firm, was hired by lawyers representing a group of CIBC shareholders who were suing the bank. She was asked to examine the bank's track record from 2007 to 2008, during the worst period of the credit crisis, and to look at whether CIBC lied to shareholders about the bank's exposure to toxic investments filled with U.S. subprime mortgage debt, and in so doing inaccurately portrayed the real value of the bank's stock. Preston concluded that CIBC inflated the true value of its shares by nearly $40 per share during this period by failing to accurately inform shareholders about the losses the bank was facing, and estimated that damages borne by the shareholders totalled US$6.6 billion. (The bank's annual revenues in 2008 were $3.7 billion.)

Despite this litany of woe, the bank's leadership became rich, very rich. Former Bay Street research analyst Diane Urquhart examined the bank's records and concluded that the combined compensation for CIBC's top ten executives between 1999 and 2007 totalled almost $600 million, which was high compared to the other banks (the bank's top five executives pocketed an average of $84 million each over that period). John Hunkin, the former CEO and the man most responsible for the bank's gusher of red ink, retired in 2005 having made $90.4 million since 1999. When David Kassie was forced to resign in the winter of 2004 as head of the bank's brokerage arm, CIBC World Markets, he left having pocketed $86 million; Brian Shaw, another head of CIBC World Markets, who was forced out in 2008, left the bank's employ with $50 million—both also since 1999. And Hunkin's successor, Gerry McCaughey, pocketed $103 million from 1999 to 2007. In 2010 alone, McCaughey's total compensation was $9.3 million, although he also cashed in 544,000 shares for an estimated payout of $42 million.

Moreover, the bank seems to have obscured some of its payouts to executives. Bob Verdun is an acerbic, blunt-spoken former newspaper publisher and take-no-prisoners shareholders' activist from Kitchener, Ontario, and in 2007 he noticed peculiar items in the fine print of an old CIBC proxy circular (a document sent to shareholders outlining important matters concerning the bank). "They slipped something through that looked like a small number of stock options," Verdun told me. "In fact, it was units in an ill-defined bonus pool that turned out to be millions of dollars." Dated March 2001, the proxy statement contained a reference to the "CIBC Special

Incentive Plan (SIP)" — a one-time bonus that, according to Verdun, rewarded ten of the bank's top executives with a total of as much as $141 million.

While the proxy statement was vague about the reasons behind the bonus, mentioning only certain merchant banking investments, Verdun suspected it was tied to CIBC's immense profits from its investment in the American telecommunications company Global Crossing Ltd. The problem was that Global Crossing went bankrupt in 2002 amidst allegations it committed a massive stock market swindle, one in which CIBC was accused of participating by Global Crossing shareholders and one of the company's former executives. "As far as I can determine, [the SIP] was their big payoff for doing such a wonderful job for Global Crossing," said Verdun sarcastically.

Mostly, Verdun was angry because the SIP reference was so oblique. "In my fifteen years of intense analysis of bank financial statements and proxy circulars, I have never seen anything as flagrantly improper. My objection is they sneaked it by the shareholders . . . It was an intentionally misleading disclosure." He took his complaints to CIBC and tried to get the OSC, Toronto Stock Exchange and the media interested in the matter, arguing that Ontario's securities laws had been broken. He met with CIBC officials and the bank brought in a heavyweight corporate lawyer, John Tuzyk, a senior partner at the Bay Street law firm of Blake, Cassels & Graydon who is an expert on corporate governance. Tuzyk assured Verdun the bank was not in violation of Ontario's disclosure rules.

Verdun was unconvinced. In his opinion the bank's senior managers were a disaster, having become wealthy while at the same time taking enormous risks that hurt shareholders. "The multi-billion-dollar writedowns due to subprime lending, the multi-billion-dollar payout in the Enron scandal . . . were not the result of clumsiness by

incompetent executives at CIBC," he maintains. "They were calculated risks taken by experienced professionals looking to line their
own pockets with huge bonuses. The problem is not the skill of
CIBC's executives, but their motivation . . . The blunders are the
worst in the industry, but CIBC executives are among the highest
paid in Canada."

Conrad Black sat on the board of CIBC for twenty-seven years,
leaving in January 2004, by which time Richard Breeden had made
public his 2003 discovery of unauthorized fees out of Hollinger
International's coffers being paid to Black and Radler and to HLG.
It seems that a degree of comfort with getting rich as the ship sinks
is something he and the bankers had in common. The fact that such
executives were profiting as they weakened or ruined their companies was not so unusual. Indeed, Canada's corporate culture was
clearly changing. There was a move away from building companies
through innovation and ingenuity (in the mould of Steve Jobs and
Apple Inc.) towards viewing business enterprises as personal piggy-
banks, and doing so at the expense of investors, employees and the
whole Canadian economy.

TWO

RISE OF BAY STREET, DEATH OF MAIN STREET

O N A FRIDAY MORNING in the fall of 2004, Denis Turcotte was working in his office at Algoma Steel Inc. when the company's chief financial officer stuck his head in the door. Sprawling along the St. Mary's River in Sault Ste. Marie, Ontario, Algoma is an integrated steelmaker sitting on two thousand acres of land that includes a blast furnace, thin slab caster, coke ovens and coal piles. "I have a guy on the line who says his name is John Paulson," the CFO told Turcotte. "He said he just bought 10 percent of the company and he would like to talk to you."

As the 43-year-old CEO of Algoma, Turcotte handled investor relations as part of his job. He took the call. "I was wondering if I could come up and have a tour of the plant and meet you guys?" Paulson asked. Turcotte agreed. It wasn't every day that a prominent Wall Street hedge fund manager was willing to travel to this hard-luck town of 75,000 located on the edge of the Canadian Shield.

Paulson arrived two weeks later. An intense man with deep lines under his eyes, Paulson ran Paulson & Co., a New York–based hedge fund with nearly US$5 billion in assets in 2004. He'd heard Algoma was a sweet investment, especially after Turcotte transformed it into the most efficient steel producer in the world, and one of its most profitable. Acting as gracious hosts, Turcotte and his managers gave Paulson a tour of the facility, talking about future plans. "We are on good, solid footing here now," Turcotte told Paulson, "Understanding where this company needs to be in five years we need to look at some things, which includes buying some companies in order to drive growth."

Paulson was cool to this news. The hedge fund manager didn't seem to want Turcotte spending money on acquisitions, a reaction foreshadowing events to come. Paulson returned to New York and promptly bought another 9 percent of Algoma, thus becoming the company's largest single shareholder. Meanwhile, Algoma stormed from success to success, paying off its $350 million debt and stockpiling $500 million in cash.

At the time of the American's visit, Turcotte didn't appreciate the sort of man John Paulson actually is. His real agenda became apparent in the fall of 2005 when he demanded Algoma hand over the $500 million in cash reserves to shareholders like himself—money Algoma was planning to use to upgrade and expand the company's operations in order to keep it growing in the notoriously cyclical and competitive steel market. "Plus he wanted us to borrow another $400 million to $500 million," says Turcotte. "That would give out $800 million to $1 billion to shareholders. But we would have no cash and $400 million to $500 million worth of debt. We said no."

Paulson then played hardball. To get his way, he attempted to kick out Turcotte and Algoma's board. A war broke out over the company's future.

———

PAULSON'S ATTEMPTED COUP exemplifies how the financial industry has changed, often with consequences lethal to otherwise healthy businesses. Traditionally, the banking and investment business provided money to entrepreneurs and companies so that they could start or grow businesses (and when those companies prospered, the investors made their money back with interest). The 2007–2009 credit crisis, however, exposed how high finance (and its extraordinary and growing capital reserves) had morphed into a dangerously unstable force. Indeed, not since the 1929 stock market crash and Great Depression has the world of high finance so altered the fates of nations and economies, and by the late 2000s and early 2010s the reckless behaviour of bankers and brokerage houses, with their exotic financial instruments, was creating global economic chaos.

Lost in the hue and cry over subprime mortgage debts, shoddy regulatory regimes, moral hazards and the size of Wall Street bonuses was the fact that finance capital was also laying waste to those sectors of the economy critical to prosperity—especially the onshore manufacturing sector. Stock markets were also influencing the behaviour of the CEOs of manufacturers, as now there was an inordinate focus on driving up stock prices even if it meant managing their companies into the ground.

For Canada, the erosion of the manufacturing base is particularly disastrous. Our economy has long relied on natural resources as its main source of prosperity. By the mid-1990s, however, Canada was beginning to break out of this box by offering a full variety of products and services to international markets (as in the case of Nortel), and our capital markets were also becoming more self-reliant. Although our economy remained heavily dependent on resource extraction and foreign investment, there were growing signs the country was becoming a more well-rounded capitalist power.

Moreover, our low currency, proximity to the U.S. market and social-ized health care system made Canada an attractive place for manu-facturers to locate their operations.

Since 2000, however, the country has suffered a reversal of these trends: a backwards slide into once again being a mere provider of raw materials for the rest of the world. More than 500,000 manufac-turing jobs (one-sixth of the nation's total) disappeared by 2009 after employment in that sector peaked in 2002. Meanwhile, high value–added exports (products that are the best in their markets) as a share of total exports have dropped from over 55 percent in 2000 to 35 per-cent in 2010. Moreover, while commodity prices in oil and minerals skyrocketed in the late 2000s and the resource sector boomed, the federal government permitted foreign multinationals to snatch up our mining, energy and other resource-based companies. These included Alcan, Inco, Falconbridge, Western Oil Sands, Noranda, MacMillan Bloedel and Addax Petroleum. In 2010, the Harper gov-ernment was even content to allow the sale of Potash Corp. in Saskatchewan to the Australian conglomerate BHP Billiton Ltd., until a national hue and cry stopped it from going ahead. (In an indication of corporate elite opinion on the matter, *The Globe and Mail* editorialized against the Harper government's decision to halt the sale.) Foreign ownership means that these companies' R & D, with its high-paying jobs, is less likely to be carried out here. Couple this with the evaporation of well-paid, unionized manufacturing jobs and Canada's employment picture is now dominated by the low-wage, non-exportable service sector.

More troubling, the financial industry has actively helped to destroy manufacturing companies in Canada and abroad. Perhaps the most pernicious development in this assault has been the rise of private equity funds—hedge funds and other large pools of mostly

wealthy people's money—that make money by engineering leveraged buyouts (LBOs) and selling off companies' assets. Hedge fund
managers swoop in on what they term "distressed" businesses, buy a
controlling or significant interest, downsize them, and invariably
leave companies weaker and laden with debt, while workers are out
of jobs and their pension plans are gutted. "Overwhelming evidence
and practical experience show that most activities [of private equity
firms] raise serious concerns and problems in the real economy,"
concluded a 2007 report presented to the European Parliament by
Poul Nyrup Rasmussen, the former prime minister of Denmark.
Included in these problems are negative impacts on long-term
investment in R & D and new technology, on jobs and working conditions and on investor protection, and as well as overall risks to the
stability of the financial markets. Meanwhile, led by India and
China, Asia continues to rise as the world's dominant economic
region, and is doing so based largely on manufacturing goods the
world wants.

The shift away from manufacturing can be seen by looking at the
sectors in which GDP and employment are generated. Manufacturing's contribution to GDP declined to about 13 percent in the 2010s
in Canada, as compared with nearly 30 percent in the 1950s, while
the finance, insurance and real estate sectors rose from less than 12
percent of GDP in the 1950s to more than 20 percent in 2010. In
China, however, manufacturing's output is more than 25 percent of
the nation's GDP, with factory production exceeding that of the
United States.

Economist William Lazonick argues that an obsession with solely
maximizing shareholder value has had a detrimental effect on the
North American manufacturing sector's ability to compete with its
Asian rivals. Indeed, after losing eight to nine million jobs in the

United States (and 486,000 in Canada) during the 2007-2009 recession, the manufacturing sector had recovered only one million by 2010 despite stimulus spending (Canada's employment bounce back was stronger, with most of the jobs lost in the recession eventually returning). By 2011, 23 million Americans who wanted to work full-time could not get a job. "The U.S. economy is fragile because of a failure of its leading corporations to make sufficient investments in innovation and job creation [during this] new age of global competition," Lazonick wrote in a 2010 paper. "Even the most innovative sectors of the U.S. economy have become highly *financialized* [his italics], with the allocation of corporate resources being driven by the ideology of 'maximizing shareholder value.'" Lazonick argues that financialization occurs when corporate executives focus on boosting share prices and distributing "value" to shareholders, especially in the form of stock repurchases, at the expense of investment in innovation and the creation of jobs. This exacerbates inequity and instability and restricts the potential for economic growth in the States, he says. "Despite the financial meltdown of 2008, there are scant signs in the 2010s of institutional changes that will constrain the destructive behaviour of financialized corporations."

I reached the Canadian-born Lazonick at his home in Massachusetts (he teaches at the University of Massachusetts). About this growing influence of Wall Street and Bay Street on the overall economy he told me, "Basically, the financial sector has been structured to extract value rather than to create value." He went on to say "the general tendency is to give too much power to the financial interests and not enough power to the community interests and to the types of managers who can figure out how you can deal with an ailing company." While building a company takes an enormous amount of time and energy, destroying one can happen in an instant, and Lazonick observed that "Wall Street has just become a gambling casino . . . Ultimately, you don't make money just out of money. You need people producing things and selling things."

WHEN JOHN PAULSON made his move against Algoma, trying to poach its cash reserves, it was a defining moment in the clash between the financial industry and the so-called Old Economy in Canada. For decades, steelmaking had been a critically important Canadian-owned industry. It was a sector that offered decent jobs and thrived during boom times and survived the lean years. Free trade made life more difficult, as the industry had to compete with offshore mills that dumped cut-rate steel into the Canadian market. In 2003, after the World Trade Organization (WTO) ruled against U.S. duties, China moved into North America with inexpensive steel, and soon enough North American steel companies were contending with global trade winds that were rarely fair and made once-profitable stand-alone Canadian steelmakers vulnerable.

In the case of Algoma Steel, the company had been lurching towards bankruptcy in the early 1990s and was saved only by an employee buyout. Then, in 1997, the company spent $440 million to upgrade its mill. Four years later, however, sagging under $300 million of debt, it filed for bankruptcy protection. In desperation, Algoma hired Denis Turcotte, a French Canadian who had grown up in Thunder Bay and ascended through the ranks of a large pulp and paper company. Now he was handed the unenviable job of turning Algoma around. He was impressed by Algoma's $1 billion in assets, as well as its production technology. Most of the company's problems were structural, he thought, and so Turcotte reorganized how the company was managed. Management welcomed advice from workers on how to improve efficiencies (among other things), and by 2003 Algoma was producing steel at much higher quantities for less money. "We had to drive productivity up and drive costs down," Turcotte says.

He expected to save $100 million within three years, but it took only two. The savings and increased production, along with an improving steel market, made 2004 Algoma's most successful year ever, with $344 million in profits. The following year the company earned $240 million and paid off nearly $350 million of debt. "Algoma went from being a dog with fleas in investors' eyes to achieving record margins and becoming the most profitable steel company in North America," says Turcotte. "The stock was back up into the high twenties and low thirties."

It was just as Algoma was turning the corner that John Paulson made his appearance. His Wall Street–based Paulson & Co. was already active in Canada, investing in oil sands development and becoming the second-largest shareholder of the gold mining company Placer Dome Inc. (which has since been bought by Barrick Gold Corp.). Investment comes to his fund through pooled investment vehicles like mutual funds. When he took his run at Algoma's cash reserves in October 2005, Turcotte responded by offering a distribution of $238 million to shareholders. Paulson was unappeased, angered because American shareholders would incur a 25 percent withholding tax on the payment (a tax he clearly had not foreseen, largely because his interest in Algoma was focused on other ways to make money from taking over the company).

His cash grab rebuffed, Paulson moved to get rid of Turcotte and the board. To accomplish this he needed to paint them as incompetent, a tall order given their extraordinary success. Nonetheless, Paulson criticized the board over the tax issue and expansion plans, and, surprisingly, for not putting the company up for sale. His aim was to remove seven of the eleven board members and replace them with his own people, and he appealed to shareholders' greed to do so, encouraging them to help themselves to the company's pantry. Then he launched a legal action that would allow him, not the company, to hold a special shareholders' meeting, scheduled for March 2006.

Turcotte, the board, Algoma's workers and the city of Sault Ste. Marie itself fought back. "You can't run a steel company like a cash machine," said Wayne Fraser, director of United Steelworkers of Ontario. His union accused Paulson of "corporate terrorism" and launched a lawsuit against him. Paulson, sensing he was not going to win, backed down, reducing his stake in Algoma to 5 percent. Turcotte told me that Paulson knew all along that the $500 million in reserves was needed by Algoma to get through the tough times. "He's a very bright and sophisticated guy," he said. "But these guys are traders. They move in and out very quickly . . . It's a very common tactic."

Nonetheless, the fight with Paulson had its consequences, and Algoma's victory was bittersweet: it revealed the company's susceptibility to takeover by foreign interests, and in 2007 it ceased being Canadian owned, sold to the Essar Group, an Indian conglomerate. Turcotte left the company and now works as a consultant.

Moreover, Paulson's failed takeover of Algoma was one of the hedge fund manager's few setbacks. Soon afterwards, noticing the huge glut of mortgage-backed securities engorging Wall Street, he bet against the housing market, expecting the bubble to burst and hoping that a financial meltdown would occur in order to make himself spectacularly rich—a gamble that paid off. When the subprime debt balloon popped in 2007, his fund earned US$15 billion and he personally pocketed US$3.7 billion. "I've never been involved in a trade that had such unlimited upside with a very limited downside," he crowed to *The Wall Street Journal*.

By 2010, Paulson's fund had grown to US$37 billion and he was raking in billions in annual compensation. But that same year his reputation took a hit when the SEC accused him of conspiring with the investment bank Goldman Sachs in an investment scam designed to rip off investors. In 2007, Paulson had instructed Goldman to create a synthetic collateralized debt obligation (CDO) which is a large pool of debt investors can buy into. In this case, the CDO that Goldman established was tied to the performance of sub-prime mortgage-backed securities. If the securities increased in value, investors would make money. If they declined, they would lose their cash. But Goldman decided to game the entire process. They told investors the bonds in the CDO would be chosen by an independent manager. In reality Goldman allowed Paulson to select the bonds, and he chose ones he believed were most likely to implode and lose value. In other words, he helped Goldman create a CDO they were pretty certain would collapse. They then secretly placed bets in the form of insurance policies that would pay out if the CDOs plummeted in value.

Goldman then sold the CDO package to investors like foreign banks, pension funds and insurance companies, which would profit only if the bonds gained value. Instead, as Paulson and Goldman hoped, the bonds tanked. Paulson and Goldman cooked this up, according to the SEC, without informing investors about the risk. "As a result, investors in the . . . CDO lost over $1 billion," says the complaint, adding that "Paulson's opposite CDS [credit default swap] positions yielded a profit of approximately $1 billion for Paulson." Despite this allegation, the SEC decided not to charge Paulson (they charged Goldman, however, which settled the case by paying a record US$550 million fine).

Yet Paulson's Midas touch abandoned him in 2011. His funds went into freefall as the markets fell, with one fund plummeting 47 percent and another 32 percent. He'd also invested heavily in Sino-Forest Corp., the Chinese forestry company listed on the TSX and exposed as a stock market scam: his hedge fund took a US$720 million bath on that investment alone.

While Algoma managed to beat back this particular carpetbagger, other steel companies were not so fortunate. Hamilton-based Stelco Inc., for one, fell victim to this new breed of predator, and this time it was one from closer to home.

THREE

PILLAGING STELCO

THE OFFICES OF UNITED Steelworkers (USW) Local 1005 reside in a shabby two-storey union hall a few blocks from Hamilton's harbour, on the south shore where the steel mills belch out smoke all day long. I was meeting Rolf Gerstenberger, the president of the local representing the few remaining workers at Stelco Inc.'s nearby Hilton Works plant. He's a throwback, a hippie, a radical and a Vietnam-era student activist who fled to Canada to escape the draft. In 1973, Gerstenberger took a job at Stelco, then Canada's largest steelmaker; at the time Hilton Works employed 13,000 workers and was producing over five million tons of steel per year.

Gerstenberger has seen the landscape change dramatically since those halcyon days. Hilton Works had once been Canada's largest steel mill, but soon after I met Gerstenberger it was shut down and 900 workers were locked out by the company. This part of town was conspicuously tattered. Just down the street, a strip of Cash Depots, seedy bars and dollar stores add to the neighbourhood's desolate, post-industrial feel.

In his mid-sixties, Gerstenberger is a tall, good-humoured (and profane) man with a baritone voice. At the time we met, Hilton Works had been operating at far below capacity for over eighteen months, its workforce down to a skeleton level. "By October 28, 2008, our blast furnace was down," Gerstenberger told me. "Literally happened overnight." By that time Stelco had become a subsidiary of U.S. Steel Corporation, the American steel giant.

The demise of Stelco has a great deal to do with Bay Street's focus on making money no matter what the damage done on the manufacturing side. It's the story of how a noble cornerstone of Canada's industrial heartland was laid low by speculators. Once a prosperous working-class city hugging Lake Ontario, and the centre of steel manufacturing in Canada, Hamilton today has the second-highest poverty rate in Ontario, its steel mills either closed or operating at below capacity, and all of them owned by foreign corporations.

What happened has little to do with fraud (at least in the legal sense), although the company's original shareholders certainly feel they were robbed. Stelco's problems date back to 1996 when it decided to take advantage of an Ontario law that allowed the company to stop putting aside money to meet its employees' pension obligations, both past and present. As a result, Stelco's contributions to its employees' plan dropped and by 2003 the company was facing a $1.3 billion in outstanding pension liabilities. By then Stelco was losing nearly $19 million a month, although the company had $173 million in the bank, was meeting payments to creditors and was by no means bankrupt.

Michael Woollcombe, a former Stelco director, told me that Stelco's board then hired Ernst & Young—the accounting firm that also acts as a bankruptcy monitor, overseeing a company's operations once it has sought creditor protection—as well as Hap Stephen, a restructuring expert, to examine options for the company. Hiring these people, says Woollcombe, "creates a self-fulfilling prophecy, because they financially benefit significantly if the company ultimately files for [bankruptcy] protection." And indeed, with the urging of Ernst & Young and Stephen, in January 2004, Stelco filed for protection from its creditors under the Companies' Creditors Arrangement Act (CCAA), Canada's version of Chapter 11, which allows corporations to reorganize while keeping creditors at bay. The accounting firm and Hap Stephen were then hired to guide Stelco through the reorganization process.

The day before Stelco's board pushed the company into CCAA protection, CIBC World Markets published a forecast predicting steel prices and demand were about to rise. Shares in steel companies were already floating upwards, and there were clear indications that North America would soon be facing a steel shortage.

With money in the bank and the market for steel warming up, why would Stelco seek creditor protection? Ostensibly it was because the company was running out of money too fast. But other theories abound. Bill Ferguson, president of USW Local 8782, which represents workers at Stelco's Lake Erie plant in Nanticoke, Ontario, believes it was "to get rid of the pension plan." Meanwhile, the company's shareholders felt it was a ploy to wipe them out so the board and anyone who purchased the steelmaker could get rich by issuing new shares. "A bad pension situation is not justification enough for throwing [the company] into bankruptcy," says Murray Pollitt, the president of a Toronto-based investment company, Pollitt & Co., Inc., which held Stelco shares. "We wanted to call a shareholders' meeting and we weren't allowed to do so. It was just terrible. The people who owned the company had no say whatsoever, they were completely disenfranchised. The people [the board] putting us into bankruptcy . . . saw a lumbering steel company and said we could grab this thing for nothing. And they did."

Bill Cara, who runs an investment firm out of the Bahamas, Cara Trading Advisers Ltd., concurs. "This was orchestrated. The board took a company down because they wanted certain assets out of it and they wanted to make a lot of money. But they took a healthy company, an icon of Canada that hadn't missed any payments. Think about it. How can you do that? How can you file for bankruptcy because your plan says you're going to have a rough year or two ahead? It was a scam from the get-go."

In fact, less than four months after Stelco sought CCAA protection, it began turning a profit: steel prices and demand had shot up as predicted. "Six months into the bankruptcy, Stelco had a record quarter and we got a bonus," recalls Gerstenberger, shaking his head in disbelief. Stelco lost $36 million in the first quarter of 2004 but made $42 million in the second, $58 million in the third and finished the year with net earnings of $65 million. But the company was now trapped. If it came out of CCAA, it would not only have to deal with the pension liability but also $550 million in other debt obligations. By seeking CCAA prematurely, Stelco's board had weakened its position by punting financial obligations down the road and making it vulnerable to a takeover by parties who didn't have the steelmaker's best interests at heart. The company was now in play, and who would control its fate was up in the air.

Ordinarily, you would assume that the only people interested in buying a steel company would be executives of other steel companies. But as an indicator of how things were changing, this was not the case when it came to Stelco's suitors. Most of them, as it turned out, were bankers, hedge fund managers and traders. And they, surprise surprise, really had no interest in running a steel company.

ONE BAY STREET ENTITY keenly watching the Stelco situation was Brookfield Asset Management Inc., a Toronto-based, $150 billion real estate and energy conglomerate. Brookfield used to be called Brascan Corp., which rose to prominence on brothers Peter and Edward Bronfman's money to become a corporate titan, once controlling a third of the TSX's value and owning parts of more than two hundred companies. It already boasted ties to Stelco: Courtney Pratt, a former executive of a Brascan subsidiary, was the new Stelco CEO, and it was he who led it into CCAA protection.

Brookfield has a division called Tricap Partners Ltd., a private equity "distress" fund that buys the cheap debt of struggling companies and engineers turnarounds before selling the companies off for a profit. I went to see the Brookfield executive who oversees this side of the company's business—senior managing partner, Cyrus Madon. I met him at Brookfield Place, two office towers standing near the foot of Bay Street. Sitting in a boardroom, Madon struck me as a quiet, unruffled man. He told me that Tricap looks for companies that have broken balance sheets or are overleveraged and need to be recapitalized. "Often they have operational challenges," he said. "The reason we look for those companies is we can buy their assets for better value. We look generally for hard asset businesses [such as manufacturers]."

Yet the track record of these "distress" funds in turning companies around is spotty at best. "What they are really doing is bleeding these companies dry," says Heather Slavkin, a policy adviser with the American Federation of Labour and Congress of Industrial Organizations (AFL–CIO), America's largest labour federation.

"[They get] half the workforce to do the work of a full workforce. And take out money from research and development that's necessary to make them competitive in a global market in the long term."

What followed was a tug-of-war over Stelco's fate, with everyone from the union, the board and shareholders to banks and private equity funds jostling to shape its future. Tricap was not alone in its interest in Stelco. Canadian investment firms including Clearwater Capital, Equilibrium Capital and Sunrise Partners, Germany's Deutsche Bank and the New Jersey–based hedge fund Appaloosa Management were all jockeying to figure out how to profit from the situation. All of these financiers were hoping to buy Stelco for a song and then dispose of it for a hefty profit. "None of these hedge fund guys have a long-term investment plan," says Peter Warrian, a professor of industrial relations at the University of Toronto and a steel industry expert. "They simply want to take what's valuable and sell it to the highest bidder."

In 2005, Michael Woollcombe, a lawyer with Equilibrium, and Roland Keiper, who worked for Clearwater, managed to get onto Stelco's board of directors. They did so because their firms controlled significant stakes in the company, and had the backing of 40 percent of shareholders, whose interests they represented. The two men were convinced the company's management was downgrading Stelco's value on purpose. "The enterprise value being talked about was absurdly low on the basis of management forecasts," Woollcombe insists. While management was saying Stelco was almost worthless, the company's main competitor, Dofasco Inc., had just been sold for $5.6 billion to Arcelor SA of Luxembourg, and a report produced by Navigant Consulting concluded that Stelco's shareholder equity should be worth between $1.1 billion and $1.3 billion (they later downgraded it to $750 million). Claiming the steelmaker had little value was a lie, but saying so would allow someone to buy it for next to nothing.

Meanwhile, Stelco was spending huge sums of money on lawyers, consultants and accountants—$80 million in the first eighteen months after it went bankrupt. Thirty-nine law firms played a role in the Stelco reorganization, charging rates of $300 an hour outside of court and up to two or three times that amount for each hour spent in court. "Once you are in CCAA, it's a cesspool, and the courts don't do a good job of managing it and the lawyers and other professionals have a vested interest in continuing it on," laments Woollcombe. "And shareholders' value gets pissed away for no benefit. It's just leakage."

THE LOGJAM OVER WHO WOULD CONTROL Stelco and bring it out of CCAA was broken in the fall of 2005 when the leadership of the steelworkers' union formed an alliance with three investment pools: Brookfield/Tricap, Bay Street's Sunrise Partners LP and the American hedge fund Appaloosa Management LP. The latter was a US$3 billion fund managed by David Tepper, who used to run the junk bond trading desk at Goldman Sachs in New York. The union got into bed with these financiers because they offered to pump money into the pension plan (then servicing eight thousand retired Stelco workers) and honour collective agreements. The union was playing a high-stakes game with Bay Street in the hopes its members' jobs and pensions could be salvaged.

With a loan of $150 million from the Ontario government, Brookfield invested $55 million of equity and offered up bridge financing of $375 million to buy the company in conjunction with Appaloosa and Sunrise. However, this sale meant wiping out the value of all the shares held by Stelco's original shareholders—a total of $167 million. "They got it for a song," says Pollitt, of the

investment house Pollitt & Co., Inc. And Gerstenberger, who broke
with his union's leadership and refused to negotiate with the Bay
Street firms, calls it "legalized theft."

To run the company, the new owners hired Rodney Mott, an
American turnaround specialist who'd made a name for himself by
resuscitating a collection of Ohio steel mills destined for the scrap
heap. He walked away from the Ohio job with nearly US$100 mil-
lion in compensation. Mott added to his fortune by working for
Stelco. When the company came out of CCAA protection in April
2006, new shares were issued. Mott bought one million at $5.50 each
and was given another million. On the day the shares were issued,
they began selling at $15 and quickly rose to more than $20. Mott
almost quadrupled the value of his shares overnight. He didn't even
bother moving to Canada; instead, he commuted to Hamilton from
his home in South Carolina. And just as well: his efforts to turn
Stelco around floundered and it began losing money again.

In late 2007, Brookfield and its partners unloaded Stelco—a mere
twenty months after buying it—to U.S. Steel for US$1.1 billion. At
the time, Stelco's new shares were selling at $38.50. For its invest-
ment Brookfield/Tricap made more than $330 million in profit,
while Appaloosa and Sunrise cashed in more than $180 million—
which was more than seven times their original equity investment,
plus profit from interest, fees and debt. Mott sold his shares and
walked away with more than $66 million. Meanwhile, about 2,000
workers had lost their jobs or taken early retirement since the company went into CCAA three years previously.

U.S. STEEL, IT TURNED OUT, was no gentle caretaker of Stelco's
ninety-seven year-old legacy. By 2008, Stelco was making healthy

profits for its new owners. In the end, though, it didn't matter. In November of that year, U.S. Steel announced it was idling Hilton Works, once the largest steel mill in Canada. In fact, that winter it said that with the slowdown in the economy it was cutting operations way back at all of Stelco's plants and would be supplying its Canadian customers from its American mills. This forced the federal government to sue the company for reneging on promises to keep Stelco open, which was one of the conditions of its being allowed to buy the company (all foreign purchases of large Canadian companies are reviewed by Industry Canada, which can impose conditions on the sale).

Then, in the summer of 2009, U.S. Steel locked out the remaining 150 workers at Stelco's Lake Erie plant, one of the most high-tech steel mills in the world, and demanded large concessions from the union. The workers were out for more than eight months, and several lost their homes. The lockout was finally resolved in the spring of 2010. It was an ironic turn of affairs for Bill Ferguson, the local's president, who'd been instrumental in negotiating with Tricap, Sunrise and Appaloosa. "In regards to being caught with our dicks in our hands by the financial industry, we did what we had to do," he says defensively. "If we had done nothing, I can guarantee you pension benefits would not be as good, wages would not be as good and working conditions would not be as good . . . Now, [U.S. Steel's] conduct since they bought it has been reprehensible, I would be the first to admit that."

In November of 2010, U.S. Steel locked out the remaining 800 workers at the Hilton Works after demanding a two-tier pension plan and a reduction to the indexing of the current pension scheme. They were out eleven months before a new deal was finally reached and the plant reopened. In 2011, the federal government settled its lawsuit with U.S. Steel after the company agreed to keep its two Stelco mills open until at least 2015. The steelworkers' union condemned the settlement as letting U.S. Steel off the hook for upholding the conditions required for its purchase of Stelco.

Indeed, the fallout of Bay Street's meddling with Stelco was disastrous. The company was now a shadow of its former self. And the steel industry as a Canadian-owned sector was also finished. In a 24-month period stretching from 2006 to 2008, every major Canadian-owned steel company was bought by Indian, European and American conglomerates—including Dofasco, Algoma, IPSCO and Stelco. This was all part and parcel of the hollowing out of Canada's manufacturing sector. More than 50 percent of all steel sold in Canada was now being imported—up from 20 percent in the early nineties.

THE ROLE OF THE financial industry in the buying and selling of companies—only to downsize or sell them off—is a sign of how far it's drifted from its original raison d'être. Bankers and hedge fund managers increasingly resemble vampires, sucking the lifeblood out of ailing or vulnerable companies, especially manufacturers, who actually make and sell things, rather than extending them lifelines. Still, there was no national outcry over the demise of Stelco, the attempted raid on Algoma or the purchase of the entire steel industry by foreign interests. And that lack of interest undoubtedly reflects a prevailing attitude that these so-called Old Economy industries are somehow passé and that the future of economic prosperity lies elsewhere, for example in the high-tech sector. And yet, when it comes to high tech, executives and their enablers in the financial industry don't view things any differently. As it turns out, high tech can also be pillaged with impunity.

FOUR

PLUNDERING NORTEL

IN HIS WILDEST DREAMS, Robert Ferchat never imagined he would find himself at age seventy-four roaming the polished hallways of Parliament Hill in Ottawa trying to save Nortel Networks Corp. from extinction. It was the spring of 2009 and Ferchat, a short man with avuncular features and boundless self-confidence, met with half a dozen top ministers in Stephen Harper's government, including Industry Minister Tony Clement, pitching them all on a plan to rescue the once-storied telecommunications company from being broken up and sold off to foreign buyers. As a former president of Nortel and a respected figure in the telecom industry, Ferchat was leading a small group of ex-Nortel executives in a last-ditch, quixotic attempt to raise $1 billion to resuscitate the company, which had slid into bankruptcy earlier that year. With government backing, Ferchat believed he could have the company back on its feet within two to three years. Yet, despite his legendary charm, Ferchat couldn't find anyone to pony up. "Nortel has a bad name in Ottawa and we're not going to do anything because they're liars and cheats," was the refrain he kept hearing.

Liars and cheats. How had it come to that? After all, Nortel was not a tobacco company, arms dealer or mafia crime family; it had once been Canada's most celebrated high-tech corporation, a global brand name and one of the nation's few genuine multinationals. At its height, Nortel employed 100,000 people, had 32 manufacturing sites, 20 R & D labs and 370 international offices and was the sixth largest manufacturer of telecommunications equipment in the world. It was hailed as a success story in a sector of the economy rooted in the Internet and cellular phone usage, and therefore destined to grow for decades to come. It was also ideally positioned: it spent $2 billion annually on R & D and spawned dozens of offshoots in the Ottawa–Gatineau and Toronto regions.

But in 2009 its pieces were being sold off to foreign companies and eight of its former senior executives had been charged with fraud. Its investors had lost a bundle; just one class action lawsuit, settled in 2006, paid out $2.4 billion, a refund of only $1 per share for anyone who bought the stock at $45. "Nortel has come and gone," lamented Ferchat, "and we have lost our intellectual base, our centre of innovation and a generation of new business in a fast-moving technology." Canada's high-tech sector has only one world-leading brand remaining: Research In Motion Ltd. (RIM), makers of the BlackBerry. By 2012, however, RIM too was in trouble, its stock in free fall and rapidly losing ground to Apple and others in the fiercely competitive market of handheld cellular devices. RIM was even being talked about as a takeover target.

Nortel's demise spoke volumes about the lack of importance Canada's business and political elites placed not only on companies that actually make things the world needs but on the high-tech sector as a whole. As the company careened towards insolvency, there was little hand-wringing over what this would mean to the country's economic fabric.

NORTEL'S TROUBLES STARTED at the top, and a primary reason its executives and CEOs lost their way lay in the financial incentives offered them, in particular a stock option plan installed in the late 1980s. A 2007 academic report entitled *Inside Agency: The Rise and Fall of Nortel* argues that Nortel's reliance on options created an unhealthy focus on pushing up the stock price to the detriment of the company's overall well-being. Although they were earning a base salary of just over $1 million, with stock options Nortel's CEOs were paid significantly more than their counterparts at U.S. telecommunications suppliers such as Cisco and Motorola. With their bonuses driven by revenue, "on a straight cash basis, there was strong inducement for Nortel's CEO to engage in an unbridled growth strategy, mostly through acquisitions," the study argued.

John Roth embraced this strategy and made a lot of money for himself as a result. A veteran electrical engineer who'd joined Nortel in the late 1960s and risen through the R & D side of the company before taking over in 1997 as CEO at age 53, Roth initiated a buying spree: over the next three years, Nortel snapped up eighteen companies, mostly start-ups, in deals worth more than US$30 billion. Nortel purchased them primarily by issuing stock. "The only thing that was important to management at the time was managing the stock price by buying companies that had ridiculous forecasts of where their revenues were going, or companies that had revenues but had no bottom line," remembers Mike McCorkle, a former Nortel treasurer. "We would go out and dilute the shares of [Nortel] by buying a company that had no quantifiable value."

Of the companies Nortel purchased, most had no revenue, few customers and only a handful of employees. It shelled out US$3.2 billion for Xros, Inc., a firm with only US$3 million in tangible assets, and another US$3.25 billion for a fledgling outfit called Qtera Corp., which had no revenues, 170 employees and only one customer. As Nortel issued stock to purchase these companies, the value of the shares diminished. "Everybody at Nortel was drinking the Kool-Aid," says McCorkle.

Nonetheless, such purchases drove up Nortel's stock price and boosted the company's "on paper" revenue picture. Soon Nortel was a darling on both Bay and Wall streets, with most of the shares being grabbed by retail investors and pension funds filled with the retirement savings of Baby Boomers. By July 2000, Nortel's shares had reached US$89 in New York and $125 on the TSE, the company suddenly constituting more than one-third of the TSE 300 composite index's value—a total of $398 billion. Meanwhile, between 1997 and 2000, the number of analysts following Nortel tripled from twelve to thirty-seven, and nearly all of them were overwhelmingly enthusiastic, blindly urging investors to buy the company's stock.

One of the few not caught up in the hype was Ross Healy, an independent telecommunications analyst who runs Toronto-based Strategic Analysis Corp. Healy read Nortel's financial statements closely and noticed alarming things. "They were paying staggering amounts of money for near-start-up companies and yet they were fundamentally trashing their own balance sheet by replacing hard equity with basically goodwill," he says. Indeed, although Nortel was paying dividends to shareholders, it hadn't actually posted an after-tax profit since fiscal 1997. By 2000, as the tech/dot-com bubble burst, orders for Nortel's equipment were drying up or being cancelled, and skeptics like Healy could see that the market for Nortel's products had hit a wall. "It was perfectly obvious to me that most of the fibre-optic systems would go broke—that Nortel's customers would go bankrupt," he says.

Yet Roth had built himself a perpetual motion machine that, if it stopped moving, would collapse. It had the hallmarks of a Ponzi scheme in that his business plan called for growth through acquisition, but the moment revenues dropped, or slowed down, the impact on Nortel's three billion shares would not be pretty. As the market for their wares imploded, Nortel began to mislead its investors about the soundness of the company. And Roth led the charge.

The CEO had his reasons. While Roth's base salary was US$1.4 million, he controlled stock that, if cashed in at one point, would have netted him $309 million. In the summer of 2000, he began selling his stocks and pocketed more than $123 million. In a single day he exercised options to buy 450,000 shares at $8.57 and sold them for $81.02, a pre-tax gain of $32.6 million.

Meanwhile, Roth was issuing statements and press releases announcing dynamic growth and terrific earnings for 2000 and the coming year. "Looking forward to 2001, we expect the overall market to grow in excess of 20 percent," he said in October 2000. "Given our strong market position and industry-leading networking solutions, we expect to continue to grow significantly faster than the market, with anticipated growth in revenues . . . in the 30 to 35 percent range." A month later, Roth claimed that for the first quarter of 2001 "we expect our revenue and earnings per share from operations will be in the range of [US]$8.1 billion to [US]$8.3 billion." Such positive statements helped push Nortel's stock up by more than $4 to nearly $60 on the TSE. Meanwhile, Roth was being feted by the media as a god among men.

In reality, Nortel was sinking fast. Behind closed doors, on September 15, 2000, Frank Dunn, Nortel's chief financial officer and someone Roth had elevated within the company, received a set of charts from one of Nortel's finance vice-presidents containing internal forecasts for its various divisions. They showed that Nortel would miss third-quarter 2000 revenue and earnings targets by over $400 million and $500 million respectively. By October 17, 2000, Nortel knew that its yearly revenues were off by more than almost $2 billion from expectations. Nortel's finance personnel described this in cryptic notes: "Lost $1.9 [billion in] 2nd half [2000] revenue over last 4 weeks" and "1st half 2001 already $1.5 [billion] off expectation." The company's sales forecast for optical equipment was at least $500 million below the $10 billion level for which Nortel had primed the market. The company's fourth-quarter earnings were at least $320 million short of the amount needed to meet earnings per share.

Neither Dunn nor Roth made this information public for months. Instead, they allowed hundreds of thousands of securities to trade at prices they must have known were artificially high. Moreover, using its inflated common shares as currency, Nortel bought a Switzerland-based subsidiary of telecommunications manufacturer JDS Uniphase for US$2.5 billion. In effect, by failing to admit that Nortel's financial situation was worse than the markets had been led to believe, Nortel bought the subsidiary at a discount that was not deserved.

Two days after announcing the purchase of the JDS Uniphase assets, on February 15, 2001, after the close of trading, Nortel issued a press release conceding that sales in the coming year were going to be lower than expected and there would be layoffs. Share prices fell sharply, from $46 per share to $24 within a month, and investors lost tens of billions of dollars. Yet before the news was made public, Nortel's top executives had cashed in. Lawsuits allege that Chahram Bolouri, president of Nortel's global operations, sold shares in January 2001 that earned him US$2.4 million, while e-business president William Connor cashed in his shares worth US$4.6 million. Bill Hawe, Nortel's chief technology officer, exercised his stock options and earned a profit of US$18.6 million. Not surprisingly, one class action lawsuit charges Nortel's senior management with insider trading and having "profited at the expense of [shareholders] as such persons were able to buy and sell Nortel common securities with the benefit of material information which had not been publicly disclosed to [shareholders]."

Soon after the bad news hit the press that winter, Roth announced he was retiring. In total, he cashed in an astonishing US$135 million in stock options before he left the building (in 2000 Roth had had the temerity to deride Canada's tax policies as hurting the wealthy). He moved into a palatial mansion in Caledon, Ontario, to lord over his collection of expensive sports cars, including a classic 1967 Corvette and a 1966 Jaguar E-type, and to build a huge model train set.

WHILE ROTH CRIPPLED NORTEL, he didn't destroy it entirely. His successors, however, picked up where he left off. And in many respects they followed the same methods embraced by the executives running Enron, the American energy giant that collapsed in 2001 due to massive fraud.

At the time Roth left, Nortel was in peril, its stock plummeting— it would become penny stock at one point, with mass layoffs under way, 60,000 over the next two years—and the company ended 2001 with sales off original estimates by more than 35 percent. By the end of 2002, its stock had lost 99 percent of its peak value. The company closed 20 million square feet of office and manufacturing space and wrote down nearly US$16 billion of debt.

However, the manipulation of the company's financials went beyond just a few misleading press releases and statements to the media; it also involved playing fast and loose with a bevy of accounting practices that had the net effect of making Nortel more attractive to Bay Street investors—which is strikingly similar to what occurred at Enron. "The problem was that Nortel was inventing its own accounting," says Al Rosen, one of Canada's most esteemed forensic accountants. "They were discarding the cost of a whole bunch of expenses so they would not have to show such huge losses and [could] get people to invest more and more."

To this end, in 1999 the company adopted a bookkeeping practice called "earnings from operations," which in effect allowed Nortel to remove from its books the acquisition costs of new companies it was buying and to show investors it was making money when it was not. In 2000, this technique allowed Nortel to claim it could "earn" 26 cents per share in the fourth quarter and 16 cents in the next.

Nortel executives also skewed the numbers through "vendor financing," whereby the company aggressively offered hundreds of millions of dollars of credit to customers so they could buy Nortel equipment. According to one shareholders' lawsuit, these vendors were "uncreditworthy" and had no real means to pay for the product. Ferchat told me this practice began on a limited basis while he worked at Nortel but became more the norm after he left the company in the early nineties. "It allows you to hit your [sales] objectives," he explained. "All of this is driven by bonuses and objectives in stock prices." In short, vendor financing means you're buying your own product to boost your own bottom line.

A third method that Nortel's executives embraced was "bill and hold," which allows you to record a sale before you've delivered the product. Nortel had banned the practice in early 2000, but by the fall of that same year, as it was apparent they weren't going to meet their sales results, the company reinstated it. This allowed Nortel to record undelivered inventory sitting in storage as revenue. The company recorded more than US$1 billion in sales in 2000 alone through "bill and hold" transactions. Worse, John Foster, a project manager with Nortel's optical unit in Texas, saw that the company was recording revenue in 2000 for products that not only hadn't been built but weren't even scheduled to be engineered. He estimated that Nortel used this strategy to record $900 million of revenue that year alone. And not long after he was laid off in 2001, Foster approached the SEC and told them of his concerns and gave them incriminating documents. But he never heard back from them. "The revenue was being misstated," Foster later told the CBC. "There were people [at Nortel] who told me when I brought this up, 'You better keep quiet about that.' It becomes part of the culture where numbers become more important than the truth."

According to the SEC, these accounting methods were all overseen by Frank Dunn, Nortel's CFO, the person the board promoted to replace Roth as CEO. According to Melanie Johannink, a former Nortel executive assistant and PR and human resources staffer, Dunn was "a very aggressive, angry man." Dunn moved into the CEO's office in October 2001 and continued to massage the company's numbers.

In the summer of 2002, Dunn told analysts from the New York and Toronto investment communities that he expected Nortel to turn a profit by the second quarter of 2003. He also touted a "Return-to-Profitability" bonus plan to encourage Nortel's employees to reach this target. "This drive to profitability is based on the targeted break-even model of the quarterly revenues of below $2.4 million," Dunn told Bay Street analysts in the fall of 2002—perhaps the only people in town who might have understood what he was saying.

Executives were now under the gun, and to ensure these profit targets were met, Dunn and his senior financial team began using another bookkeeping scheme. While it was common practice to keep large cash reserves to deal with "worst-case" scenarios, the reserves were not, according to U.S. accounting laws, allowed to sit on the books indefinitely as a rainy day slush fund, as this would distort the picture of the company's health to investors and lead to stock manipulation. Just the same, Dunn and his senior management team set aside excess reserves in various silos so that the money could be released at a later date in order to help the company meet the profit targets they'd promised Wall Street. "That was certainly being done," says former Nortel treasurer Mike McCorkle. "In the cold light of day, it's managing earnings in order to manage the stock price."

At the end of 2002, Nortel discovered that it was going to earn a profit in its last quarter. This would have triggered payouts to Nortel staff through its return-to-profitability plan. Dunn thought investors would be unhappy with this quarterly payout, since the company had in fact lost $3 billion from overall operations across the whole year. So the profits were stashed away in excess reserves and the books manipulated to show nothing but the overall loss for year-end. By then, the company was sitting on US$453 million in reserves.

Nortel's leap into profitability was short-lived anyway, and early in 2003 it looked as if the company would continue to lose money, despite promises to become profitable by that summer. In fact, Nortel should have reported a loss of $124 million in its first quarter. Nonetheless, Dunn was eager to pay his top executives bonuses to ensure his management team stayed together, so he used the cash reserves to magically return Nortel to "profitability" even as the internal forecasts were worsening.

Dunn and his top executives then released US$274 million in reserves, and on April 24, 2003, Nortel announced a first-quarter "profit" of US$54 million. Dunn touted his success, stating that he was "extremely pleased to have achieved profitability in the first quarter of 2003 and reached [his publicly stated] goal one quarter early." Dunn publicly attributed Nortel's positive showing to nothing more than a well-run company: "I'm delighted with the results," he said. "We're profitable for the first time in three years, over three years, and we met our profitability objective one quarter early." Nortel executives pulled the same stunt when they released second quarter results for 2003, again releasing excess reserves to give a false picture of the company's overall health.

One result of this bit of bookkeeping flim-flammery was to trigger an outlay of over $90 million in bonuses, $19 million of which went to forty-three top executives while the remainder was spread out over the 30,000-person workforce. Of the $19 million, $5 million went to Dunn and Nortel's CFO, Douglas Beatty, and controller, Michael Gollogly. Dunn himself received $3.6 million in bonuses and a chunk of stock, which paid him an additional $2.9 million.

But Nortel's auditors, Deloitte & Touche, noticed the unorthodox use of reserves and began asking questions. They brought their concerns to Nortel's audit committee, who in turn hired a Washington, DC, law firm, WilmerHale, to investigate the matter. Meanwhile, Dunn continued to announce strong earnings. In January 2004, he gave interviews in which he touted the fourth-quarter results as showing a huge profit. The stock price rose on the TSE with the news and newspaper headlines trumpeted NORTEL SURGES ON STRONG RESULTS. "We expect to grow faster than the market in 2004," said Dunn.

WilmerHale's investigators combed through balance sheets, collected hundreds of thousands of emails from Nortel's financial employees, and eventually produced a report to the board. It was bad news. Very bad. Forensic specialists they'd hired concluded that the company's finance team "conveyed the strong leadership message that earnings targets could be met through the application of accounting practices that finance managers knew or ought to have known were not in compliance." The fallout was swift. The executives who had received return-to-profitability bonuses were forced to return them, and on April 28, 2004, the board sacked Dunn and Nortel's CFO and controller. At the time, Dunn was building a 10,800-square-foot lakeshore mansion in Oakville, Ontario, estimated to be worth up to $15 million. He and his lieutenants were later charged by the OSC, the SEC and the RCMP for securities violations (Dunn denied the fraud allegations levelled against him).

Nortel was forced to revise its earlier financial statements—which it would ultimately have to do four times between 2004 and 2007—and this latest scandal, coming so close on the heels of the 2001 disaster, placed the corporation in an even deeper hole. "The company was taking [so] much time working on the restatements that they lost track of the path of technology," says Melanie Johannink. "The financial restatements, the company transitions, the hardship the company was going through was more of a focus than the technology."

Nortel's board continued making poor personnel decisions, too. After a caretaker CEO took over from Dunn in 2004, the board hired Mike Zafirovski the following year. Zafirovski was an American who'd once worked as a top executive for Motorola, the telecom industry giant. When I asked Ferchat about Zafirovski's abilities as an executive, he was derisive: "It was really above his pay grade. He had never operated a stand-alone company in his life." Moreover, Zafirovski refused to move to Toronto, insisting on commuting from his home in Chicago. "So he flew around in the corporate jet, which is not cheap, and treated himself very well," Ferchat said. Furthermore, after Zafirovski took the Nortel job, Motorola sued him for breaching the terms of a nondisclosure contract he had signed with them. Nortel agreed to shell out $11.5 million to Motorola to settle the matter, and then proceeded to pay Zafirovski handsomely: a base salary of $1.2 million plus stock options. In 2007 alone, he made $10 million in total compensation, although he was laying off workers and not making much headway in reviving the company.

To be fair, Zafirovski was handed a badly listing enterprise whose technology was becoming out of date and whose competition had become stiffer than ever. On top of that, Nortel had to keep spending great sums due to the fallout from the Roth and Dunn years. Between 2005 and August 2009, Zafirovski estimated Nortel spent more than $400 million on outside auditors, management consultants and other accounting specialists. To settle the biggest investors' class action lawsuit, Nortel spent $2.4 billion and admitted to inflating revenues by $3.4 billion.

In the end, Zafirovski failed, and after the Harper government refused to rescue Nortel in the fall of 2008, the company announced it was seeking creditor protection.

Robert Ferchat and a group of other former Nortel executives tried to save the company in the spring of 2009, but the federal government refused to help. Soon afterwards, RIM was denied the right to bid on some of Nortel's biggest assets. Again the Harper government refused to intervene in the auction process to ensure a Canadian company benefited from this technological know-how, instead allowing the company's crown jewels to be sold to foreign companies.

As a Canadian corporation, the company was officially dead, its divisions gone to European and American high-tech multinationals. Investors had lost billions, and as the economy became ever more rooted in technology, Canada found itself without its biggest player. Three years after it had gone bust, Canadian companies were still spending less on research and development than they did in 2007—a decline often blamed on Nortel's disappearance.

In the spring of 2011, Nortel's portfolio of patents—covering six thousand inventions in every corner of the mobile computing and telecommunications landscape—was sold for $4.5 billion to a consortium made up of Microsoft, Apple, Ericsson, EMC, Sony and RIM. It was a price that revealed the true value of the company's assets and ingenuity. "Nortel used to hire three hundred to four hundred graduates a year," Ferchat lamented before he passed away from cancer in 2011. "That's gone. Nortel actually helped professors to stay up to date. It was like having a great teaching hospital, and if you have a great teaching source in emerging technology, your knowledge base grows exponentially. Nortel was a font of knowledge of physics and a hell of a lot of software, plus it provided the architecture of making large telecommunications systems. And that's just gone."

In January 2012, former CEO Frank Dunn, CFO Douglas Beatty and Controller Michael Gollogly went on trial in the Ontario Superior Court for two counts of fraud each.

With Nortel's death came the gnawing sense that our economy, beyond cutting down trees and pulling ore out of the ground, was increasingly based on thin air—a paper economy rooted in people trying to make money out of nothing but other people's money.

FIVE

HOW TO CORRUPT A STOCK MARKET

"I'D LIKE YOU TO meet someone."

"Who's that?"

"Semion is here."

They were seated at the hotel bar, and upon hearing this news, Joseph Groia turned to his legal assistant and coolly instructed her to go upstairs to her suite and wait for him.

Groia then followed Igor Fisherman, the 46-year-old chief operating officer of YBM Magnex Inc., through the modernist restaurant of the Marriott Hotel in Budapest, Hungary, to a large round table. There, presiding like a pasha, was Semion Mogilevich, a short, fat, balding, 52-year-old man with rounded shoulders and a salt-and-pepper moustache. Eating breakfast with his wife and son, Mogilevich was being watched over by a clutch of heavy-set eastern European bodyguards.

The sight of Mogilevich scared Groia stiff. It was July 1998, and the tall, imperious lawyer with the Montreal-based corporate law firm

Heenan Blaikie LLP had been hired by YBM's board and sent to Hungary to find out whether the industrial magnet manufacturer was a legitimate enterprise or an elaborate hoax. There had been allegations from regulators and the media that YBM was a front for the Russian mafia, a claim supported by an FBI raid on the company's Newton, Pennsylvania, head office two months earlier. YBM was listed on the Toronto Stock Exchange (TSE), with valued market capitalization amounting to the better part of a billion dollars at its peak.

Despite having its head office in the U.S.A. and its magnet factory on the outskirts of Budapest, as a corporate entity YBM was entirely Canadian. It first appeared on the markets in Alberta and its board was dominated by Canadian businessmen, financiers and corporate lawyers—most notably David Peterson, the Liberal premier of Ontario from 1985 to 1990. Weeks into a fact-finding mission that had already taken him from Toronto to Pennsylvania to London, Groia was attempting to unravel the company's secrets, and by his second day in Budapest he was certain YBM was a fraud. Any notion to the contrary was dashed as soon as he was introduced to Mogilevich, a godfather of the Russian mafia. Nicknamed the "Brainy Don," the "Billion Dollar Don" and, more ominously, "The Grave" for his ruthless methods, Mogilevich was thought by law enforcement to be the puppet master behind YBM.

"I've heard a lot about you," Mogilevich grumbled. "You're obviously a smart guy, and I have a lot of investments in Canada and the United States and I am always looking for smart guys. Perhaps you can help me?"

Groia assured the Russian mobster he would send him material about his law firm and would be delighted to assist him with his business affairs. Inconsequential chatter followed, and forty-five minutes later Mogilevich rose, shook Groia's hand and headed for the door, a dozen or so large men escorting him to a caravan of black SUVs waiting outside.

Groia told Igor Fisherman he was feeling jet-lagged and asked if he could postpone the day's business. He then rushed upstairs, told his assistant to pack, and together they sped to the airport, grabbing the first plane out of the country. Soon after arriving in Toronto, he broke the bad news to YBM's board: the Russian mob indeed controlled the company. David Peterson immediately resigned as a director. The YBM scandal, however, was only picking up speed. Enraged investors, lawsuits and charges of fraud soon entered the mix.

IF CANADA'S ECONOMY was increasingly based on chasing paper profits in the financial industry, then the YBM Magnex scandal says much about the ethical underpinnings of this flourishing sector.

While manufacturing declined as a source of employment and prosperity, high finance grew in significance, employing roughly 750,000 Canadians by 2010. In Toronto alone, more than 300,000 people were working for the financial sector, making it the third-largest financial services centre in North America, behind only Chicago and New York. In fact, one-third of the city's lawyers and accountants work for this industry in some capacity. And the wealth thrown off by Bay Street, especially through annual bonuses, visibly manifests itself in neighbourhoods such as Forest Hill and Rosedale. Houses already filled with fine furnishings and artwork, with the ubiquitous Mercedes, BMWs, Maseratis, Ferraris, Range Rovers and Jaguars parked in the driveways, are regularly renovated for millions of dollars. Moreover, as Wall Street and other financial centres around the world roiled from the body blows dealt by the credit crisis, Bay Street emerged as a shining star of financial prudence and propriety. Consequently, the Ontario government was designing its economic policy around the hope the financial industry would grow and make up for the loss of manufacturing jobs and the tax revenues they once generated. "In the new economy, Ontario doesn't make stuff anymore," *Toronto Life* magazine remarked in 2009. "We let other places do that; our new job is to lend, invest, and manage people's money." Canada's banks were now among the strongest on the continent and the TSX began aggressively wooing American entrepreneurs to raise capital on our capital markets.

But as the economy made this transformation, Bay Street's moral relativism came sharply into view. In the world of investing, the question always is whether you can trust the investment product, your broker, the financial institution standing behind it, the credit rating agencies and the regulators.

The financial industry likes to pride itself on being a white-shoe, respectable part of the economy. Banks and brokerage houses spend an inordinate amount of money on advertising campaigns portraying themselves as founts of investment wisdom who have investors' best interests at heart. When you speak with bankers, investment brokers and the corporate lawyers who work for them, their sense of authority (and of themselves) is palpable. Questioning their integrity is akin to suggesting they have fleas. In 2009, I was assembling a short CBC television documentary called "Can You Trust Your Broker?" and when I contacted the brokerage industry's lobby group, the Investment Industry Association of Canada (IIAC), for an interview, I was rebuffed out of hand. After the story ran, a Bay Street brokerage house filed a nuisance lawsuit against the CBC. The suit did not claim there were any factual errors with the piece, but the president of the firm dismissed it as "yellow journalism." (The CBC settled out of court for a small sum.)

The YBM Magnex scandal suggests that this haughty sense of integrity and trustworthiness in Bay Street could very well be misplaced. As Earl Cherniak, a respected Bay Street lawyer who later represented YBM investors in a legal action, told me: "There were all kinds of indications that this was not a kosher deal. [But] there were huge fees involved . . . The brokerage houses made enormous amounts of money, the law firm made all kinds of money, as did the accounting firms. There was money to be made." The deal in question was YBM's effort to raise money on the TSE for a company that was actually a front for organized crime. In the process, YBM exposed just how easy it is to corrupt Canada's capital markets.

"It's a cultural issue in my judgment," observes Michael J. Hershman, CEO of the Fairfax Group, a Virginia-based investigation firm that played a part in the YBM saga. "And the YBM case is indicative of a Canadian business environment which is a little Wild West in nature."

YBM HAD ITS ORIGINS in the collapse of the Soviet Union and the emergence of a class of Russian gangsters taking advantage of the post-socialist chaos. Semion Mogilevich, a Ukrainian who studied economics at the University of L'viv, began his criminal career in the 1970s and made his first millions by fleecing fellow Jews. In the mideighties, when tens of thousands of Jewish refugees fled to Israel and America, Mogilevich bought their assets on the cheap, promising to exchange the goods for fair market value and send them the proceeds. Instead, he sold the valuables and pocketed the profits.

In 1989, Mogilevich left Moscow, settled in Israel and became an Israeli citizen. Then, a year later, he married a Hungarian national, which allowed him to move to Budapest, where he began to build the foundations of his global empire. He bought a string of night-clubs in Prague, Riga and Kiev—they were called the "Black and White Clubs"—that were fronts for a flourishing trade in prostitution. Allegations of Mogilevich's crimes are extensively detailed in FBI and Israeli intelligence reports, which assert that he's trafficked in nuclear materials, drugs, prostitutes, precious gems and stolen art and engaged in extortion. He smuggled goods out of Moscow's Sheremetyevo International Airport, bought a bankrupt airline in a former central Asian Soviet republic to haul heroin out of the Golden Triangle—a densely jungled area that overlaps Thailand, Burma, Laos and Vietnam—and allegedly purchased much of the Hungarian armaments industry. In one deal, Mogilevich sold pilfered Warsaw Pact weapons—including ground-to-air missiles and twelve armoured troop carriers—to Iran for US$20 million.

Mogilevich does not shrink from using violence either. "[His] contract killers are trained by Russian members of the Afghan war," says a 1996 declassified FBI report. "Victims are repeatedly tortured and stabbed to death, rather than shot." During the 1990s, Mogilevich's organization had two posh villas outside the small town of Říčany, near Prague, where anyone who crossed him was savagely murdered. In 1998, after the American journalist Robert Friedman wrote an exposé about his criminal career for *The Village Voice*, Mogilevich put out a US$100,000 contract on his life. Friedman went into hiding. "He was a smart don," says Jim Moody, the head of the FBI's organized crime division from 1989 to 1996, "and his people were really vicious."

By the early nineties, Mogilevich was making so much money that he needed to launder it through legitimate companies in the West. Initially he focused on the U.K. and a London law firm then known as Blakes Solicitors. Posing as a businessman, he washed

US$50 million via the lawyers' trust accounts. In 1995, the London police raided their homes and seized US$2 million from their accounts in the Royal Bank of Scotland.

Mogilevich then shifted his attention to North America and its stock markets. Public companies are ideal vehicles to wash dirty money: they transform cash into stock and then increase its value by attracting investor interest. "They wanted a capacity to launder a lot of money," says Jay Naster, a former Ontario Securities Commission lawyer, "and putting it through a securities market is a wonderful way to do it."

Mogilevich realized the best way to access the North American markets was through Canada, "a better place because the U.S. had a lot of legislation that Canada didn't have," says the FBI's Jim Moody. The gangster's vehicle was YBM Magnex Inc., a Hungarian company that claimed to produce industrial magnets. Among its top officers were two Mogilevich associates, Igor Fisherman and Jacob Bogatin.

Getting YBM onto the North American markets took some ingenuity. Mogilevich set up the company's head office in Pennsylvania in early 1994, with Bogatin as its sole director and president. Fisherman soon joined the board. Meanwhile, a Mogilevich-controlled shell company, Pratecs Technologies Inc., was registered in Alberta at the same time (Pratecs merged with YBM Magnex in 1995). It was no accident that Alberta was selected: the province had a stock exchange that made it easy for anyone to establish a shell operation due to its poor due diligence over companies it agreed to list.

In the spring of 1995, British authorities launched a legal action against Mogilevich related to his money-laundering scam, and when Alberta Stock Exchange (ASE) officials learned of this, they halted trading in Pratecs shares. Still, due to lack of co-operation from

Russian authorities, the case against Mogilevich collapsed, and the ASE immediately allowed Pratecs to resume trading, even though British authorities considered Mogilevich so unsavoury that they banned him from entering the U.K.

In fact, Mogilevich's name was quietly listed with the Alberta Securities Commission as an original YBM shareholder in 1994, at the very time he was becoming notorious in Russian organized crime circles. The FBI were fully aware of his activities by then, including his ties to North America.

In 1996, Mogilevich and five of his associates owned nearly one third of the company's shares and his own people filled key executive positions. In March of that year, the company was listed on the Toronto Stock Exchange (TSE) and its shares posted for trading. Stamping YBM with an imprimatur of respectability was critical, especially as the company's board consisted of an odd collection of retired scientists, a realtor and controversial Howe Street speculators. Two key people were then approached and agreed to sign on: Owen Mitchell, a vice-president and director of First Marathon Securities Ltd., and David Peterson, the former premier of Ontario.

Mitchell invested his own money in YBM (he had as much as $2 million wrapped up in the company at one point), and First Marathon, a Toronto-based brokerage house, became one of YBM's underwriters (whose job is to encourage investors to buy a company's stock). Peterson, who invested $50,000 in YBM, was chairman of Cassels Brock & Blackwell LLP, one of the powerful "Seven Sisters" Bay Street law firms, and Cassels Brock became YBM's corporate counsel. Another senior Cassels Brock partner, Lawrence Wilder, was brought in to offer legal guidance. Other blue-chip companies also gave their seal of approval to YBM. The investment dealer Griffiths McBurney & Partners joined as an underwriter, and

Pennsylvania-based Parente, Randolph, Orlando, Carey & Associates, a certified public accounting firm, became YBM's auditor. The air of respectability was in place.

From all appearances, this collection of people and institutions were swayed by YBM's claims of being a legitimate magnet manufacturer, but nobody bothered to look any closer to see if this was actually the case.

IT WASN'T LONG BEFORE a series of alarm bells went off. The first occurred in January 1996, when two YBM employees from Hungary, who had already worked in the United States, were denied visas to re-enter America. Explaining the move, the U.S. State Department said they had information YBM was conducting some "illegal activity." YBM hired a law firm to investigate why the visas were denied. They soon learned that the U.S. Attorney General's Office was involved in a highly sensitive investigation of the company.

A board meeting was convened and the directors received the bad news. The lawyers also informed the board about a 1995 article in the Russian newspaper *Izvestia*, linking the company to organized crime. YBM's board struck a special committee, chaired by Owen Mitchell, to look into the rumours swirling around the company. A corporate investigation firm, The Fairfax Group, a reputable Virginia-based outfit whose staff included an ex-governor of Rhode Island and former personnel from KPMG, FBI, the CIA and Scotland Yard, was hired to find out why was YBM being investigated by U.S. authorities. Just one month into Fairfax's investigation, they heard from intelligence sources that YBM and Mogilevich were connected.

In March of 1997, two Fairfax investigators, Clayton McManaway, a former State Department official and diplomat, and William

Larkin, a forensic accountant, briefed Mitchell on their findings to date, telling him known crime figures were involved with YBM's management and the company was under investigation by the FBI. McManaway later told the OSC that he "was struck by the lack of reaction" by Mitchell to their findings and that Mitchell never asked any significant questions. McManaway claimed he offered the YBM director typed notes of his findings, but Mitchell refused to accept them.

Fairfax then conducted meetings with YBM's special committee, attended by Mitchell and board members Harry Antes, Michael Schmidt, Jacob Bogatin and Cassels Brock counsel Lawrence Wilder. The Fairfax investigators told the directors that the founding shareholders, including Mogilevich, were all tied to or were members of Solntsevskaya, a Russian organized crime group. They said that these shareholders retained significant ownership of YBM and exerted considerable influence over the company. While they found no evidence of money laundering, indications of it were present in the company's European operations.

Fairfax also said they had been unable to confirm whether companies that were supposed to be YBM customers were real, that they had found "a lack of inventory" and suspected "possible cooked books." They also identified five employees—including CEO Jacob Bogatin and COO Igor Fisherman—as cause for alarm. "Our concerns about the current relationship between the original investors and the company are stock ownership, influence through Fisherman and others, difficulty dislodging them . . . [and] possible covert intelligence operations," said Fairfax's briefing notes. In Hungary the Fairfax investigators found records kept in milk cartons in a damp basement, receipts for equipment purchased from the original investors that appeared brand new even though the transactions had occurred years earlier, and invoices for large dollar figures that were addressed to post office boxes.

Fairfax also outlined concerns that YBM magnets were being used in weapons production, which, given Mogilevich's ties to organized crime and the arms black market, might be a problem for the board and YBM's investors. "Most ominous is [a] possible triggering device for nuclear weapons," they said, and expressed further misgivings over firms with which YBM allegedly did business. One, a supposed customer in Israel, "does not exist," their notes declared. Fairfax checked out two other magnet buyers and found "offices of an attorney" and no sign of either firm. "We didn't pull any punches and we certainly didn't tell them anything we didn't have reason to believe was correct," recalls Michael J. Hershman, the CEO of Fairfax. "The report raised some very serious red flags, unavoidable for anyone to have ignored."

At that point, the prudent thing for the directors to do would have been to shut down YBM and never attempt to raise money from investors. But they chose not to. Strangely enough, the special committee did not even ask for a formal written report from Fairfax. Instead, Mitchell and Lawrence Wilder compiled their own report to present to the board based on Fairfax's findings.

In April 1997, Mitchell sent a draft of this report to Fairfax, seeking comment. When Fairfax investigators reviewed it, they grew alarmed, telling Mitchell his report was inaccurate and did not reflect what Fairfax had discovered. In court documents Fairfax investigator William Larkin would later say the special committee's report "reads as if the work conducted [by Fairfax] never took place . . . Mitchell failed to include in his draft report the information which [Fairfax] had provided to Mitchell: it was a white-wash." Philip Stern, the most senior Fairfax investigator and a former U.S. special prosecutor, called the report "spin-doctoring." The report Mitchell presented to the full board did discuss the connection of YBM's founding shareholders to organized crime, including Mogilevich, but dismissed it as being unimportant with no evidence supporting the allegations. The report also said that there was no evidence that senior management of YBM was "in any way involved in any illegal or improper activities." Overall, the report gave YBM a clean bill of health.

To this day, Fairfax remains shocked at how YBM's special committee responded to their findings. "I have to tell you that this is probably the most egregious example of a company ignoring information that would have an adverse effect on investors and stakeholders," says Michael J. Herschmann. "From time to time we might issue a report that clients might take issue with parts of: they might ask us to go back and clarify certain things or do additional work. But when we come up with information that indicates the involvement of organized crime in a company, I have never had a situation where that was simply ignored."

YBM began efforts to raise money from investors. As this plan gained momentum, Canadian stock market regulators did little to stop it.

THE RCMP HAD BEEN KEEPING YBM under observation since 1995 and was receiving information about the company from the FBI. In the spring of 1997, knowing that YBM was assembling a prospectus for equity financing, the FBI asked the Mounties to inform the Ontario Securities Commission (OSC) about their concerns regarding YBM and the likelihood it was a front for the Russian mafia. "We were trying to warn [the OSC] not to approve it, or stall it, or hold off or investigate, but don't allow the prospectus because we had reason to believe it's a fraud," Thomas Fuentes, the head of the FBI's organized crime division from 1997 to 2002, told me. "And they didn't believe us."

To be fair, the FBI and RCMP had not furnished any substantive proof to the OSC, and had refused to be identified as the source of the warnings—standard operating procedure in cases where no charges have been laid and they're relying on intelligence sources for information (the RCMP refused to admit that they were even investigating YBM and would only say that they were monitoring the company). The U.S. Attorney's office also wouldn't officially admit that YBM was under investigation.

In the summer of 1997, YBM filed its preliminary prospectus with the OSC. The plan was to raise $100 million on the markets. The document made no mention of the special committee, the Fairfax investigation or its findings. Three days after the prospectus was filed, the OSC received a memo from the Toronto Stock Exchange (TSE) describing a conversation between Michael Haddad, one of the TSE's chief investigators, and an official from a French bank. The memo said the bank had had dealings with YBM and it believed the company was "obviously involved in money laundering." French officials were investigating the matter. Attached to the memo was a report from the French bank entitled "Some Strange Facts About YBM Magnet Business," which detailed irregularities with YBM's sales and volumes, including boasting huge sales without having any significant customers in Europe. A TSE official warned the OSC not to approve the prospectus because it would be "worse than Bre-X"— the Canadian gold mining scam that cost investors $6 billion when it blew up in 1997.

The OSC began meeting with YBM personnel, informing the company about the allegation YBM was involved in money laundering. In the end, the OSC pressured YBM into hiring the accounting firm Deloitte & Touche LLP, to conduct a full audit before the prospectus would be approved.

In October 1997, YBM released the results of Deloitte's audit. Though it identified a number of irregularities in reported sales, it too gave the company a clean bill of health. The audit, however, was strangely limited. YBM hadn't given the auditors any material from the Fairfax investigation (or even told them of its existence); furthermore, though Deloitte was capable of carrying out a forensic audit—a specialized look at YBM that could potentially uncover a money-laundering scam—neither OSC nor YBM asked it to do so.

Nonetheless, with the Deloitte audit in hand the OSC faced a dilemma: does it allow the prospectus to go ahead or continue to stall? Meanwhile, the OSC kept on receiving bad news about YBM. In early November, OSC lawyer Jay Naster heard from another unidentified source that YBM's sales figures and profit statements were inaccurate. His superior, Kathy Soden, the OSC's manager of market operations, also received damning information from the RCMP. And yet, despite having "serious concerns about the integrity of the company," she decided the OSC had no grounds to prevent the prospectus from proceeding "without evidence to back up the allegations."

"Maybe regulators *should* work on rumour and innuendo and based on allegations denied by the company," says Naster, in justifying the OSC's decision to approve the prospectus, "but you would have a hard time defending that in a court of law."

Joe Groia, a former head of enforcement at the OSC, disagrees, saying the commission was under no obligation to approve YBM's prospectus. "There is no fucking way the OSC should have given that receipt for that prospectus," says the lawyer. He points out that if the company had been denied and had asked for a hearing, whatever law enforcement was telling the OSC could have been aired at that time. Instead, no doubt influenced by the corporate heavyweights lined up behind the company, on November 20, 1997, the OSC allowed YBM to proceed. Underwritten by First Marathon Securities, Griffiths McBurney & Partners, ScotiaMcLeod, Canaccord Capital Corp. and Gordon Capital, YBM immediately became a favourite among a group of Canada's most prominent analysts and money managers, who promoted it heavily to investors as the Bay Street hype machine went into overdrive. YBM quickly raised $100 million. Buoyed by reports of rapidly increasing sales and profits, the stock rose to $20 in March 1998. The company suddenly had a market value of nearly $1 billion.

AND THEN THE WHOLE THING came unstuck very fast. When Deloitte & Touche started auditing YBM's 1997 financial records, it found extraordinary irregularities regarding a series of transactions. Deloitte's staff met with YBM's audit committee and directors and told them they would have to complete a forensic audit. The accounting firm refused to sign off on the previous year's figures until this was carried out.

Instead of coming clean about the breadth of Deloitte's concerns, YBM released its first quarter results for 1998, despite the fact that the audit for the previous year was incomplete. Nevertheless, the stock price began to unravel. In May 1998, FBI agents raided the company's head office in Newtown, Pennsylvania, and the OSC finally issued a cease trade order. Still, according to a lawsuit later filed by the court-appointed receiver, Griffiths McBurney continued to trade a significant quantity of YBM shares for its Russian clients as much as nine months after the stock had been halted. For example, the brokerage house, the lawsuit said, netted over $400,000 in commissions for selling $27 million worth of YBM shares in one day. In other words, while investors were losing their shirts, the brokers were making a fortune.

In 1999, the OSC charged the company's directors and top executives and underwriters with failing to provide proper disclosure when they submitted YBM's prospectus and with failing to publicize Deloitte's refusal to finish the 1997 audit. David Peterson made the audacious but unsuccessful move of trying to get the charges against him dismissed by launching a lawsuit against the OSC. He claimed that because the commission had "superior knowledge" about YBM's ties to organized crime, they should never have okayed the prospectus in the first place—a tremendously galling stance to take.

Scattered over three years, the OSC hearings into the YBM scandal took up 124 days of testimony, with the commission finally coming down with its verdict in 2003. It levied fines totalling $1.2 million (which most observers saw as a pittance) and banned five of the company's officers from working for publicly traded companies, some permanently. Peterson escaped punishment, although in its decision the OSC clearly felt he should have done more to stop the scandal from happening: "While Peterson meets the legal test of due diligence, the panel remains disappointed that he did not offer more insight and leadership to the board in these circumstances." Afterwards, *The Globe and Mail*'s business columnist Eric Reguly caustically summarized the former premier's role by saying the OSC's findings suggested that "membership on YBM's board was just another job for Mr. Peterson. He testified at the OSC hearings that he did not take notes or keep a file while he was a YBM director, but insisted he tried to determine the truth about the company's alleged mob links . . . He did not attend any meetings of the Fairfax group, the investigator hired by the special committee to gather information about YBM's background and status with the U.S. State Department."

And investors? How much did they lose? They launched lawsuits against YBM's directors, its underwriters and Cassels Brock. Estimates of their losses ranged as high as $875 million. To settle the suits, the defendants collectively shelled out $120 million in 2002 — or about 14 cents on the dollar, depending on how you calculate the losses. One indictment said the Russian mobsters used companies and bank accounts in more than 20 countries to shuffle money about, defrauding an estimated US$150 million from shareholders. The U.S. government estimated that Mogilevich personally pocketed over US$18 million, while Jacob Bogatin took US$10 million and Igor Fisherman US$3 million. Only Bogatin was arrested and jailed. In 2009, the FBI finally put Mogilevich on its "10 Most Wanted" fugitive list. He remains at large, living in Russia.

DEFENDERS OF CANADA'S CAPITAL MARKETS will claim YBM was an aberration, a perfect storm of criminality combined with a lack of regulatory oversight that is a once-in-a-lifetime occurrence. But the manipulation of Canada's capital markets and banks by organized crime to launder money is actually commonplace. In the 1980s, Montreal crime boss Vito Rizzuto controlled Penway Explorers Ltd., a junior resource company listed on the Alberta Stock Exchange that was used in a pump-and-dump scam (whereby criminals buy a listed company, attract investors by overhyping the stock and then disappear with the cash they raise). Police also found that the Rizzuto and Caruana-Cuntrera crime families laundered at least US$35 million through Montreal's City and District Savings Bank (now Laurentian Bank of Canada) and two other financial institutions. In the 2000s, the Rizzutos used the Montreal-based hedge fund Norshield Financial Group to invest profits in offshore accounts. In 2007, police tied Rizzuto associates to Financement Malts Inc., a Laval, Quebec, loan and mortgage company that police say was the centre of a money-laundering web.

That same year, I was in Italy researching a story about the Calabrian mafia, the 'Ndrangheta, which has a powerful presence in Canada's underworld. The 'Ndrangheta is one of the world's largest criminal syndicates, with estimated annual revenues of $68 billion. I went to see Alberto Cisterna of the National Anti-Mafia Directorate at his offices in downtown Rome. The scholarly-looking young magistrate has spent over twenty years investigating the Calabrian mafia and he told me that the 'Ndrangheta loves Canada, especially because of our banks. "Over the years there have been investigations in Italy that proved the Calabrian mafia was using Canadian banks to launder money they earned from drug trafficking," he said.

In British Columbia, the Hells Angels have a track record of laundering money through publicly traded companies listed on the Vancouver Stock Exchange, and of employing lawyers to help set up such companies.

Most Canadians, of course, are not mobsters or bikers, nor do they associate with them or invest their money in mob-influenced companies. Most Canadians' connection to the financial industry lies through their own broker or investment adviser. And it's at that entry point where Bay Street's proclivity for thieving and deceiving investors begins.

SIX

PAUPERISM BY A THOUSAND CUTS

L ARRY ELFORD HAD A talent for ticking off his bosses and colleagues. He sometimes made them look bad, and often publicly
so. In 2000, Elford was earning a very handsome salary as a top investment adviser at RBC Dominion Securities in Lethbridge, Alberta,
and had every reason to lay low and carry on. And yet, perhaps
against his better judgment, he felt compelled to pen a column for
the local paper, the *Lethbridge Herald*, divulging how brokers quietly
charge their clients fees that are hidden. "If you're a salesman, you
could juice the thing, squeeze the thing, for three or four types of
compensation for selling certain types of product," explains Elford.
"And then of course you would be on the vice-president's list of your
(brokerage) and they would call you a big swinging dick." His bosses
and fellow brokers were not amused with his candour in print. "It
really pissed off the troops," Elford told me.

Elford is that rarity, a thoughtful refugee of the financial industry
who talks openly about his experiences, if not a Don Quixote figure

trying to ram his lancet through the heart of a business he worked in for twenty years. Like most brokers and investment advisers, Elford was a guide for his clients into the financial services industry, helping them understand a mysterious world where people speak an arcane language, blind faith is assumed and necessary, and the reasons why you prosper or lose your shirt are rarely understood.

Most people's involvement with the financial industry begins and ends with their broker or financial adviser. These relationships are based on trust, even friendship, and are rooted in the belief that your professional representative has your best interests at heart. In Canada, 130,000 investment professionals peddle a bewildering array of products, including mutual funds, guaranteed investment certificates (GICs), stocks, bonds, RRSPs, income trusts, asset-backed commercial paper and exchange traded funds (ETFs). Inside the business, ordinary working- and middle-class people, known as retail investors, are the lowest priority, the truly affluent receive considerably more attention, while those treated with the greatest care are institutional investors such as pension funds, hedge funds and the banks themselves.

Most Canadians are retail investors, and whether or not their broker or financial adviser makes those investors money, they do make bountiful livings for themselves. Rain or shine, bull or bear market, says Elford, "the financial industry is sound as a dollar on the banking side because they can gouge you by a few percent a year." In fact, when bank profits fall in one area of their business, they keep their coffers full by increasing fees in another area. For instance, in the summer of 2011, as capital markets and investment banking profits fell among Canada's chartered banks, they moved to boost earnings by collectively raising mortgage rates.

The financial services industry takes your money and says it will do its best to earn you more by investing it. Sometimes you make money, sometimes you lose it, but the banks and brokerages themselves don't really engage in the gamble; instead, to ensure themselves a steady stream of income, they hit you with fees and commissions each step of the way—fees and commissions and penalties that are buried in the fine print of everything you buy from them.

Ultimately, this is why Larry Elford became so disenchanted with the business. He joined the industry in 1984 at age twenty-four, taking an entry-level position with Dominion Securities Pitfield in Lethbridge, Alberta, a city of 75,000 near the American border. To be able to sell investment products and give advice, he took the Canadian Securities Course—a correspondence course which takes, on average, just three months to complete. "The education to be a financial adviser or stockbroker is, in fact, very limited," explains Chris Robinson, a professor of finance and accounting at York University's School of Administrative Studies. "You don't need a university degree, a grade twelve education is it." Consequently, says Robinson, the industry has "a large number of investment advisers with very limited education and with strong incentives to do things that are in not the best interests of their clients. That's the iceberg not showing up."

For Elford, getting established as a young broker in Lethbridge meant either finding clients or cleaning out his desk. The credo was "achieve or leave" and "eat what you kill." Unconnected, he had little choice but to make cold calls and knock on doors to find investors. "It's very difficult for a mid-twenty-year-old kid to convince people that they should trust him with their money," he remembers, and for the first five years he struggled, earning as little as $13,000 a year. Twice he received letters from his bosses warning him he would be let go if he didn't perform better.

But then his luck changed. He discovered a mutual fund that offered clients tax deductions, and his career was saved. His turnaround coincided with a major upheaval in the industry: in 1987, Canada's financial services sector was deregulated, allowing the chartered banks to buy and own brokerage houses, something they'd previously been forbidden to do.

AFTER THE GREAT DEPRESSION, bankers and brokers were prevented from co-existing under the same roof due to the reckless behaviour of traders bringing the banking system to the edge of total collapse. Also, as stand-alone operations, brokerage houses were owned by their partners—like law firms—and so there was little incentive to sell clients toxic investments, according to Diane Urquhart, who joined the industry in the 1970s. "The ethics were much higher," she insists. "If the investment analyst felt this product was not sound, the investment house and CEO would inevitably say we're not going to enter the market with it. They were concerned about reputational damage to the firm if their customers lost money. They were worried the partners would lose their own net worth invested in the firm."

After deregulation, the chartered banks gobbled up most of the big investment houses, and today the sector is dominated by bank-owned outfits: the Royal Bank of Canada owns RBC Dominion Securities Ltd.; the Bank of Nova Scotia runs Scotia Capital Inc.; the Bank of Montreal has BMO Nesbitt Burns Inc.; the Canadian Imperial Bank of Commerce owns CIBC World Markets Corp.; the Toronto-Dominion Bank operates TD Securities Inc.; and the National Bank of Canada owns National Bank Financial Inc. Once the big banks took over, says Elford, the culture changed towards selling the banks' proprietary products, whether they were any good or not. Brokers became "investment advisers," and their focus was volume—finding as many clients as possible and getting them into as much investment product as possible. Their role, Elford says, was reduced to that of salespeople, of "product pushers."

Urquhart reached the same conclusion while working at Scotia Capital during the 1990s. "Thirty years ago," she says, "the brokers were very involved with the research operations in identifying quality investments for customers and then servicing them. Today, you need not take any personal responsibility for the losses borne by your customers."

Elford feels that the banks are not interested in training their staff to make wise investment decisions, and a lack of knowledge far too often means that your average broker doesn't know what's contained in the complicated and exotic investments he or she is selling. (Collateralized debt obligations and asset-backed commercial paper, which were at the heart of the 2007–2009 global financial meltdown, are good examples. Many brokers had no idea what these "instruments" really were or contained.) "Brokers who work for investment houses do not have the education or the skill or the time to be able to determine whether an income product with structured features is safe and suitable for customers," says Urquhart. "They are in the same position as the customer in that they're not receiving any transparency on the product."

Christopher Thomas also saw this sell-at-any-cost culture take over during his thirty-five years toiling for Bay Street brokerage houses. Old-school and genteel, he joined the business in the 1960s and remembers brokers being strongly motivated to ensure their clients prospered. He left the industry in 1997 to set up Measuredmarkets Inc. in Port Hope, Ontario, a company that tracks insider trading on the markets. Thomas remembers that when the banks took over the industry, "there was massive pressure to gather assets, find clients, bring the money in and worry about the investment decision later . . . When I worked for a large bank-owned investment firm, they said, 'Oh, you don't even need to read the newspaper, we will tell you what to give your clients.'" Thomas once attended a luncheon with colleagues in Toronto where a mutual fund company representative made a presentation claiming his products performed better than their competitors. "You're making unfair comparisons using a different type of scale than your competitors," Thomas told the representative. His bosses were not pleased. "I was reprimanded for having embarrassed the mutual fund company . . . although what was being presented was fraudulent. The pressure upon the brokers to follow the company line is immense."

IN ELFORD'S CASE, Dominion Securities Pitfield was snapped up by the Royal Bank of Canada, becoming RBC Dominion Securities. With markets booming during the nineties, Elford produced as much as $1 million in annual commissions and oversaw $100 million in assets. (His salary was a comfortable $300,000 a year.) He acquired a staff, sold a range of investment products and became a member of the firm's coveted Chairman's Council, reserved for the top 5 percent of salespeople in the country. He was rewarded with a vacation to Rome, and in 2001 he was given a prize by the Better Business Bureau for being one of the most ethical businessmen in Lethbridge.

Yet Elford kept seeing things that made him very uneasy, and he grew increasingly vocal with his complaints. One big irritation was how fees were levied on customers. The investment industry is chary of educating clients about what they are being charged—you have to read the boilerplate fine print on documents to glean this informa-tion—and these fees are not tallied up or otherwise apparent on your bank statements. In the case of mutual funds, the commissions are disclosed, but usually only once a year."You are being charged this fee that you can't see," says York University's Chris Robinson. "You have to pay for it and you don't realize how much they are taking away."

Most people would assume that brokers or investment advisers make money only if their clients make money. Not so. Their com-pensation is based less on profits they generate for clients and more on chargeable fees and the amount of clients' assets they have under management. In short, by the mere act of investing your money—whether that investment pans out or not—the industry prospers. In fact, it's not uncommon for brokers and advisers to generate extra fees through "churning," the daily or weekly buying or selling of securities just to earn commissions. To make matters worse, brokers have a built-in incentive to sell instruments with the highest hidden charges. "You could make twice the commission by putting your cli-ents in a more expensive plan," explains Elford.

These hidden fees can put a serious crimp on your savings and retirement plans. In 2010, a *Daily Telegraph* investigation in the U.K. found that over £7.3 billion (or C$11.6 billion) was being "skimmed off" by Britain's bankers from eight million investors every year in the form of hidden fees and levies. Your average British investor was losing $1,275 a year to such fees. If they put $80,000 into a fund pro-viding typical returns over twenty-five years, they would pay $172,000 in unnecessary charges, the paper found.

The exact same phenomenon exists in Canada. A study commis-sioned in 2007 by the University of Toronto's Rotman International Centre for Pension Management compared the average returns of

Canadian equity mutual funds with the equity component of pension plans between 1996 and 2004. By then, Canadians had $650 billion of their savings in mutual funds. And yet, year over year, it found that pension plans generated more returns for investors than mutual funds—3.8 percent more on average. The reason was simple: the fees attached to mutual funds were so high that you would have to plough twice as much money into a mutual fund than a pension plan to end up with the same amount when you retire. "I am effectively robbing you of half of your retirement," says Elford. Indeed, as much as $25 billion a year of investors' money goes directly into the pockets of brokers and other financial industry folks in mutual fund fees that investors would otherwise keep if they were in pension plans. "No matter how objective these people try to be, there is a natural underlying incentive to sell product for which they make the highest fees. It's as logical as night follows day," says the study's co-author, Keith Ambachtsheer, director of Rotman's pension management centre and a globally respected authority on the subject. And fees levied on investors in Canada are among the highest in the developed world. "The fee-based products in Canada, such as mutual funds, have fees that are often two times what retail customers in other countries would pay," says Urquhart.

This is true. A study conducted in 2009 by Morningstar Inc., a Chicago-based independent investment research company, found that a typical front-end load fee for a Canadian mutual fund is 5 percent—often paid because investors were unaware it was a negotiable sum (in the U.S. it was as low as 2 percent). A typical investor in a Canadian equity mutual fund pays a fee of 2 to 2.5 percent of their total assets to the fund manager. In comparison, the study found, an American would pay less than 1 percent. Moreover, unique to Canada are so-called "trailer-fees" paid directly to investment advisors as a sort of maintenance tax. Morningstar found that fees on Canadian mutual funds were "notoriously high."

"Canadian investors do not pay much attention to fees," the study concluded. "Canadian investors are comfortable with fees because they don't know how low these fees should actually be. Assets tend to flow into average- or higher-fee funds because Canadian investors use financial advisors to help them make decisions. Advisors direct client assets to funds that pay better trailers. And since the trailer is included in the (management expense ratio), the result is that assets flow into higher-fee funds."

Just how much fees and commissions can add up was revealed after the collapse of Portus Alternative Asset Management Inc., a Toronto-based hedge fund set up by two financial neophytes, Michael Mendolson and Boaz Manor, in 2003. Portus managed to raise $800 million from 26,000 investors before it was shut down in 2005 amidst fraud allegations. Of the total raised, Mendolson and Manor diverted $110 million to run the hedge fund and pay fees and commissions to investment advisers who'd recommended to clients they invest in Portus   ›

IN 2002, ELFORD QUIT RBC Dominion Securities and took a job with the Bank of Nova Scotia's brokerage house, ScotiaMcLeod. He sued RBC for constructive dismissal, claiming they forced him out because of his vocal complaints about ethical problems within the industry. Elford was seeking $13 million in damages. RBC countersued and those lawsuits were still ongoing by 2012.

His life at ScotiaMcLeod wasn't much better — "I found one bank was really no different from the other," he told me — and two years later he quit the business altogether. Now retired, he's been a vocal critic ever since, producing documentaries and articles and writing letters to newspapers, usually emphasizing that the real danger facing investors is not the odd rogue broker. "I think rogue brokers are a bit of a distraction. They can say they caught this guy doing something and it allows our entire system to get away with crime and financial abuse far greater than any rogue broker or group of them would do. I think we have a rogue system. We don't have a few bad apples — we have a bad barrel that allows people to be misrepresented and misinformed and misled to an awful extent."

Nevertheless, when brokers and investment advisers do go rogue and become outright thieves, the damage they cause can be enormous.

SEVEN

BROKERS GONE WILD:
A ROGUES' GALLERY

J UST DAYS BEFORE IAN Thow fled to the United States, one step ahead of the RCMP, Shirley Garwood and her sister Helena "Dolly" Kells drove up to the gates of his estate. The mutual fund salesman owned a 6,500-square-foot mansion near the coastal village of Brentwood Bay on Vancouver Island, with cedar beams, vaulted ceilings, rough-hewn stone and floor-to-ceiling windows. From there, Thow could gaze out over his $100,000 wharf and enjoy the sight of his $1.5 million Sea Ray yacht bobbing gently on the waves. In addition to the house, which was worth $4.6 million, Thow owned a helicopter, two executive jets, a Hummer, a Porsche Boxster, two Mercedes-Benzes and a Cadillac. It was August 2005 and Garwood and Kells arrived highly agitated.

Thow was a senior vice-president of Berkshire Investment Group Inc., a member of Berkshire's advisory board and manager of the firm's Victoria, B.C., branch. Owned by the Jamaican-Canadian billionaire Michael Lee-Chin, Berkshire sold mutual funds. Thow had convinced the two sisters to invest $405,000 with the firm and to take out a $200,000 mortgage on their home to do so. It was their entire retirement savings (plus their equity), and, given their ages— Garwood was in her late sixties, Kells nearly eighty—they could ill afford to lose it. When the women heard that Thow was under a cloud and was about to declare bankruptcy, they tried to reach him. They wanted to know what was happening to their savings. But he wasn't picking up his phone, so they showed up at his doorstep.

"We drove through the gate and he told us on the intercom to stop right there," recalls Garwood. "He came to us on a motorcycle. He never let us further onto the grounds, just left us near the gate."

In his mid-forties, Thow was six foot three and weighed well over two hundred pounds, an imposing, gregarious figure with a firm handshake. He liked to call Garwood and Kells his "favourite ladies" whenever he dropped in on them at their Victoria home, gift basket in hand. On this day, when they asked Thow if their money was at risk, he was reassuring, saying, "No, no, this is just a big misunder-standing. Don't believe what you hear because it's all false. I'll take care of you because you're my two favourite ladies and I wouldn't want anything to happen to you."

Thow was a fraud artist. He had systematically ripped off the sav-ings and retirement funds of long-time friends and seventy-three of his clients—including Garwood and Kells—to the tune of $32 mil-lion over a three-year period. His crimes bear special scrutiny because they illustrate just how long scammers like him can get away with their deceptions—with little punishment meted out if they are caught—because checks and balances in the industry are so weak. Moreover, these are often people who work for the leading banks and brokerage houses in Canada.

Gary Logan, a former Toronto Police Service investigator, believes that many more rogue brokers exist in the financial industry than is acknowledged because the mechanisms designed to catch them so often fail, and because investment houses often make huge profits from the fraud artists in their employ. Logan, who spent sixteen years investigating frauds on Canada's capital markets, points out, "These firms rely on the activities of the investment advisers to generate base income and bonuses at the end of the year," and this creates a disincentive to closely scrutinize these employees' behaviour when they lose sight of the line between being aggressive and being a criminal.

IAN THOW WAS BORN in California in 1961 and moved as a boy with his parents to Vancouver. As a young man he tried his hand at being a travel agent before becoming a mutual fund salesman in 1988 with Investors Group, a Winnipeg-based investment management outfit. By the mid-nineties, Thow was earning over $600,000 a year as Investors' regional manager in Victoria. In 1998, he quit Investors to set up the Victoria branch of Berkshire, an investment company established by Lee-Chin in the early nineties that would eventually have over $12 billion of assets under management. Thow continued to prosper, and soon became a fixture on Victoria's charity circuit while making a host of celebrity friends, including Patrick Duffy (of *Dallas* fame), who would join him on gambling, drinking and fishing excursions to vacation destinations like Las Vegas and Jamaica.

Shirley Garwood and Helena Kells first met Thow in the late eighties when he was at Investors, and followed him to Berkshire. He utterly charmed them and they relished his frequent house calls over the years. "I always said to him, 'I wish our daughter would meet someone like you,' because he was such a nice and sincere family man," says Garwood. But things began to sour for the sisters in 2004 when several of their mutual funds lost money. Thow suggested a plan to make back the cash: invest in the mortgages of real estate developers. The fact the sisters had little cash didn't faze him. Thow told them to liquidate their Berkshire account, cash in their RRSPs and borrow against their house. He also arranged a line of credit for them with the Bank of Nova Scotia. The sisters handed over $405,000, and shortly thereafter Thow stopped visiting. The two women never received a single document detailing where their money had actually gone. "I feel like an idiot that I didn't ask him for paper," moans Garwood. "We trusted this man. That's all I can tell you."

Thow had perfected a model of separating investors from their cash. He was superb at beguiling people with his visible trappings of success—the mansion, private jets, luxury cars and yacht—all of which suggested security and success, while he engendered enormous goodwill through his charity work. If necessary, he would also pull out his trump card: Michael Lee-Chin. Thow pressed his clients to attend the billionaire's speeches whenever he was in town. Investors fell for it in droves.

Daryl Goodwin was one. An Air Canada pilot Thow had met when they were teenagers at flight school, he bumped into Thow years later at a hockey game in Victoria. Thow set out to woo Goodwin and his relatives by taking them on trips in his private jet, boasting he earned $7 million a year at Berkshire and that he was worth $350 million. He flew them to a fishing lodge in Langara, B.C., and to Jamaica, where they stayed at a villa Thow said belonged to Lee-Chin. Thow convinced the Goodwin family to invest $2.5 million in Lee-Chin's National Commercial Bank of Jamaica (NCBJ). Within months, they had lost $1 million, although they wouldn't realize this for some time.

Thow had no scruples about targeting the very elderly, either. Gloria and Gerry Boudreau were Victoria retirees in their eighties.

They met Thow in 1998 and he recommended they leverage their savings—considered one of the riskiest things to do in the investment world—and pushed them to borrow money to further increase their investment pool. The couple reluctantly agreed, saying they would borrow $50,000. Instead, Thow pressured them into taking a $200,000 loan. In 2004, he told the Boudreaus that the value of their holdings had declined below the amount they'd borrowed and in order to make it up to them he would offer them an investment in three-month mortgages, a "bulletproof plan," as he put it. The minimum investment was $350,000, he said, so Thow suggested they increase their line of credit and redeem their Berkshire mutual funds. All told, the Boudreaus invested over $426,000, and lost $350,000 of it.

By the summer of 2005, Thow's world was beginning to implode. Many of his clients, including Garwood and Kells, were demanding their money back and the RCMP's Integrated Market Enforcement Team (IMET) was onto him. So Thow bolted across the border to Seattle. "He was racking up huge debt," says Dave Ackermann, an IMET officer assigned to the case. "He had two jets, he had a yacht, but it was basically all on loan. He had a house that was mostly mort-gaged. His credit cards were racking up thousands of dollars. He once blew $70,000 on one meal in Las Vegas." The bankruptcy receiver hired to find out where Thow's money went estimated that his lavish lifestyle cost him more than $25 million, including $13.5 million spent maintaining his aircraft and about $5.5 million in credit card bills. "We ended up proving that $12 to $14 million of the $32 million was of a criminal nature," says Ackermann. "It was incredible the amount of money he was burning through."

Given all of this, plus the fact that Thow neglected to send *any* financial statements to his clients, how is it that Berkshire didn't twig that one of their stars was essentially a thief? In fact, Berkshire's compliance department had been warned as early as September 2004 that something was seriously amiss, and sworn affidavits by a Berkshire manager indicated that in 2004–2005 a growing number of Thow's clients were cashing out their Berkshire accounts, and Thow's assets under management were declining faster than those of any other financial adviser at the branch.

Thow was forced to return to Canada in 2009 under an extradition order, pled guilty to a series of fraud charges and was sentenced to nine years in prison. He expressed no remorse for his behaviour and will be out of jail in 2012.

Many of Thow's former clients will never recover. Helena Kells had a heart attack after she and her sister learned their $405,000 was gone. Shirley Garwood became addicted to sleeping pills and Ativan because of acute anxiety. "[Thow] made his victims addicts," she says. The sisters are financially strapped, living day to day on their pensions, unable to maintain the upkeep and pay the debts on their home, and worried about the future and their failing health.

OF COURSE, NOT ALL brokers who run up against the law are thieves. But even the industry, its own watchdog and the provincial securities commissions can't always agree on what constitutes acceptable behaviour—nor, seemingly, are they particularly capable of determining whether rules have been broken. In the instance of one very successful B.C. broker, the IDA and its successor agency, IIROC, have charged her three times and found her guilty of professional misconduct, only to have two of their rulings overturned by the B.C. Securities Commission.

Originally from Montreal, Carolann Steinhoff moved out west as a pharmaceutical rep before entering the brokerage industry with ScotiaMcLeod Inc. (now a division of Scotia Capital Inc.) in Victoria in the late eighties. She put in twelve-hour days, and focused on signing up professionals—lawyers, surgeons, professors, wealthy retirees and other high-net-worth clients. She would cold-call them as late as eleven o'clock at night, encouraging them to invest with her.

Steinhoff married a doctor, joined the Royal Victoria Yacht Club, lived in a $1.8 million waterfront home, drove a Porsche, took exotic holidays and donated a lot of money to charity. By 1999, she had about 500 clients, managed nearly $300 million in assets, and earned more than $4 million a year in commissions. Her bosses loved her. Like Larry Elford, she was made a member of Scotia's elite Chairman's Council.

But then a handful of clients started complaining that Steinhoff had engaged in discretionary trading—trading with a client's money without their permission. This is a practice forbidden by the industry's rules; you must obtain a client's okay before you trade or invest their money in the markets. According to the disciplinary records of the Investment Industry Regulatory Organization of Canada (IIROC), one of the industry's self-regulatory bodies, discretionary trading is one of the most common complaints made by clients against brokers and investment advisers.

In May of 1999, ScotiaMcLeod fired her for breaking the terms of her supervision. Office politics might have played a part—Steinhoff was apparently unpopular among her fellow brokers (Scotia even lied to Steinhoff's clients after she was dismissed, saying she'd left their investments in worse condition than she had). She sued the firm for wrongful dismissal and a settlement was reached. She then moved to a smaller, Vancouver-based brokerage firm, United Capital Securities Inc. (UCS).

Following her dismissal, the Investment Dealers Association (IDA), the governing body of the brokerage industry at the time (IIROC's predecessor), pursued a complaint from one of Steinhoff's former clients and ruled that Steinhoff had executed an unauthorized trade on her client's behalf. The body fined Steinhoff $5,250 and ordered her to rewrite a conduct course.

She appealed and in 2004 the B.C. Securities Commission (BCSC) overturned the ruling, finding that the IDA had rejected material facts and had failed to produce compelling evidence that Steinhoff had committed trades without authorization. The BCSC said IDA had erred in law and relied too much on speculation. By then Steinhoff had left UCS to join Wellington West Capital Inc., an investment services firm. There, she continued to flourish, becoming a branch manager.

In 2007, new allegations arose. Wellington discovered that Steinhoff and her staff had appeared to have altered clients' documents without the clients' permission. The firm conducted a review of the branch's files and found evidence suggesting that Steinhoff had instructed her assistant to alter a client's guarantee form, including an email Steinhoff wrote, saying, "Just go to the file and get the guarantee and change the date on it, and fax it to them, thx." Another email said, "Just get a new form; cut out his signature from something we have already and paste it on form and fax."

In 2009, IIROC charged her and, after a hearing in 2010, penalized her with a one-year suspension, a fine of $60,000, costs of $45,000 and a three-year prohibition from holding any directorship or senior position within a brokerage firm.

Again, Steinhoff appealed to the BCSC, and again the provincial regulator cleared her of any wrongdoing. Steinhoff said that if any documents were changed it was carried out by her staff on their own volition and without her knowledge or approval. She also said her emails (one of which ended with a winking emoticon) should be interpreted as part of an inside joke within the office. Moreover, the emails were never acted upon and no clients were harmed.

The BCSC agreed and found that IIROC had relied upon evidence that was not clear, cogent or convincing, that it had overlooked the testimony of assistants who said that Steinhoff had not asked them to cut out and paste signatures, and that the IIROC panel was biased in how they weighed her testimony. The BCSC believed her side of story—that where it appeared Steinhoff had instructed her staff to alter documents, she had indeed done so in jest. In 2011, it threw out IIROC's entire ruling.

Perhaps familiarity with the problem of unauthorized alteration of paperwork was driving regulatory agencies' repeated interest in Steinhoff. They had no doubt seen more than their share of disdain for the industry's rules in the past. As it turns out, forging or doctoring a client's signature on documents is surprisingly commonplace in the investment world. Further investigation by IIROC of Wellington's Victoria office illustrated just how common the practice can be. Investigators found 132 letters of direction from clients to staff which bore client signatures that had been copied from other documents. Forty-two such letters had instructions written over whiteout and a photocopied signature attached. Some of these had been altered and faxed as originals more than once.

Warren Funt, the IDA's vice-president for western Canada, admitted this goes on in 2007 when he was quoted in an online article saying, "A forgery is not always a forgery." Funt clarified this by claiming that there are two types of forgery issues—one involving fraud and the other a matter of a dealer filling in a missing signature for his or her client. But former Bay Street derivatives trader and investors activist Robert Kyle disagrees. "Very often in the securities industry clients' signatures are forged as a matter of convenience," he says. "It's still wrong, it's still illegal and can lead to great complications down the road between the dealer and investor."

Following a complaint from two of her clients in late 2008, new allegations against Steinhoff emerged. A complaint had been filed with IIROC by a young couple in their thirties who lived in Victoria. They'd been Steinhoff's clients since 2004. Four years later they were selling their home and were planning to move to a new house that was yet to be built. They would be renting for a few months until construction was complete. In the interim (about four months), the couple wanted to park the money from the sale of their home in a secure investment, specifically a high-interest bank account offered by ING Direct.

The couple contends that when they went to see Steinhoff she convinced them to open a "margin account" instead, allowing them to borrow money against the security of the investments in their account. Buying stocks on margin can enhance profits or exacerbate losses, depending on which way the market goes. Steinhoff allegedly recorded their investment objectives as "growth" and their risk tolerance as quite aggressive, which would be unusual for people wanting to safeguard cash for a down payment on a home.

After their home was sold, the couple deposited $125,000 (their entire net worth) into the brokerage account and Steinhoff used all of it and the leverage to buy securities in twelve different companies. According to IIROC, she failed to obtain prior authorization to buy these stocks and used the margin account to leverage the couple's investments. If true, that was a violation of industry rules.

Throughout 2008, the stocks plummeted in value along with the rest of the market, a situation that was worsened by the multiplying effect of the margin account. Because the couple had borrowed for their investment, they were also losing from the value of the loan. Concerned about their losses, the young couple contacted Steinhoff, who allegedly assured them the market would bounce back. She was wrong. When the couple needed the money to pay for their new home, Steinhoff sold all the stocks. They'd lost nearly $70,000, and yet Steinhoff had made $6,800 in commissions. In order to buy their new home, the couple had to deregister their RRSP accounts and borrow $65,000 from family members. When they reported all of this to Wellington, Steinhoff described their complaint as "revisionist chronology" and claimed it was they who had raised the idea of opening a margin account. In the fall of 2011, however, IIROC found that Steinhoff was guilty of failing to obtain prior approval before making stock purchases in their account, and of purchasing the stocks on margin inconsistent with the couple's wishes, and that she had recommended they continue with the investments even as the portfolio declined. Steinhoff has said she would appeal this ruling.

By early 2012, Steinhoff was working at her fourth investment house, Queensbury Securities Inc., where she is listed as a vice-president.

PERHAPS NO CASE BETTER reveals the damage a rogue broker can inflict than that of Harry Migirdic. A Montrealer of Armenian descent, Migirdic began working in the industry in 1980, initially at Merrill Lynch Canada's Montreal offices before the firm was absorbed ten years later by Wood Gundy, a brokerage owned by CIBC. Merrill Lynch had promoted Migirdic to "vice-president," a meaningless honorific used as a marketing tool to impress investors (by 2000, the brokerage house had two hundred of these "vice-presidents"), and he kept the title when CIBC Wood Gundy took over.

After the Wood Gundy takeover, Migirdic spun out of control, making disastrous investments with his clients' money. One of his first victims was Rita Luthi, a Quebec businesswoman who entrusted him with $150,000. By early 1993, only $18,000 was left, a fact Migirdic hid from Luthi when she sought to withdraw $60,000. To cover up the loss, Migirdic needed a guarantee from a solvent third party so that he could "go in the red" with Luthi's account without the bank intervening. He selected Haroutioun Markarian as his patsy.

Markarian had been Migirdic's client since 1986. Also of Armenian heritage, Markarian had arrived in Montreal from Egypt in 1962 with $300 in his pocket. He co-founded a mechanical company, and by the time he sold the business and retired in 1993, he'd built himself a $4.5 million nest egg. Migirdic went to Markarian and showed him a form, saying he must sign it for bureaucratic reasons related to his account. What he failed to tell Markarian was that he was actually signing a guarantee agreement that provided collateral for the losses in other clients' accounts. Migirdic could now drive Luthi's account into debt and CIBC Wood Gundy would look away, knowing that someone was going to cover it.

Every year for the next seven years Migirdic had Markarian sign updates on the guarantee, deflecting Markarian's increasing anxiety and anger by blaming CIBC's bureaucracy for demanding his client's signature on the documents. Migirdic also opened an account under the name of an unsuspecting uncle living in Turkey so that he could play the stock market with it. When this account too went deep into the red, owing $250,000 by 1994, Migirdic got Markarian to cover this loss as well.

He used the same ploy on others. In 1993, an elderly widow named Kiganouchi Papazian unwittingly signed a similar guarantee, also convinced by Migirdic that it was a bank form regarding her own account. She worked in a store in the basement of the building that housed Migirdic's branch. Her salary was about $25,000 a year, she spoke neither French nor English, and her assets were modest. In 1998, when Papazian's son saw the guarantee and complained to him, Migirdic promised to rescind it within 48 hours. He never did. In 2001, CIBC Wood Gundy seized $300,000 of Papazian's money, claiming the guarantee was valid. She went to her grave heartbroken and penniless.

Overall, Migirdic made 1,400 unauthorized discretionary transactions. He cost another client $900,000, and lost nearly $1.3 million from other accounts. Migirdic committed just about every infraction of securities law you can as a broker: unauthorized investments, unauthorized changes in client profiles, day trading, transactions with insufficient coverage, excessive speculation, illegal compensation of clients, you name it. All of which raises two questions: why didn't Wood Gundy's compliance department notice Migirdic's misbehaviour, and why wasn't he fired for losing so much of his clients' money? At one point, the bank ordered him to pay back $250,000 after he removed money from an account without authorization; and when he accepted a power-of-attorney document with a false signature, he was caught and fined $30,000. Despite such transgressions, investor activist Robert Kyle suggests that the brokerage kept Migirdic on staff because he was a big earner and his superiors would have "received a cut of everything. If Migirdic is one of their top salespersons, they would be making a piece of that. Do they want to turn their own guy in if he's making millions?" Between 1991 and 2000, Migirdic billed $11 million in commissions, of which he took home as much as $5 million.

In the end, Migirdic turned himself in. By December 2000, the account under Migirdic's uncle's name alone was almost $1 million in the red, a time bomb waiting to go off. Stressed by his web of deceit, he contacted Wood Gundy's top executive, Thomas Monahan, in February 2001 and admitted there were "problems" with certain accounts. Monahan told Migirdic to write down the details of what he had done, and Migirdic did so, admitting (among other things) that he had deceived Markarian about the documents he was asked to sign. When Migirdic met with his superiors, he reiterated that Markarian never knew he was guaranteeing the debts of perfect strangers. Incredibly, at this point, events took an even darker turn, one that speaks to systemic corruption and bullying tactics at the highest levels of the investment industry.

In March 2001, CIBC Wood Gundy called Markarian and his wife to a meeting with Migirdic's immediate supervisor, Thomas Noonan, and a lawyer employed by the bank. Noonan showed the Markarians the signed guarantees and they confirmed that it was Haroutioun who had signed them. Noonan then told the Markarians that they owed the bank $1.35 million. Their accounts were frozen. Noonan and the lawyer never uttered a word to the elderly couple about Migirdic's fraud or confession.

Markarian, sixty-eight years old at the time, went into shock. At the end of the meeting, he was unable to stand up and had to be helped from the room. He could not speak for fifteen minutes, but then asked his wife, "Is it a dream, Alice? Is it true?" He was in such a state that a doctor was called to his bedside. Markarian soon hired a lawyer, who told the bank the guarantees were signed under false pretences and they couldn't seize the money. The bank ignored these appeals and refused even to meet with the Markarians or their attorneys.

And Migirdic? He was fired by CIBC Wood Gundy but was never charged with fraud. The RCMP and Montreal police refused to investigate the matter and Migirdic kept all of his profits. The Investment Dealers Association did slap him with a $360,000 fine and banned him for life from selling securities, but Migirdic never paid a cent of these penalties because they're not legally binding.

THOMAS MONAHAN HAD MADE the decision to seize Markarian's money, but he would later testify that when he received Migirdic's confession he didn't know whom or what to believe. He conferred with his superiors and lawyers from CIBC and the corporate law firms Heenan Blaikie LLP and Torys LLP. They all concluded, despite what Migirdic and Markarian had told them—let alone the sheer implausibility of Markarian guaranteeing the losses of people he didn't know—that it was okay to empty Markarian's account.

The beleaguered investor sued CIBC, which fought him every step of the way. For example, in 2004, the IDA produced a report on Migirdic which should have put an end to the bank's contention that Markarian knew he was signing guarantees. Not only does the report document Migirdic's litany of crimes and frauds, it insists that Migirdic obtained Markarian's signature "under the false pretence that it was required for account maintenance." Wood Gundy responded months later, offering to return a mere $250,000 to Markarian—in effect treating the whole affair as a nuisance suit and attempting to wash its hands of the matter. In fact, the bank was unwilling to give any of the clients who'd been ripped off by Migirdic full compensation for their losses. On the eve of trial, however, in November 2004, the bank finally agreed to pay back all of Markarian's money, though it refused to cover his legal bills (by then in excess of $300,000), accept liability or pay the interest that had accrued. Markarian turned down the offer.

The case went to trial in January 2005. CIBC Wood Gundy argued that Markarian was a "sophisticated businessman" and must have known that he was signing guarantees for strangers' accounts, an allegation that imploded once Markarian's lawyer, Serge Létourneau, got Monahan to admit on the stand that the "sophisticated employees" in his own compliance department had not caught Migirdic.

"Why is it a big problem for Mr. Markarian to have been deceived since he is a very sophisticated businessman, and not for you?" asked Létourneau.

Monahan finally admitted that Markarian "was deceived by Mr. Migirdic."

Still, when Létourneau asked Monahan whether he felt justified in taking Markarian's money, Monahan responded, "Yes."

"You still maintain it today?"

"Yes."

The trial dragged on for four months, and it would take more than a year for Justice Jean-Pierre Senécal to issue a verdict. But when he did, it was a blockbuster. Not only did he award Markarian $1.5 million based on the money Wood Gundy took from him and the costs he'd incurred, the judge also gave him $1.5 million in punitive damages, the largest award of that type ever handed down in Canada. Senécal found Migirdic guilty of fraud and said CIBC Wood Gundy contributed to his crime by failing to properly manage him. The judge wrote that after Migirdic's fraud was discovered, the brokerage firm treated the Markarians with "profound contempt. It cruelly dropped them and even went after them as if they were responsible for the dreadful turn of events. It was as if the employer of a thief—the one responsible for fraud—made the victim responsible for his misfortune."

Still, the decision had little effect on Migirdic. Because Markarian's lawsuit was in civil court, the finding of fraud by Senécal carried no criminal weight, and Migirdic remains untouched by the law to this day. Meanwhile, Monahan kept his job and in 2009 was appointed CEO of another CIBC subsidiary, asset service provider CIBC Mellon Trust.

EIGHT

BANKERS BEHAVING BADLY

WHILE THE GLOBAL BANKING system was going up in flames between 2007 and 2009, Canada's five chartered banks seemed to be facing down this once-in-a-generation conflagration with equanimity. None of them appeared to be teetering on the verge of collapse, and their brokerage houses remained solvent. Indeed, in the midst of this financial tsunami, the World Economic Forum released its annual Global Competitiveness Report, ranking Canada's banks as the soundest in the world, partly because Canadian regulators had the good sense to force the sector to put aside more capital reserves of a high quality than their American counterparts and not become overleveraged.

By 2009, as measured by assets, four of the ten largest banks in North America were Canadian. A decade earlier, none were in the top ten. In 2009, just seven banks in the world were awarded a Triple-A rating from Moody's, and two of them—RBC and TD Canada Trust—were Canadian. That same year, Canada's five chartered banks earned combined profits of $14 billion. Meanwhile, the fact that the big Bay Street brokerage houses were owned by the banks meant they survived the global meltdown far better than Wall Street investment firms like Bear Stearns, Merrill Lynch and Lehman Brothers, which had overleveraged, lacked deep pockets and therefore collapsed or were sold off to banks. While manufacturing in southern Ontario's Golden Horseshoe was being decimated by a strengthening dollar and overseas competition, Canada's financial industry was flourishing, and the perception that Canada had a sound (and clean) banking sector was *the* drawing card for attracting foreign investment.

But was this reputation for fiscal prudence really warranted? First, it's not true that Canada's big banks hadn't been bailed out during the credit crisis. In the fall of 2008, through the Canada Mortgage and Housing Corporation (CMHC), the federal government created a unique program that allowed the banks to move tens of billions of dollars of mortgage assets off of their balance sheets–anywhere from $69 billion to $125 billion, depending on whose estimates you believe. (Originally, the amount was supposed to be just $20 billion, a figure that had to be ratcheted upwards—and substantially so—once it was clear this was not going to be enough to help the banks.) The plan was designed to ensure the banks had enough liquidity to keep lending— although it's unclear if they actually loaned out any of that money. Banks were also called upon to honour their financial commitments to all of the subprime mortgage debt they had insured through credit default swaps (CDSs—insurance contracts that promise to pay for the credit losses on subprime mortgage and other "toxic" debts). These "margin calls" happened just as the banks were facing write downs on other risky forays into the U.S. subprime mortgage market, bringing their losses from the credit crisis to roughly $17 billion.

A closer look reveals that the vaunted stability of Canada's banks obscures a long track record of reckless risk-taking and corporate malfeasance. Not only does this "stability" owe much to the industry's charging Canadians some of the highest banking and investment management fees in the world, a practice they can get away with because they constitute an oligopoly—a cartel, if you will—but the industry is rarely held to account for its most egregious scandals. "Finance is a dirty world," says Yves Michaud, a former Quebec politician and the founding president of the Association des petits épargnants et investisseurs du Québec (Association of Small Savers and Investors of Quebec), an organization that has won some significant victories against the banks. But just how badly behaved are Canada's chartered banks?

In 2008, the Royal Bank of Canada (RBC), the country's biggest bank, was sued by five Wisconsin school boards who claimed the bank took US$200 million of their money and sank it into "synthetic" CDOs stuffed with obscure credit default swaps (a synthetic CDO technically has no mortgage debt behind it, just insurance contracts paying premiums, making them even more suspect). After the credit crisis struck, US$195 million of the school boards' investment disappeared, leaving them strapped for cash.

The boards had ventured into the capital markets because they needed to find new sources of money to meet obligations, including paying retired teachers' health care benefits. They were convinced by RBC and the St. Louis–based brokerage firm Stifel, Nicolaus & Co. to borrow US$163 million from a European bank with the idea of investing it in a synthetic CDO constructed by RBC. The CDO was a witch's brew of complexity, containing portfolios of credit default swaps pegged to corporate bonds. The school boards said the bankers led them to believe this was a safe and secure investment when, in fact, it was quite risky. Indeed, the corporate bonds were linked to subprime mortgage debt. Sure enough, after the credit crisis struck, the investments tanked and the foreign bank seized the school board's collateral underlying the investments. "[The] Royal Bank of Canada was responsible for . . . providing a suitable investment for the districts," says Stephen Kravit, one of the lawyers for the school boards, "and they failed miserably." Moreover, the boards allege that RBC deliberately moved toxic mortgage assets off its own books and transferred the risk onto the school boards. Thus, if the assets turned sour, the school boards would be left holding the bag.

RBC fought the lawsuit through the Milwaukee courts, trying to get it tossed out. The school boards successfully beat back these efforts. And in the fall of 2011 the bank agreed to pay more than US$30 million to the SEC after the commission charged the bank with failing to explain the risks of the CDOs to the boards. The SEC also sued Stifel, citing fraudulent misconduct in its role in the deal.

RBC was in trouble on other fronts too. In 2011, the state of Massachusetts' securities division sued RBC Capital Markets LLC and one of its traders, Michael Zukowksi, demanding it reimburse investors for nearly US$800,000 in losses incurred as a result of Zukowksi convincing them to sink their money into a particular kind of exchange-traded funds (ETFs), highly leveraged and unstable investment products. ETFs are investment funds traded on stock exchanges; similar to mutual funds, they hold assets such as stocks, commodities or bonds, and are attractive to investors because of their low costs, tax efficiency and stock-like features. In recent years they've become all the rage in investment circles. The suit charged that RBC Capital Markets, starting in 2007, sold high-risk ETFs to residents of Massachusetts who didn't fully understand what they were or the risks involved. The suit noted that "since at least 2006, and certainly after January 2009, RBC knew that . . . ETFs were not suitable for all clients. However, RBC did not implement proper supervisory procedures reasonably designed to prevent and detect unsuitable sales" until after the damage was done. Zukowski testified that he received no training from RBC about ETFs and that the bank's research department had approved of ETFs being sold to investors, which is why he believed they were sound enough to peddle to his clients.

Canada's fourth largest bank, BMO, has also had its fair share of scandals. In 2008, David Lee, a star commodities trader working out of BMO's New York offices, pled guilty to inflating the fair market value of natural gas option positions in his derivatives trading portfolio from 2004 to 2007. Lee's trading contributed to an $853 million loss in the bank's commodities trading business for 2007, which saw profits plunge by $440 million. Lee also admitted to charges of conspiracy, making false bank entries and destroying evidence after an inquiry was launched by the U.S. Commodity Futures Trading Commission.

YET THE CHARTERED BANK that seems to get into the most hot water is CIBC. With revenues of $12 billion and profits of $2.4 billion in 2010, CIBC remains a cornerstone of Canada's banking sector. The bank's problems originated in the 1990s when Al Flood, then its chairman and CEO, decided it should have a global presence, especially in investment banking. CIBC had bought the brokerage house Wood Gundy in 1988 and expanded into the American market in the early nineties when it purchased Argosy Group, a New York–based investment firm founded by three alumni of junk bond dealer Drexel Burnham Lambert. In 1997, CIBC snapped up Oppenheimer & Co., another New York investment house, and in 1999 all these outfits were collected under the umbrella of CIBC World Markets, run by CEO John Hunkin, who'd come up through the investment banking side of the business.

CIBC wanted to play with the big boys of international finance, and yet Canada was such a tiny player in the world's investment market that becoming a global force in this milieu was a tall order. Driven by a desire to prove itself, CIBC was overly eager to please high-profile customers—including Enron Corp., the Houston-based energy conglomerate. During the nineties, Enron became one of the world's biggest corporations and was a highly prized client for the banking community. By 1998, CIBC had forged a close relationship with Enron, just as the energy company began embracing accounting measures designed to hide losses and post non-existent revenues, a strategy engineered by senior Enron executives including Kenneth Lay, Jeffrey Skilling and Andrew Fastow, and assisted by the company's accounting firm, Arthur Andersen LLP.

While the actions of Enron's senior executives and of Arthur Andersen were pilloried after the company collapsed in 2001, what is often overlooked in the scandal is how Enron's bankers contributed to the company's downfall. CIBC loaned Enron more than US$3 billion and helped it raise an additional US$3 billion from investors through selling securities. It garnered huge fees and interest payments from these deals. And CIBC's partnership with Enron was so close that the bank's senior managers were in almost daily contact with Lay, Skilling, Fastow and other Enron senior executives. But the bank did much more than finance Enron: it helped the company mislead investors about the true state of its finances.

The bank acted as an underwriter of stock Enron issued. One lawsuit launched by the University of California, an Enron investor, accuses CIBC of publishing statements about this stock that contained false and misleading information about Enron's financial health. The bank's analysts did the very same thing, says the lawsuit. The effect was to artificially inflate the trading price value of Enron's shares.

For example, Enron announced a joint venture with Blockbuster in 2000 to sell movies on demand through customers' televisions. But this deal enabled Enron to improperly report more than (US) $110 million in phony profits. CIBC is accused of reassuring investors that this entire venture was sound, even if "behind the scenes . . . CIBC knew that the [video on demand] project was very risky and was plagued by technical and legal problems that made it likely that it would never advance past a pilot project stage," claims the lawsuit. Indeed, the project was quickly abandoned, although the phony profits remained on the books. This bookkeeping sleight-of-hand allowed Enron to inflate its stock to an all-time high of US$90.

According to court documents, CIBC helped Enron structure and finance illicit special purpose entities (SPEs) that were used to manipulate the corporation's financial statements. (An SPE is a legal entity that is typically used by companies to achieve a very specific goal, such as holding assets destined for a particular project. In the case of Enron, the SPEs were used to hide its debt and thereby give a false picture of the company's health.)

Between June 1998 and October 2001, CIBC and Enron structured thirty-four transactions that were purportedly assets sales but were in fact loans made by the bank to the corporation. These were known as FAS 140 transactions and allowed Enron to record as much as US$585 million in profits from the sales of assets that did not in fact exist. These transactions also permitted Enron to record fictitious cash flow and understate its debts. "Had these transactions been accounted for properly as financing transactions, Enron would have recorded [US]$3.5 billion in debt and [US]$3 billion as cash flows for financing instead of cash flow from operations," says Helen Hodges, a lawyer with Robbins Geller Rudman & Dowd LLP, a San Diego, California, law firm that sued Enron's banks on behalf of investors in 2003. "These transactions were [about] hiding debt," continues Hodges. While FAS 140 transactions generated fake profits for Enron, the company's bankruptcy examiner found that CIBC knew these transactions were fraudulent but helped Enron's executives carry them out anyway, even though it meant misleading Enron's shareholders about the health of the company.

In December 2001, Enron declared bankruptcy, wiping out US$38 billion of creditors' money in the largest corporate insolvency in American history. Enron shareholders lost another US$60 billion from its peak share price. The SEC and U.S. Department of Justice investigated CIBC's role in the collapse, and two years later the bank signed an agreement with the DOJ admitting its role in the fraud, accepting responsibility for its employees' actions, and acknowledging "that Enron's purpose in entering into these [FAS 140] transactions was to remove assets from its balance sheets and book earnings and/or cash flow at quarter- and year-end."

After Enron's investors sued CIBC, the bank dawdled, costing the bank's shareholders even more money. "The [culprit] who came forward first paid less," remarks Hodges of the inevitable settlements. "The longer you drag it out, the more you paid. CIBC was the last to come to settle." Finally, in 2005, the bank was forced to shell out US$2.4 billion, the most of any bank that had conducted business with Enron. (It also paid US$80 million to the SEC in fines.)

———

ENRON WAS HARDLY THE ONLY suspect company to do business with CIBC during this period. In 1996, American investment banker Gary Winnick wanted to get into telecommunications, hoping to establish a company that would lay fibre optic cable beneath the Atlantic Ocean to take advantage of growing Internet and phone usage. Winnick had worked in Los Angeles for Drexel Burnham Lambert—alongside Michael Milken, the junk bond king who went to jail for securities fraud in the 1980s and was one of that decade's premier symbols of reckless trading and greed—but Winnick had since left Drexel to run his own investment firm.

To get his fibre optic company off the ground, Winnick phoned Bruce Raben, an old Drexel colleague, who was working for CIBC World Markets (Winnick's son also worked for CIBC). CIBC liked Winnick's idea and put up US$41 million for 38 percent of the common stock in Global Crossing Ltd., Winnick's new company. Fifteen months later, when Global offered its stock to the public, CIBC's stake in the company had a market value of US$926 million. CIBC also raised capital for Global and spearheaded a group of banks who lent US$482 million to the enterprise as well as providing US$850 million in financing for its first undersea cable. Beyond receiving fees, CIBC also filled and controlled five of the nine seats on Global Crossing's board.

Throughout the late 1990s, CIBC played a major role in raising US$9.2 billion for Global through offerings of debt to investors. And yet, despite the ease with which cash was found on Wall Street, there was a big hitch: Global was not generating enough revenue and had weak cash flow. Its fibre-optic network was also not working very well. It was, in effect, a big company built on a tiny and shaky foundation.

This didn't prevent Winnick from adopting a lavish lifestyle and paying himself generously. He received US$10 million a year in salary and bonuses, played golf with President Clinton, dined with King Constantine of Greece, and spent a rumoured US$90 million for the former Hilton estate in Bel Air, California. Global Crossing's executive offices were located in Beverly Hills in two extravagant white stone buildings, one resembling an Italian villa. Winnick spent US$7 million renovating the place, turning his own office into a replica of the Oval Office, with added touches including a painting by Pablo Picasso (valued at US$15 million). He repeatedly made *Forbes* magazine's list of America's richest people and spent heavily on politicians and those he deemed politically connected. He and his staff travelled on five corporate jets, including a Boeing 737 and a Gulfstream.

By 1999, Global Crossing had built too much fibre optic capacity for its customers, who had discovered that Internet and phone traffic was not as heavy as predicted. And the company was now facing serious competition. With high levels of debt and falling revenues, the company was teetering while hiding its true financial state from investors. With CIBC owning such a large stake in Global Crossing and its employees controlling the company's board, it is difficult to believe the Canadian bank didn't know the wheels would soon fall off.

CIBC decided it was time to bail. "We have made enough money," Al Flood said in the spring of 1999 before asking the bank's New York office to offload its stake in Global. CIBC sold the first of its Global shares in June of that year, and lawsuits would later accuse it of disposing of its holdings while "the CIBC Directors and the other insiders continued to lend their affirmative support to misleading statements about Global's financial condition." In the end, the bank made a killing, turning its original US$41 million investment into almost US$2 billion profit, while CIBC's five directors on Global's board quit the company, cashed in and became multi-millionaires.

Global Crossing filed for bankruptcy in January 2002, the fourth-largest corporate collapse in U.S. history, costing investors over US$40 billion, with lawsuits soon painting the company as a massive fraud designed to enrich its senior executives at their expense. "The company and its purported multibillion dollar revenues and strong, substantial cash flow were a complete sham," said one. After Global Crossing went bust, it was discovered that one of the company's former vice-presidents of finance, Roy Olofson, had tried to warn senior management about accounting practices that gave an inaccurate picture of the company's health. His tip-off, however, had been ignored.

CIBC got off pretty much scot-free. In 2006, it settled the major investors' lawsuit against the bank for its role in the collapse for just $20 million. Global Crossing, by contrast, was forced to settle a class action lawsuit, brought by investors and employees who lost retirement funds, to the tune of US$325 million. Winnick's proceeds from selling his Global Crossing stock exceeded US$800 million. Meanwhile, over his own staff's objections, the head of the SEC dropped charges against Winnick. The company's critics believe that Winnick's political connections saved his hide.

To this day, within CIBC, its investment in Global Crossing is viewed as a huge success. For insiders, it clearly was.

AND THEN THERE'S THE CASE of Pay Pop. While this scandal involved much smaller sums of money than the fiascos of Enron and Global Crossing, it speaks volumes about the bank's corporate culture.

In 1998, Robert Zaba, a stock promoter based in Vernon, British Columbia, snapped up Pay Pop, Inc., a Nevada shell company with

no assets or business activity but which claimed to be in the telecommunications business. Zaba's partner-in-crime was Daryl Desjardins,
a convicted drug dealer who lived in Abbotsford, B.C. Although Pay
Pop operated in British Columbia, it traded on the U.S. National
Association of Securities Dealers' Over-the-Counter Bulletin Board,
and from the summer of 1998 to March 1999 it sold more than 55
million shares to the public. "It was a pump-and-dump," says Bud
Cramm, an RCMP stock market fraud investigator who spent four
years investigating Pay Pop.

One part of the scheme called for Zaba and Desjardins to obtain
a ready source of "free" Pay Pop stock, shares they didn't actually
have to pay for, and then find a transfer agent willing to issue this
stock and convert it into a tradable form. In the summer of 1998,
Zaba approached Alnoor Jiwan, the manager of CIBC Mellon
Trust's Pacific region, to make him a tempting offer. A subsidiary of
the bank, CIBC Mellon Trust is an asset servicing company and
Jiwan supervised its B.C. operations and Vancouver office. In return
for a bribe made up of Pay Pop shares, Jiwan agreed to help Zaba and
Desjardins, permitting CIBC Mellon Trust to issue the free stock
certificates without a proof-of-registration statement. In total, Zaba
and Desjardins gave 820,000 shares of Pay Pop to Jiwan as payment
for his role in this scam. Most of the money from the sale of Pay Pop's
stock to investors went to Zaba and Desjardins. Desjardins once
boasted it was his own "printing press" for money, and using the
proceeds bought himself several exotic cars and an ownership stake
in a thoroughbred horse. (The RCMP later claimed that Pay Pop
had ties to the Hells Angels motorcycle gang.) In total, Zaba and
Desjardins pocketed over US$3 million from the scam.

Did CIBC Mellon Trust know what Jiwan was up to? Apparently
not. On two separate occasions, Pay Pop's American lawyer, Warren

Soloski, wrote to Jiwan to say he was in violation of American securities laws by issuing the free stock. "NEVER DO THIS AGAIN," he said in one letter. In the summer of 1999, after Soloski learned that CIBC Mellon Trust had ignored his instructions and issued more stock, he flew to Vancouver and met with Jiwan and another manager. Soloski, in the other manager's presence, bellowed at Jiwan, telling him his actions violated U.S. securities laws.

Jiwan had no intention of turning himself in, perhaps knowing something about CIBC Mellon Trust's lax internal controls and that he was unlikely to be caught. "CIBC Mellon Trust's inadequate policies and procedures permitted Jiwan to carry out his portion of the fraudulent scheme," the SEC later concluded, noting that in order to issue Pay Pop stock, proper protocol demanded that CIBC Mellon's lawyers and other staff sign off on it to ensure laws were being followed. This never happened. Moreover, the amount of Pay Pop stock being issued was too large to have been overlooked. "In essence, CIBC Mellon Trust allowed stock to be issued without satisfying itself that all United States regulatory requirements had been met," said the SEC. "[CIBC's] internal control system wasn't working, because they would've spotted it if they had any type of system," adds Bud Cramm.

Pay Pop collapsed in late 1999, and the SEC finally wrung a settlement out of CIBC Mellon Trust in 2005, whereby the bank paid $6 million in penalties. Jiwan was fired while Desjardins was arrested in 2006 for helicoptering marijuana from B.C. into the United States and was slapped with a four-year prison sentence. Zaba was arrested in Houston that same year for his role in a Nigerian-style letter-writing solicitation fraud. Investors in Pay Pop lost millions.

———

THESE TRANSGRESSIONS BY CANADA'S BANKS, while troubling, were merely precursors to the role they played in the 2007–2009 global financial meltdown by marketing and selling investments based on toxic U.S. subprime mortgage debt and credit default swaps. It was in this arena that they displayed all manner of recklessness and lack of regard for basic fiscal prudence and simple common sense.

— NINE —

SUBPRIME HORROR:
THE CANADIAN CONNECTION

IRIS PEARCE IS A victim of America's subprime mortgage crisis even though she's a Canadian living in Canada, has never had a subprime mortgage on her home and never knowingly invested in other people's debt.

I first met Pearce in the summer of 2008, and we sat in the living room of her small white clapboard house in St. Catharines, Ontario. It's well appointed, filled with dark wooden furniture, a place befitting a retail worker in her early sixties. Pearce is a ruddy-cheeked, handsome woman with a warm personality who still retains her British accent. I wanted to know about her troubles with Bay Street and asset-backed commercial paper (ABCP), an obscure investment product that generates income for investors from pools of commercial and housing mortgages and other forms of debt (such as car loans and credit cards). It gained notoriety in August 2007 when $32 billion of investors' money tied up in ABCP was frozen after the U.S. subprime mortgage meltdown crashed into Canada's capital markets. Pension funds, big companies, governments and 1,800 retail investors, including Pearce, couldn't get their hands on their own money. Pearce had sunk $135,000 into ABCP, and by the time we met she'd gone an entire year cut off from her savings. She was more than upset about it. "I can't buy new windows for the house or go on vacation. They have taken away my power to do what I want with my own money," she fumed. "And I don't know when I will get it back."

Pearce, it turned out, was one of the lucky ones. Of the investors who had their money frozen that summer, only retail investors like her eventually got it returned, a figure amounting to $187 million. The rest received promissory notes that mature in 2017—these included various Canadian government entities, like the Caisse de dépôt, Ontario Treasury and the Alberta Treasury Branch, and major corporations, such as Domtar's pension fund, Magna International, Canadian Pacific, Sun-Times Media, Air Canada, Ontario Power Generation and Canada Post. The losses to these investors caused by this delay are estimated to reach upwards of $7 billion. This was not supposed to happen. After all, ABCP was Triple-A rated, meaning it was considered a very safe product, and investors like Pearce were told it had the backing of the big banks. Furthermore, subprime mortgages were not even available in Canada. So how were retirees like Pearce, not to mention Canadian companies and governments, victimized by a financial product based on subprime mortgages and credit default swaps that resided outside our borders?

To ANSWER THIS QUESTION, you have to step back and look at the broader forces that have shaped the global economy in recent years.

The U.S. subprime mortgage crisis was rooted in the growing income gap between America's rich and poor. In the United States, the Congressional Budget Office estimated that between 1979 and 2007, the inflation-adjusted income of America's poorest families rose a mere 18 percent (and less than 40 percent for the middle class), while over the same period the income for the top 1 percent rose by 275 percent. As wealth from the working and middle classes shifted into the hands of the most affluent during the three decades leading up to 2007–2009, that money was not going to sit around in bank accounts or under mattresses. Instead, through the wizardry of financial engineering, the wealthy realized that their new-found riches could be transformed into even larger sums, and the first step was to lend this money back to the very people who were now scrambling to pay everyday bills.

The rapidly growing income divide was not limited to the U.S.A. Virtually all Western countries were seeing the rich get richer while most others experienced diminishing financial prospects. In Canada, between 2001 and 2009, the personal debt of the average Canadian adult almost doubled, from a little over $20,000 to more than $40,000 when adjusted for inflation; and by 2011, Canada had the dubious distinction of ranking first among twenty OECD countries in terms of consumers' debt-to-financial assets ratio, and seventh in debt-to-income ratio. In a survey published by TD Canada Trust in the spring of 2011, 30 percent of respondents reported that they did not have enough money to cover basic living expenses; 38 percent said they had no savings at all.

Thus, by the 2000s, two realities were converging to cause a perfect storm. One was the fact of credit becoming increasingly easy to obtain for average people aspiring to join the middle class. At the same time, the working and middle classes were growing more impoverished and needing greater quantities of credit in order to buy things like homes, cars and other utilities. These two realities met on the trading floors of brokerage houses and banks around the globe.

The credit crisis came about because mortgages and other forms of debt (credit cards, car and student loans, and so on) were converted into investment products which were then sold to investors. This was done through the process of "securitization," whereby debt is bundled together into things like collateralized debt obligations and offered up to investors as a viable investment, with the debt producing income for investors by way of interest and principal payments. Banks and investment houses became packagers of this debt and sellers of the securities based on it. Unfortunately, securitization also meant that it was investors, not the financial institutions themselves, that bore the risk when the underlying debt went bad.

Starting in the 1990s, as borrowing money became easier, people in Canada and the United States began buying homes in greater numbers than ever before. The religion of home ownership is a potent force in North America, and the financial industry greased the skids by offering loans that required less and less in the way of collateral, a down payment or evidence you would ever be able to pay the money back. In the United States, this took the form of subprime mortgages, which permitted people to buy a house without putting any money down and without having to prove they had any savings or a job. In 2005 and 2006, US$350 billion worth of subprime or near-subprime loans closed in America. And because this mortgage debt could be securitized, Wall Street wanted as much of it as possible. (The subprime mortgage industry arrived in Canada through Xceed Mortgage Corporation. This Canadian company's funding sources dried up when the bottom fell out of this U.S. market in 2006–2007 and no such mortgages were sold in Canada.) A speculative bubble soon emerged, based largely on the widely promoted notion that housing prices never fall.

"Most people within the industry knew that these mortgages were structured to fail," says Bruce Marks, the president of the Neighborhood Assistance Corporation of America (NACA), a Boston-based mortgage lender that has fought Wall Street's predatory practices. "It was only a matter of time." The reason they would fail was that subprime mortgages contained built-in interest payment hikes that made them virtually impossible to pay off. Furthermore, they were invariably sold to low-income earners who simply didn't have the means to keep up with the ever-burgeoning payments. Default was inevitable. Investors who bought mortgage-backed securities from brokers around the world had little idea that their investment rested on the ability of poor Americans being able to make their monthly mortgage payments, which they increasingly were unable to do.

Upon this rickety foundation sat the entire global banking system.

Moreover, brokers and bankers either turned a blind eye to the fact that mortgage-backed securities were on shaky ground or they simply out-and-out lied, telling their clients that because housing prices never fall and people don't generally default on their mortgages, these investments were safe and sound. And to prove it, they paid large fees and commissions to credit rating agencies so they could slap Triple-A ratings on mortgage-backed securities, giving investors a false sense of confidence about their safety.

The investment products based on all of this toxic mortgage debt were not sold only to Americans. Indeed, in this day and age, wealth flowing through the financial industry is not bound by national borders, and neither are banks and brokerages in regards to where they seek out opportunities. So Canadians who parked their money in an investment product like ABCP or CDOs soon discovered that their cash was tied up in the mortgage debt and credit default swaps of another country, which explains why the financial meltdown was not isolated to those countries where mortgage lending practices had gone berserk.

Ironically, one of the clearest indicators that this mountain of debt and fraudulent behaviour would ultimately produce catastrophe appeared in Canada a full two years before the crisis blew up in 2007 around the world.

"THE WHOLE SUBPRIME MORTGAGE craziness really began, in a sense, in Canada," explains Dimitri Lascaris, a lawyer and partner in Siskinds LLP, a London, Ontario, law firm that sued the owners of FMF Capital Group Ltd. on behalf of investors. "It was not that [subprime mortgage] lending was going on here, but the first public company loaded down with this kind of debt to explode was listed on the Canadian stock exchange. Its business was in the United States, but it was listed on the Canadian stock exchange." Which meant that the demise of FMF Capital, the first indication that the subprime market was doomed to failure, was burning Canadian investors well before the subprime meltdown began in the U.S.

FMF Capital's origins go back to Robert Pilcowitz and Edan King, brothers-in-law who practised real estate law in Southfield, Michigan. In 1992, the pair founded Michigan Fidelity Acceptance Corporation (MFAC), a company that sold subprime mortgages to aspiring homeowners. MFAC bundled this debt and passed it on to American loan purchasers, and it was then moulded into investments by Wall Street. With Americans buying houses in record numbers, MFAC flourished. By 2003, it was packaging US$724 million worth of subprime loans in more than twenty-five states. "These guys were lending to anyone who was prepared to take out a mortgage loan," says Lascaris. "The growth of the company was insane.

They started off in Michigan but were soon all over the United States, especially the areas later hit the hardest, such as Florida or California."

To increase their wealth, Pilcowitz and King decided to take MFAC public, choosing Canada and the TSX to make their initial public offering (IPO). If the choice seems odd, their reasoning was simple. "American securities authorities wouldn't allow them to list in the States," explains Lascaris, suggesting that authorities in the U.S. found MFAC too risky. "They were more likely to get a listing in Canada." And sure enough, Pilcowitz and King were soon talking to the Bank of Montreal and its investment firm, BMO Nesbitt Burns Inc., about gaining access to the pocketbooks of Canadian investors.

Meanwhile, MFAC's volume of subprime mortgage loans tripled to over US$2 billion by 2004, and the company's ability to track the loans soon broke down. ("Throwing darts in the dark," was how one former MFAC employee described trying to obtain reliable information from the company's data system.) MFAC was growing on the shaky foundation of bad mortgages, and its collapse was inevitable, a fact later conceded by one of the firm's own lawyers, who said to at least two MFAC executives that Pilcowitz and King fully expected "the bottom to fall out of the [company's] business" after it went public. "As I read it, what they were trying to do is time it perfectly so they could paint a picture to investors of explosive growth of the business and make a credible argument that they would continue to grow massively," says Lascaris. "But then they would get out before the interest rates rose to a level where mortgage holders began defaulting en masse. Their timing, admittedly, was impeccable. Impeccable."

In order to take MFAC public on the TSX, they needed a new company that was, on paper at least, headquartered in Canada. This led to the creation of three new shell companies, one of which, FMF

Group, was incorporated in Ontario. Pilcowitz and King then transferred MFAC's assets and liability related to its mortgage lending business to the FMF group of companies.

FMF's Canadian operation was a shell corporation, its "head offices" listed at the same address as Goodmans LLP, a corporate law firm that acted as its counsel. But the company's senior officers continued to work out of Michigan. FMF was designed to shield the principals from any lawsuits, a fact baldly conceded in its own prospectus: "It may be difficult for [investors] to commence legal proceedings in Canada against [Pilcowitz and King] . . . In addition, it may not be possible for [investors] to collect from MFAC or these other non-Canadian residents judgments obtained in courts in Canada . . . It may also be difficult for [them] to succeed in a lawsuit in the United States, based solely on violations of Canadian securities laws." In other words, if FMF tanked as a result of fraud, Canadian investors would have to sue them in Michigan—and good luck with that.

IN LATE 2004 AND EARLY 2005, Pilcowitz and King recruited numerous top Canadian brokerage houses to help them raise money from investors. One of the roles of brokerage houses is to act as underwriters, which involves bringing a new security issue to the investing public in an offering and, in return for a fee, commit to sell securities. Before it does this, however, the brokerage house must investigate a company to ensure it's a viable business run with integrity. In the case of FMF Capital, this due diligence was woefully inadequate. "[Underwriters such as BMO Nesbitt Burns] showed reckless indifference to the truth," says Henry Juroviesky, a Toronto lawyer who worked with Lascaris on the FMF case. "In other words, a little lawyer like me reading the prospectus in several hours knew this was a house of cards. You would think that after ten or twenty hours of due diligence they would have discovered the business model was flawed. But [the underwriters] didn't. Or they didn't care either way."

Along with BMO Nesbitt Burns, FMF attracted some of Canada's other top underwriters, including National Bank Financial Inc., TD Securities Inc., Canaccord Capital Corp. and Sprott Securities Inc. Fees paid out by FMF to the underwriters were over $11 million, of which BMO Nesbitt Burns received $4.4 million. In March 2005, a preliminary prospectus was filed and distributed to investment advisers and Canadian investors. Pilcowitz and King and the brokerage houses then put on dog-and-pony shows for investors, declaring in their presentation, "The quality of our loans is fantastic! They perform well and that is why institutional investors buy them . . . [Our] industry is thriving today . . . and will continue to be great going forward." A final prospectus, which claimed that full disclosure of material facts had been made, was then submitted to the OSC. Nearly 20 million shares were offered to Canadian investors at $10 a share. The IPO closed in March 2005, having raised nearly $200 million in cash, which was then transferred to Pilcowitz and King in Michigan.

Why were investors attracted to FMF? The answer seems clear: the reputation of the underwriters involved, in particular BMO Nesbitt Burns. Even sophisticated investors were swayed. Rebecca Bekhor, an investment adviser in Montreal working for Refco Inc., a futures broker, bought FMF shares for her clients and herself. "You figure that BMO must've done their homework, and if BMO says it's okay, it must've been okay," she told me, before adding, "Very silly of me to think anything of the kind."

Bekhor says none of the investors knew that FMF's business was based on subprime mortgages offered to people without jobs, income or assets. Regarding underwriters like BMO Nesbitt Burns, she observes: "There is an incentive maybe to not look too hard. If it's something that's not glaring, you just pass over it." The incentive, Bekhor believes, is the fees garnered by underwriting the stock. She remains bitter towards BMO. "You have to ask BMO, what were they doing?"

As soon as FMF's shares began trading on the TSX, they began falling in value. The company's unmanageable mortgage loan volume and poor information system had brought it to the brink of collapse, and despite a series of effusive press releases from FMF, Bay Street grew increasingly alarmed. In November 2005, Pilcowitz and King finally admitted that they were losing major institutional clients and that there was a dramatic rise in the number of mortgage loan losses. Within two days, FMF's single share price plummeted 76 percent, to trade at less than $1. By May 2006, it was down to 65 cents, a 94 percent decline in value from when the IPO was first introduced.

What BMO understood about the soundness of FMF Capital remains a mystery, but what's beyond dispute is that the brokerage house relentlessly promoted FMF shares to investors. Lawsuits claim BMO and one of its analysts, Atul Shah, were being persistently upbeat about FMF in the face of overwhelmingly contradictory evidence, and of rating the stock as "outperform," suggesting that it would do better than the market return. The lawsuit accuses Shah of knowing that "the value of said IPS [Inflation-Protected Security], as outlined in the prospectus, was intentionally inflated." Shah spouted the "outperform" rating right up until the bitter end, and then when brokers challenged him during a conference call, asking him, "Who pressured you to cover these shares?" and "You were dead wrong! What were you thinking?" Shah replied, "I would rather keep this between us, so let's take this offline."

In 2006, after FMF imploded, a major class action lawsuit was launched against Pilcowitz and King and all of the underwriters. Filed in the Michigan courts, it accused Pilcowitz and King of secretly dismantling "MFAC's underwriting standards and practices in order to enable MFAC to experience extravagant growth in loan originations," a charge tantamount to securities fraud. It was apparent that MFAC had allowed potential homeowners to be loaned money without having to provide evidence of their income, and according to one former MFAC executive, Pilcowitz and King were "always pushing staff to close loans. You couldn't close enough loans to satisfy them," regardless of the creditworthiness of their clientele. In addition, according to the lawsuit, the lawyers "incentivized MFAC's underwriters to focus strictly on loan volume and to disregard loan quality."

The suit was settled out of court in 2007 for a mere $29 million of the nearly $200 million investors lost. "Legally, we couldn't have done any better," says Henry Juroviesky. The underwriters had to pay only $4.5 million of the settlement. BMO paid out less than $1.8 million to cover its portion of the lawsuit. And Pilcowitz and King? Their insurers covered 90 percent of the two partners' portion of the settlement. The lawyers were forced to cough up $10 million between them but otherwise kept most of the $200 million they'd originally raised from Canadians.

So egregious was BMO Nesbitt Burns's behaviour over FMF Capital that the OSC conducted an inquiry. In 2010, the commission found that the brokerage house carried out inadequate due diligence before agreeing to underwrite FMF shares. The OSC fined the brokerage house $3.3 million (an amount that garnered this headline in The Financial Post: OSC SLAPS BMO WITH A FEATHER). "It's quite laughable when you think about it," vents Juroviesky.

"Essentially, two lawyers in Michigan had full access to the Canadian capital markets . . . with a risky business that burnt out in flames just months after it was offered. And they walked away scot-free."

DESPITE THE FMF CAPITAL FIASCO, Canada's banks eagerly waded into the U.S. subprime mortgage market. Some sold CDOs, and when those CDOs collectively turned toxic — meaning too many people were defaulting on the mortgage payments that were supposed to provide an income stream for investors — their collapse triggered the global financial meltdown. In the end, Canada's banks lost nearly $12 billion on bad subprime mortgage debt.

Hardest hit was CIBC, for two reasons: after 2005, it had created its own CDO filled with subprime mortgage debt, getting stuck with US$1.7 billion that it could not sell to investors. It also insured the CDOs of Wall Street investment houses, which contained subprime debt valued at nearly US$10 billion. To protect itself in the latter case, CIBC bought its own form of insurance from a group of mostly small bond insurance companies and American International Group (AIG), the world's largest insurer, which would itself soon need to be bailed out by the American government. CIBC executives put the whole bank at grave risk as its entire equity amounted to only $10 billion and these insurers were under-capitalized. According to Toronto class action lawyer Joel Rochon, this meant "they knew they'd basically bet the farm and they didn't disclose it to shareholders." On behalf of some of the bank's shareholders, Rochon's law firm sued CIBC in 2008 over losses incurred due to the bank's forays into the subprime debt market.

In 2006, the bank claimed it was exposed to losses of only US$729 million due to its involvement with CDOs containing subprime debt—a far cry from $11.5 billion. Still, the bond insurers were ill equipped to back even this amount as they had tiny insurance reserves. One of the companies was a New York–based outfit called ACA Financial Guaranty Corp., which was "only single A-rated and vastly undercapitalized. Accordingly, CIBC . . . knew . . . that ACA did not have the capacity to provide an effective [insurance]," says Rochon's lawsuit. "ACA did not provide meaningful protection against risk of default on CIBC's CDO portfolio." Or, as the lawyer put it to me: "It was like going to your mom-and-pop convenience store and asking them to back $11 billion."

The signs of a gathering meltdown within the subprime mortgage securities markets emerged in 2006 and early 2007. Through the spring and summer of 2007, indicators suggested that the debt funding the securitized packages of mortgages was turning toxic. But CIBC continued to mislead Bay Street and shareholders about the extent of its exposure. Brian Shaw, then head of CIBC World Markets, the bank's brokerage arm, said during a May 31, 2007, conference call with analysts that their exposure to the subprime residential mortgages market was "not a major risk issue" for the bank. Curiously, on that very day, the bank's board dumped its chief risk officer, and when analysts asked about the curious timing of this personnel change, the bank's CEO, Gerry McCaughey, denied it had anything to do with the bank's subprime exposure problems. In July 2007 the bank denied that it had US$2.6 billion worth of U.S. subprime mortgage exposure. Soon enough, though, it admitted it *was* sitting on US$1.7 billion worth, although it rejected any notion the investments were in danger of curdling.

As the subprime markets continued to implode, the bank focused on reassuring Bay Street and investors that losses would be minimal. By the fall of 2007, however, it was apparent that ACA Financial

Guaranty did not have enough money to cover the insurance on CIBC's subprime exposure. That December, CIBC disclosed for the first time that it was on the hook for U.S. subprime residential mortgage debt amounting to US$11.5 billion and facing a meltdown, but McCaughey again dismissed any concerns about the stability of these assets. Over the ensuing weeks the news for the bank worsened, and in February 2008 CIBC announced writedowns on its subprime mortgage debt of nearly US$3.5 billion, on top of the US$759 million written down in 2007. Even then, the Rochon-led investors' lawsuit says, the bank continued to mislead investors and the public about the extent of its losses. The bank's shares were now in free fall. As of fiscal 2007 they were $102 per share; by the end of the following year they were down to $55. The bank embarked on a series of further massive write-downs. "CIBC did not lose approximately $11 billion in a day, a week, a month or a quarter," says the lawsuit. "In reality, the losses were continuous throughout [2007–2008]" and the bank's refusal to make this clear in its financial statements was "negligent misrepresentation."

Rochon's law firm hired experts to examine the bank's record of disclosure and eventually produced a 65-page report by Dr. Gordon Richardson, a professor of accounting at the University of Toronto's Rotman School of Management, who concluded that the bank "failed to comply with Generally Accepted Accounting Principles (GAAP) disclosure requirements . . . and the information provided pertaining to credit risk was, prior to December 6, 2007, wholly misleading to the market in general and to class members who invested in CIBC." With the bank's stock overinflated at its peak by as much as $40 per share because its subprime debt exposure was not taken into consideration, the experts hired by Rochon estimated that CIBC's shareholders lost US$6.6 billion from the spring of 2007 to the winter of 2008. By July 2008, CIBC's market capitalization (the total dollar market value of all of a company's outstanding shares) was down to $20 billion, from a high of $36 billion a year earlier.

SUBPRIME MORTGAGES WERE ALSO a part of asset-backed commercial paper (ABCP), "a very dangerous security," says analyst Diane Urquhart. "Like selling a tin of tainted tuna. When the credit crisis occurred, the dealers knew the product had gone bad, and rather than take the loss and discard the tuna, they decided to sell it to Canadians."

ABCP arrived in Canada in 1989, and two basic types were soon being offered to investors. The first was created and sold by Canada's chartered banks. Then, in the late 1990s, a group of independent investment firms led by a small firm called Coventree Inc. arrived on Bay Street. These securitization shops began peddling what was soon called "third-party ABCP," so labelled because it did not originate from the banks. Nevertheless, the investment banking arms of CIBC, the Royal Bank of Canada, the Bank of Nova Scotia, Bank of Montreal and National Bank began selling third-party ABCP too, as did foreign outfits including Deutsche Bank and HSBC. The only major Canadian bank that refused to touch it was TD Canada Trust, which deemed the instrument unsound.

Both bank and third-party ABCP became enormously popular. By 2007, of the $360 billion sitting in Canada's money market, an astonishing 32 percent was made up of ABCP, and of that sum ($115 billion), $35 billion was in the deeply flawed third-party ABCP.

Investors were told that third-party ABCP was safe because it was backstopped by the guarantees and collateral of the big banks. This was a rather gross overstatement. Firms such as Coventree didn't have much equity of their own, and as such, if their ABCP went bad, they risked going bust. To circumvent this problem, the banks and their brokerages and the new small investment shops arranged for liquidity agreements to be drawn up stipulating that firms such as Coventree could access cash from the big banks in order to bail out investors if third-party ABCP had no buyers when they matured. (Essentially, the liquidity agreements were quasi insurance policies designed to reimburse investors if something went wrong.) Such agreements are rooted in a Canadian federal regulation called B-5, introduced by the federal Office of the Superintendent of Financial Institutions (OSFI) in 1994. The regulation said the agreements would kick into effect in the event of a "widespread market disruption," at which point the banks would step in. But there was a big hitch: "widespread market disruption" was too vaguely defined. In fact, these Canadian liquidity agreements were so weak that the U.S. credit rating agencies—Standard & Poor's, Fitch Ratings and Moody's—refused to rate Canadian third-party ABCP at all.

Then there was the matter of transparency. Provincial securities commissions allowed third-party ABCP to be marketed without a prospectus, which made it virtually impossible for investors to find out what assets lay behind the paper. "What you were told of commercial paper is that it was a pool of loans," says Daryl Ching, an investment banker who once worked for Coventree. "But not enough to do your own due diligence. There wasn't enough information to do it." In other words, if ABCP contained subprime mortgages or credit default swaps, investors couldn't find out.

As demand for ABCP grew, Coventree's staff began looking at dodgier assets to underlie it (ABCP, after all, generates income from various forms of mortgages, other kinds of loans and credit default swaps). "We had the dealers calling us and saying, 'There's just not enough, we need more, we need more,'" recalls Ching. Still, those marketing ABCP continued to tell investors that it was a very safe product. As a result, small investors, many of them vulnerable senior citizens, bought $5.8 billion worth of this toxic product in their money market funds and brokerage accounts. One of these was Iris Pearce. "I believed my broker," she says simply, who told her it was so safe the entire banking system would have to collapse before ABCP went bad.

BY THE END OF 2006, it was common knowledge within the investment industry that the subprime mortgage debt market was overextended and about to implode. J.P. Morgan abandoned it at the end of that year, as did Goldman Sachs. Deutsche Bank was now only tenuously involved. Mortgage delinquency rates were rising sharply as homeowners defaulted on their loans. In Canada too, there were growing concerns. In November 2006, the Canadian credit rating agency Dominion Bond Rating Service Ltd. issued a letter to its clients warning that investments such as ABCP would be more stringently graded in the future.

In January 2007, 6,600 investment bankers gathered in Las Vegas for the American Securitization Forum (ASF), the biggest global securitization event of the year. Many Canadian bankers attended. Elizabeth McCaul, the former superintendent of banks for New York, delivered the keynote address. She warned her audience, "We are seeing the consequences of some loan origination practices and undetected fraud that has taken place in the past few years. Mortgage delinquency now stands at its highest level in five years."

As spring turned into summer, the clouds gathering over the global markets blackened. Fears were mounting about subprime mortgage debt, as was anxiety about third-party ABCP and its exposure to toxic debt. On July 24, Judi Dalton, a Coventree executive, sent a note to all of the Canadian banks that sold its ABCP and updated them on the amount of subprime mortgage debt backing Coventree's $16 billion of trusts: 7 percent on average, with three Coventree trusts having more than 10 percent exposure. Instead of soothing worries, the memo had the opposite effect: the bankers discussed whether they should tell investors about the subprime debt exposure. They decided against it.

Still, word soon seeped out that RBC had stopped selling the paper, and confidence in ABCP began to dwindle. Yet even after the July 24 Coventree memo, the industry continued to sell third-party ABCP without informing investors of the possible risks. In the summer of 2007, Deutsche Bank Securities Ltd. sold more than $86 million worth of ABCP containing heavy U.S. subprime exposure to three different clients. Scotia Capital, the brokerage owned by the Bank of Nova Scotia, was accused in a lawsuit of publicly pooh-poohing concerns about ABCP as it sold the product to clients while, at the same time, it was dumping $337 million of its own ABCP inventory into the marketplace because of suspicions it was all going bad.

Trumping these cases was that of Barrick Gold Corp., the world's largest gold mining company, and CIBC World Markets (CWM). On CWM's recommendation, Toronto-based Barrick bought ABCP in a trust called Ironstone. James Mavor, Barrick's treasurer, said that when Barrick executives spoke to Gloria Graham, the executive director of CWM's money market group, they told her they wanted a high-quality, highly rated investment. In July 2007, as concerns about exposure to subprime assets grew, Barrick telephoned CWM and asked whether their investment had exposure to subprime assets. Mavor later wrote in an affidavit: "Graham *expressly* confirmed to

Barrick that its money market investment *did not* have exposure to sub-prime assets" (italics in original). Barrick then bought $33.3 million more ABCP, bringing their total to $66 million. As it turned out, Ironstone Trust was filled with subprime mortgage debt.

EVENTS CAME TO A HEAD on August 13, 2007. By then, the global markets were in free fall because of decaying subprime mortgage assets. "In August, what happened is investors began asking about subprime mortgages and what is in ABCP," recalls former Coventree banker Daryl Ching. "When they became aware [of the exposure] they began panicking . . . There was chaos and fear that caused an abandonment of the market." Indeed, on that August morning, $1 billion worth of ABCP had to be rolled over; that is, existing or new investors would have to buy an equal amount of new paper if sellers were going to be able to raise enough money to repay the maturing notes. But no one was buying any new ABCP. One of the most popular segments of Canada's debt markets had had a seizure.

The banks moved swiftly to reassure investors that the ABCP they'd created—$83 billion worth—was sound by promising to ensure the investments were safe. It was the $35 billion worth of third-party ABCP that was left languishing. The liquidity agreements were supposed to kick in at this juncture to rescue investors and get the market moving again, but CIBC, Deutsche Bank and other international banks balked, claiming the meltdown did not constitute a "widespread market disruption." In short, they reneged on their promise to rescue third-party ABCP investors. Consequently, $32 billion wrapped up in this investment was suddenly frozen, and more than 400 financial institutions, governments, companies, universities, pension plans, airlines and cities across Canada could no longer access their own money. Neither could 1,800 retail investors, mostly seniors like Iris Pearce, many of whom were now facing financial ruin.

Sorting out the ABCP disaster was going to take years, not months, but in the immediate aftermath of the meltdown, this much was revealed: Canada's banks had been eager to encourage investors to buy products the bankers themselves knew to be unsafe, and then they threw those clients under the bus when it all went south. Ironically, such reckless disregard was occurring in the so-called "regulated" and reputable sector of the financial industry. What the credit crisis also revealed was that investors were increasingly being victimized by a powerful unregulated "shadow banking" industry. While growing in size, it's a sector few people know much about, although it can destabilize entire economies.

TEN

TALES FROM THE CRYPT:
THE RISE OF SHADOW BANKING

O N NOVEMBER 25, 2005, John Xanthoudakis swept into the offices of Hart, Saint-Pierre LLP, a law firm on the twenty-first floor of Place Ville Marie in downtown Montreal. Dressed in a dark pinstripe suit, sky-blue shirt and red silk tie, Xanthoudakis looked the part of a successful businessman. The reality was quite different: his wife had left him, his mansion had been sold off and the hedge fund he'd operated since the mid nineties, Norshield Asset Management (Canada) Ltd., had collapsed six months earlier under mysterious circumstances. With nearly $1 billion in assets under management, Norshield had been one of the largest hedge funds in Canada. Yet it had vanished into thin air overnight.

Xanthoudakis had come to his lawyer's office to meet with some investors who'd lost money in Norshield's demise. He was running late and, unbeknownst to him, the three "investors" were, in fact, emissaries of the Rizzuto crime family—at the time the most feared and powerful Mafia organization in Canada. After Xanthoudakis finally arrived and sat down, Francesco Del Balso, a heavy-set man with cold, eerie eyes, and an ambitious underboss within the Rizzuto operation, didn't mince his words: "We represent a group of people who aren't very happy. Now, you've got about $350 million and we want $5 million of it, because we don't want these people unhappy anymore."

Taken aback, Xanthoudakis insisted that he was broke, a statement that hardly mollified the Rizzuto soldiers. "You've helped people sneak money out of this country for decades," snapped Del Balso. "I know you've got a stash 'cause that's your business."

As Xanthoudakis tried to counter the allegations, he didn't pay close enough attention to one of the Rizzuto henchmen, who rose and moved swiftly around the boardroom table. "He spun John in his chair and sucker-punched him," recalls William Urseth, an American businessman and one of Xanthoudakis's friends who worked with him prior to Norshield's collapse. "Beat him up pretty good."

"I'll be calling in the next few days," Del Balso told the bleeding Xanthoudakis as the mobsters took their leave. "You had better know then when we're getting the $5 million."

Unfortunately for the Rizzuto gangsters, the RCMP had wiretapped their cellphones as part of an investigation into the Mafia family. After the men left the law firm, the Mounties caught Del Balso on tape regaling another underboss about the beating, saying Xanthoudakis was "pissing blood over there" and joking that the hedge fund executive had "opened up like a crepe."

DEL BALSO'S ACCUSATION that Xanthoudakis was adept at moving other people's money out of the country was true. While Norshield's head office was based in Montreal, the hedge fund parked its cash in the Bahamas and other offshore banking outposts, likely the reason the Rizzutos invested with Norshield in the first place.

Investment products like ABCP, CDOs and hedge funds like Norshield are all part of a shadow banking system, a global network of non-depository banks and pools of capital that cater to primarily wealthy investors and remain stubbornly beyond the purview of government regulators. By 2008, in the United States, this shadow system was about the same size as the traditional depository banking system, and its influence was so immense that it could upend entire economies. And so, while investors complain about the failings of enforcement over the traditional banking and securities sector, no rules or regulations, and hence no recourse, apply in the shadow world—making it rife for fraud. The 2007–2009 credit crisis and ensuing global meltdown pushed shadow banking into the limelight, largely because of its role in causing the catastrophe.

For example, Wall Street hedge funds, pension funds, banks and insurers had bought credit default swaps totalling some $62 trillion by the time the crisis was at full bore (an amount that was twice the size of the U.S. stock market). CDSs are an entirely unregulated non-transparent market, and hedge funds purchased CDSs to "insure" the vast pools of subprime mortgage debt Wall Street and the rest of the global financial industry had been stockpiling during the 2000s. They believed, reasonably, that if subprime debt plummeted in value, they would make money because (under that scenario) the CDSs would pay out like any insurance policy would. And this is exactly what happened. In the summer of 2007, subprime mortgages began defaulting and the unfolding crisis in the global markets began to trigger the credit default swaps. This caused an unexpected problem, however: the sums involved were so immense that the financial institutions that sold CDSs couldn't cover the outlay needed to satisfy the margin calls. AIG, the giant American insurance company, for example, had sold US$440 billion in CDS coverage—money it simply didn't have in 2008—and the U.S. government had to step in to rescue it.

The shadow banking industry also exists to hide rich people's money from government tax collectors in offshore tax havens such as Monaco, the Cayman Islands, Bermuda, the Bahamas, and the Turks and Caicos. Or to hide the money of gangsters like the Rizzutos with their investment in Norshield. As *The Financial Post's* Diane Francis once summed it up, "Thousands of fabulously wealthy Canadians sit on yachts in tax havens without paying any taxes on wealth made in Canada." Many banks are set up in countries like these specifically to hide the assets of North Americans, particularly Canadians.

Brian Trowbridge, a Canadian lawyer from B.C., caters to this clientele. He's the CEO of Lochaven Financial Ltd. and Hallmark Trust Ltd., both located in the Turks and Caicos. David Marchant, the editor of the Florida-based newsletter *Offshore Alert*, says people put their money in such financial institutions because no one asks probing questions. "Let's say you're a Canadian and you committed a fraud and there might be a lawsuit against you, and you need to move your money," he explains. "These banks would accept it. They may not even ask you if you're being sued. They would ask the minimum amount of questions and do the minimum amount of due diligence, while a legitimate bank wouldn't accept it."

Hallmark, in particular, has been caught in a number of scandals in recent years. A Ponzi scheme was run out of it by David Smith, a Jamaican national who pled guilty in 2011 for masterminding a US$220 million scam that defrauded six thousand investors (he received a thirty-year sentence). In a civil lawsuit filed in 2007 in

Hawaii, the U.S. Internal Revenue Service alleged that two American accounting firms advised clients to evade taxes by moving money out of the country by means of MasterCards issued by Hallmark. "Hallmark is a completely rogue organization," says David P. Rowe, a Florida lawyer who is suing the bank over Smith's Ponzi scheme. "We now know that it was set up to assist people in hiding money."

Hallmark's sister bank, Lochaven, is linked to Ronald Weinberg, the former CEO of Cinar Corp., who was arrested in 2011 for defrauding the Montreal-based animation company. Weinberg parked nearly $2 million in Lochaven—money that was being sought by Cinar's new owners, who claimed it did not belong to Weinberg.

In 2009, then Minister of National Revenue Jean-Pierre Blackburn, said that 106 wealthy people had used RBC Dominion Securities Inc., the brokerage house of the Royal Bank of Canada, to set up offshore accounts in the European principality of Liechtenstein. As much as $100 million in total was sitting in these accounts. One account alone held $12 million. They did this, Blackburn contended, to hide their taxes. An investigation by Canada Revenue Agency (CRA) discovered that at least three RBC Dominion Securities advisers had helped people hide their money in Liechtenstein. The federal government eventually managed to collect $6 million in taxes from these accounts, but nobody was charged or fined. In fact, Canada permits its citizens to pay a one-time departure tax—a 25 percent capital gains tax—and then they never have to pay tax again on their nest egg as it accumulates in these havens. The use of offshore tax havens has been so pervasive that the CRA established a voluntary disclosure program to pressure tax cheats to come forward, and is devoting more resources to hunting down money in foreign jurisdictions. "In 2009–2010, the CRA identified $1 billion in federal tax from hiding assets and accounts offshore or through other international transactions," says Philippe Brideau, a spokes-person for CRA. "In fiscal 2010–2011, the CRA processed almost 4,000 offshore disclosures and identified over $166 million in unreported income."

ONE PERSON WHO'S TAKEN ADVANTAGE of this parallel financial system is Paul Eustace, an American who lives in Oakville, Ontario, a bedroom community just down the highway from Toronto. He grew up in Connecticut, studied at the University of Pennsylvania, and in 1990 hooked up with a childhood friend, Monroe Trout, who'd founded a Chicago-based hedge fund, Trout Trading Co. In 1994, Trout sent Eustace to Toronto to set up a subsidiary, and Eustace moved to Oakville with his wife and two children.

He soon met a 21-year-old stripper, Denise Nadeau, at a Mississauga, Ontario, strip joint called the Locomotion Cabaret, and Nadeau became his lover. Eustace began buying her expensive gifts, paying for breast implants and taking her on trips to New York and Bermuda, where Trout had an office. The stripper's presence in the Bermuda office apparently rankled Trout so much that he fired Eustace in 1998.

Eustace eventually set up his own hedge fund, Philadelphia Alternative Asset Management Co., LLC (PAAM), which he ran from an office in Oakville even though the fund had operations in Pennsylvania. The company managed to attract some prominent people to its board, including a vice-chairman of the Philadelphia Stock Exchange and a former president of Drexel Morgan, and lured Canadian and American investors with the promise of trading their money in an offshore fund in the Cayman Islands. PAAM collected nearly US$300 million from investors, which Eustace used to trade mostly in commodity futures and options.

Meanwhile, Eustace's affair with Nadeau went sour and she threatened to expose their relationship to his wife. Eustace had bought her a house equipped with the latest mod-con appliances and had spent as much as $1 million of investors' money on his paramour. (He also allegedly gave $87,000 to a man who threatened to kill Nadeau unless she repaid a loan to Eustace.) Overall he used roughly $2 million in cash from his clients to spend it on a host of luxury items.

But in 2005, PAAM hit a snag. A big one. Eustace had gambled incorrectly on American interest rates going up and promptly lost an estimated US$202 million of the $300 million in the hedge fund. Instead of coming clean to investors about the disaster, he covered up the losses and began issuing false monthly statements indicating strong growth, *and* Eustace continued to pocket investors' money to pay for his salary and lavish lifestyle. At the same time he was enticing clients to invest in a fund that did not exist.

After PAAM went bust in the summer of 2005, U.S. regulators demanded that he hand over his wealth and issued a restraining order to prevent him from transferring or disposing of any of his personal assets. The regulators claimed Eustace defied the order within two days of it coming into effect, selling his 1988 Porsche 911 Turbo Slantnose convertible for US$48,000 and having the cheque endorsed to one of his Canadian attorneys "in a blatant attempt to hide assets" from a court-appointed bankruptcy receiver. This was the first of many instances where he ignored the restraining order by selling assets and pocketing the proceeds, and using Canadian banks and his lawyers to assist him.

By 2012, Eustace was a fugitive from U.S. justice, working at one of his lawyers' offices in Oakville as a bookkeeper for $25 an hour. Canadian investors were suing him, while American authorities obtained a court order demanding he pay back US$279 million to his victims and hitting him with over US$12 million in civil penalties.

HEDGE AND PRIVATE EQUITY funds—big pools of money usually provided by wealthy and institutional investors (such as pension funds)—are rogue forces within the shadow banking system. Generally, retail investors cannot invest in these funds due to minimum wealth restrictions. The term "hedge" refers to, basically, taking equal and opposite positions in two different markets (such as cash and futures markets). Yet, in layman's terms, hedging often entails putting yourself in a position to cash in on a market catastrophe. It's profiting from other people's loss and seen as a terribly cynical way to make money.

Run by investment gurus and fund managers, hedge and private equity funds invest in any opportunity that suits their fancy, and according to Heather Slavkin, a financial expert with the American labour trade-union organization, the AFL–CIO, they remain unregulated because "if you're only selling to the super-rich who can afford to pay professional managers and take the hit if things go bad, they don't have to apply the same stringent laws as when you are selling to retail investors."

An early indicator of their burgeoning power dates back to 1988, when the American tobacco and food giant RJR Nabisco Inc., then the nineteenth-largest corporation in the U.S.A., was bought for US$25 billion by the private equity fund Kohlberg Kravis Roberts & Co. (KKR)—a business that few people outside of Wall Street had ever heard of. The takeover was immortalized in the bestselling book *Barbarians at the Gate*. Over the next twenty years, as trillions of dollars poured onto the global markets, private equity and hedge funds became increasingly popular, partly because, says Slavkin, pension plans and university endowment funds were being hit hard by low interest rates and needed a new option to make money. "A lot of pension funds were not getting the returns and funding that they needed from employers," she explains, "so they were chasing yield and they saw hedge funds as an opportunity to make up for the lack of contributions."

Today, there are over 8,300 hedge funds worldwide, and their total assets have risen from US$39 billion in 1990 to as much as US$2 trillion by 2011, growing at a rate of at least 15 percent a year. Hedge fund managers are now Wall Street's highest-paid professionals. In 2009, the top twenty-five were paid a collective (US) $25.3 billion in personal compensation. That year, David Tepper of Appaloosa Management made a whopping US$4 billion; George Soros of Soros Fund Management took in US$3.3 billion; James Simons of the Renaissance Technologies fund earned US$2.5 billion; while John Paulson of Paulson & Company pocketed US$2.3 billion, up from US$2 billion in 2008. (In Canada, hedge funds are a small but growing sector of the financial industry. Only 4 percent have assets of more than $5 billion, and 30 percent have assets between $10 million and $49 million. Since the late nineties, more than 200 hedge funds have set up shop in Canada, with at least $32 billion under management.)

Scandal and controversy have dogged the funds, and not only because of the credit crisis. Former German vice-chancellor Franz Müntefering describes them as "locusts," while Poul Nyrup Rasmussen, prime minister of Denmark from 1993 to 2001 and a member of the European Parliament, claims they destabilize markets and destroy companies and jobs by taking over vulnerable businesses, stripping them bare of assets and downsizing workforces (a reality seen in the cases of Algoma and Stelco). Rasmussen has become one of the most vocal critics of hedge and private equity funds because they're not subject to regulation despite having become so powerful. He wrote in 2008, "These funds are largely tax-exempt, often because they are registered offshore, although they operate from the world's major onshore financial centres."

Ironically, hedge funds often generate poorer results than other kinds of investments. "If you look at the long-term returns from these funds and at studies which don't just look at the top twenty performers—which is often what you see—[the returns are] actually lower than what you see from an indexed fund," explains Slavkin. "The fees they charge are too high for these sorts of investment strategies." Comparing their returns to the Dow Jones Wilshire 5000 and Lehman Aggregate, a study reproduced in a 2007 report for the European Parliament suggests that a simple portfolio comprising 50 percent bonds and 50 percent equities produced better returns than hedge funds in either bull or bear markets.

THE STORY OF JOHN XANTHOUDAKIS and his hedge fund, Norshield, offers insight into more than just gangsters operating within the financial system. The son of Greek immigrants, Xanthoudakis grew up in Montreal and became interested in investing while studying engineering in the 1980s at Concordia University, developing proprietary software that would give him an edge in the derivatives markets. After leaving Concordia, Xanthoudakis set up a firm called Ultron Technologies Corp. and put his trading system to the test. While his software appeared to produce terrific results, on two occasions the Quebec Securities Commission (QSC), then the province's market watchdog, stopped the sale of Ultron fund units. The first time was because Ultron was offering units in an investment fund without a prospectus. The second time, in 1987, the QSC obtained a Superior Court injunction against Xanthoudakis because he was selling an investment that had not been approved by the commission. These setbacks did not slow him down, however, and he went on to establish what would become Norshield.

As a hedge fund, Norshield was different in that it also raised money from retail investors, and was thereby partially under the purview of provincial regulators. I say only partially because Norshield had a Byzantine offshore structure. Investors' cash passed from one fund and offshore bank account to another, commingling with investments received from Canadian pension funds and financial institutions, before finally pooling in one big pot. At the bottom of this structure was a Royal Bank of Canada (RBC) call option funded by an RBC loan that allowed Norshield investors access to the performance of a basket of RBC portfolio investments. As the investors' money flowed from one entity and jurisdiction to another, the cash disappeared, sucked up in redemptions, unexplained third-party payments and the costs of maintaining the structure itself. All told, from 1993 until its collapse in 2005, $159 million belonging to 1,900 retail investors was pumped into Norshield's various funds. Another $350 million came from pension plans and financial institutions. Most of this money, except for a little over $30 million, would eventually vanish.

THE FIRST CRACK IN THE fund's foundation occurred when a scandal overtook one of its biggest clients, Cinar Corp., the Montreal-based animation studio. Founded in 1984 by the ambitious husband-and-wife team of Ronald Weinberg and Micheline Charest, Cinar was a huge success story by the late 1990s, producing children's cartoons such as *Arthur*, *The Busy World of Richard Scarry* and *The Adventures of Paddington Bear*. By then, it had a market capitalization approaching $1.5 billion and, naturally, the golden couple were seeking help in investing their cash. Hasanain Panju, Cinar's chief financial officer, stumbled upon Norshield International, one of Norshield's many entities, which managed an offshore hedge fund called Globe-X out of the Bahamas.

In 1999, Cinar invested US$108 million in cash with Globe-X. John Xanthoudakis was over the moon with his good fortune and his famous new clients. There was one glaring problem, however: Weinberg, Charest and Panju failed to inform Cinar's board about the transaction, let alone get its approval. In fact, the Cinar founders were playing a game of high-stakes poker. Cinar owed part of its success to grants and tax credits the company received during the nineties on the condition they were used to employ Canadian writers; instead, Cinar had simply pocketed the cash and hired Americans. When the tax credit abuse issue hit the media in late 1999, Cinar came under police investigation. It didn't take long for investigators to find the US$108 million that Weinberg, Charest and Panju had parked offshore in Globe-X. Outraged, Cinar's board demanded the money be returned and forced the now infamous trio to resign.

John Xanthoudakis's beloved hedge fund was suddenly under siege. At this point, he turned to an old friend, Lino Matteo, for help. The two men had met when they toiled together as orderlies at a Montreal hospital during the early 1980s. The business relationship between them revolved around Mount Real Corp., a business services company that was spun off from Norshield in 1993. Matteo ran Mount Real while Xanthoudakis was a director and principal shareholder. The company would eventually attract $130 million of investors' cash.

Tall, profane and aggressive, Matteo was notorious for his violent temper and abuse of employees and clients alike. One businessman who dealt with him claims that when Matteo lost his cool, he would shout at people, "Are you stupid? You think I'm stupid!" before grabbing a carpenter's hammer from his desk, yelling, "Put your hand on this desk, you coward, put it on the desk!" and proceeding to pound the desk with the full force of his 240 pounds.

It was this to man that Xanthoudakis turned in his hour of need.

A DEAL WAS EVENTUALLY brokered between Cinar's board and Norshield whereby the US$108 million sitting in Globe-X would be returned to Cinar. But this plan eventually went off the rails. Globe-X defaulted on returning all of the money (US$30 million was not returned) and the fund was put into bankruptcy by the Bahamian courts. This opened Norshield up to investigation. According to court documents, a bankruptcy liquidator soon reported that of the US$108 million, only US$21 million was invested in securities, a significant portion was not invested at all and the rest was "simply disbursed related to the Globe-X Companies and Norshield." The same documents cite further fraud, reported to the liquidator by former CFO of a Norshield subsidiary, Robert Daviault. A few years earlier, Globe-X had announced a shortfall and asked Cinar to cover the debt. Cinar did, to the tune of US$7 million. But the money didn't go to Globe-X; it was instead transferred to a company called Killington Holdings Ltd., controlled by Weinberg, Panju and Charest. Daviault said the bogus loss and transfer was a way for the three former Cinar officers to divert funds into their own pockets.

In 2004, Cinar was sold to a consortium and the new owners strongly suspected that Weinberg, Charest and Panju had hidden as much as $100 million in various offshore accounts. They set up a three-person committee, led by Toronto securities lawyer G. Wesley Voorheis, to hunt for the cash. "For a few years, I chased around for anyone who had money and I thought was responsible," says Voorheis. One person they spoke to was Daviault, who testified that Xanthoudakis and Matteo had a hand in a shuffling of assets to make it appear where Cinar's money ended up had assets commensurate with the level of the company's investments. Daviault went on to say that documents, accounting records, investments and transactions were "reconstructed . . . to justify and prepare a paper trail that would support the transactions that took place." Daviault also said that Xanthoudakis arranged for Weinberg, Charest and Panju to receive "kickbacks" from the gains generated from Cinar's investments.

Naturally, all of this was bad news for Norshield and Cinar. By 2005, according to one source, Matteo was hoping that "Norshield would be bombed to rubble because it would keep everybody's eyes off Mount Real." In the end, because investors' funds were vanishing as they passed through Norshield's various entities, it's believed the hedge fund's directors artificially inflated the underlying value of the assets to investors. As time went by, there was not enough money in Norshield to meet redemptions, especially as assets had been overvalued. (Not unlike a Ponzi scheme, new investors' cash was being used to pay for redemptions.) The hedge fund finally collapsed in June 2005, and depending on whom you talk to, anywhere from $108 million to $500 million of investors' money simply vanished into a maze of offshore entities. Norshield's retail investors were destined to received 6 to 9 cents on the dollar.

——

AFTER NORSHIELD'S DEMISE, a court-appointed receiver began investigating where the money went, and the Ontario Securities Commission launched an inquiry. The receiver found unexplained payments of huge sums flowing within Norshield, all largely controlled by Xanthoudakis. For example, a Barbadian bank linked to Norshield made unexplained payments of $60 million to "third parties" for which there was inadequate documentation. Indeed, in case after case there was no paperwork showing where money ended up, and no audited records were kept after 2003.

Hovering in the background was the Royal Bank of Canada. In 1999, Xanthoudakis struck a deal with the bank that gave him a line of credit. For every $15 million in assets Norshield held, RBC would advance the hedge fund $85 million. Thanks to this arrangement, Norshield's funds under management ballooned to as much as $1 billion. Why did RBC get into bed with Norshield? Investors' lawsuits claim that because chartered banks in Canada are forbidden from operating hedge funds, the deal that RBC struck with Norshield gave it a backdoor access to a section of the shadow banking industry in which it was legally prevented from engaging. "Norshield was nothing but a front for RBC to be in the hedge fund business, which they were not legally allowed to be in in Canada," says William Urseth, who helped Xanthoudakis with his PR strategy and then published a book in 2009 about the Norshield–Cinar–Mount Real debacle. "This was a way they could be in it."

Moreover, two separate investors' lawsuits filed in Canada and the United States against RBC allege the bank knew and understood the precise health and overall structure of Norshield's funds, did its due diligence and approved transactions designed to mask the fund's financial problems, including its overstated assets. The suits claim that RBC wielded significant control over Norshield, including the selection of investment advisers and managers and the allocation of risk in the portfolio, and was therefore culpable in any wrongdoing. They say RBC profited handsomely from its role as a financial intermediary, receiving compensation in excess of $60 million, and then triggered Norshield's collapse when it invoked the early termination provisions of its option agreement in June 2005. "RBC was the *de facto* investment manager of the funds although it concealed its role and the extent of its control over the investments," reads the U.S. lawsuit.

"Our complaint is saying the money went somewhere," says Lee Squitieri, a New York lawyer representing Norshield's American investors. "Did it go to assets under control or go into someone's pocket? Or go to Xanthoudakis? We don't know. The paper trail is incomplete. What we do know is that Norshield in the middle of 2004 starts going off the rails, starts doing things that had to be signed off [by] or have been known to RBC. But the bank let things unfold. Under American law, that compliance is fraud."

Urseth says when he was working with Xanthoudakis he found eighty-two boxes of documents in Norshield's Chicago offices in the spring of 2006. After reading their contents, he came to the conclusion that RBC made off with all of the hedge fund investors' money. "All of the liquidity of the funds was taken by RBC in June of 2005," he claims. "They just plain took it and everybody stood around and watched. No one dares fight RBC." (Two RBC Dominion Securities brokers were fired in 2006 as a result of their involvement in the Norshield scandal, although the bank refused to say why they were let go.)

In 2006, the OSC filed charges against Xanthoudakis and two of the company's officers. Testimony was heard from the court-appointed receiver (accountants whose job it is to find out where the money went) and investigators over eighteen days of hearings, held in 2008 and 2009. Of the $159 million placed in Norshield by retail investors, the receiver was only able to retrieve $31 million.

Meanwhile, Lino Matteo also found himself in hot water. In the fall of 2005, Mount Real collapsed and, along with it, $130 million belonging to 1,600 retail investors vanished. Matteo was charged with ethical violations by the Quebec Order of Certified Management Accountants (CMA). In a scathing judgment, he was ordered to pay $18,000 in fines after being found guilty of swindling hundreds of investors out of millions of dollars. Calling Matteo a "danger to the public," the disciplinary committee revoked his CMA accreditation.

In 2010, the OSC found Xanthoudakis and another Norshield officer guilty of breaching securities law by making false statements, failing to keep proper records and dealing in bad faith with investors. The commission imposed penalties of $2.2 million on each of the men and $295,000 for the cost of the OSC's investigation, and banned them from working in the securities industry for life.

Finally, in 2011, Quebec police arrested and charged Xanthoudakis, Matteo, Weinberg and Panju with fraud over transactions involving Norshield and Cinar and the loss of millions of dollars of investors' money. None of this proved much comfort to Norshield investors. "There has been no investigation yet of the $500 million still missing," says Toronto retail investor Chris Ouslis, who ploughed $1 million of his money into Norshield and lost all of it. Ouslis's frustration with the mere fines levied against Xanthoudakis and at least one of his co-conspirators was evident when we spoke: "These guys were in charge of $500 million and it's gone, and all you can say [is that] we're going to charge him under the securities act and fine them and that they are both bad boys. This has to be some sort of bizarre joke . . . It's not like you are dealing with your kids who spilt a cup of milk!"

AND THAT ASSAULT ON XANTHOUDAKIS in 2005 by the Rizzuto gangsters? One would think a reputable businessman would immediately go to the police to report such an incident. The Norshield founder did not. The Rizzuto goons had demanded $5 million and immediately applied pressure on Xanthoudakis to come up with the cash. Finally, in February 2006, Xanthoudakis filed a complaint with the police about the shakedown. He claimed he hadn't done so earlier because he feared for his safety. The three Rizzuto enforcers were arrested and charged with assault, but Xanthoudakis soon withdrew the complaint and the charges were dropped.

The revelations of the Xanthoudakis assault came out in *Projet Colisée*, a vast wiretap operation overseen by the RCMP aimed at the Rizzuto organization that culminated in ninety-one arrests of the crime family's top leadership and its soldiers in 2006. When I spoke to one of the RCMP officers who worked on *Colisée* and who was familiar with the beating of Xanthoudakis, I asked him whether the Mounties were interested in finding out if the Rizzutos ever laundered money through Norshield. He said, "That wasn't the focus of our investigation. We were more interested in the assault." In fact, the RCMP refused to investigate the whole Norshield affair, and to this day it's unknown whether Norshield was being used to wash the cash of the most powerful Mafia family in Canada.

Such lack of concern about the activities of the shadow banking industry is epidemic. As a result, it allows those with criminal intentions the leeway to run amok for years. No case illustrates this troubling reality better than that of George Georgiou.

ELEVEN

THE GHOST THIEF

The Philadelphia Ritz-Carlton is a five-star hotel, a neo-classical greystone edifice with a facade that resembles the Pantheon in Rome. In one suite, on September 17, 2008, George Georgiou was meeting a man he knew only as "Charlie," and they were there to put the final touches on plans for a massive pump-and-dump fraud. A 39-year-old Canadian stock promoter, Georgiou was using a cluster of Ontario-based shell companies to attract investors, manipulate stock prices and disappear with the cash.

This was not the first time Georgiou had met Charlie. A few weeks earlier, they'd come together to discuss details of the scheme. Georgiou had explained that he controlled an Ontario company called Northern Ethanol, Inc., and his plan was to boost the company's stock price from $2.50 to $3, ensuring it was "revved up" properly, meaning it would be artificially boosted. To accomplish this, he wanted Charlie—who said he controlled a group of corrupt brokers—to buy $5 million to $10 million worth of the company's shares. He would then pay Charlie and his brokers a kickback.

At the Ritz-Carlton, the men continued to hammer out the particulars. At one point, Georgiou joked that he might need to be in a "hot tub" with Charlie so no one could hide a recording device, and sought assurances there was no "cop" involved in their operation. The joke was on Georgiou. Charlie *was* an undercover FBI agent. And as the Ritz-Carlton meeting wrapped up, the FBI crashed through the door and arrested Georgiou. Under interrogation at the FBI's Philadelphia offices, Georgiou claimed he wasn't responsible for manipulating the stock, that he was merely cashing in on a plot hatched by others. "There is no better way to make money from these scumballs, mailers or promotions than to prey upon them," he said.

The FBI didn't buy it, and Georgiou was charged with running a massive stock market fraud. It was the end of the line for the former stockbroker. Not only had he bilked countless investors out of tens of millions in one of the greatest frauds engineered on Canadian soil, but he'd brought down an entire Bahamian brokerage house to boot. The story of Georgiou and his white-collar crime spree exposes a different face of the shadow banking world. While hedge funds and credit default swaps and offshore banking may seem like difficult-to-grasp abstractions, the damage he caused is much more tangible. His case reveals how easy it is for an incorrigible thief to slip in and out of both the so-called legitimate world of finance and the shadow banking sector, committing fraud and yet going undetected for nearly two decades by law enforcement. And thus underlining why the shadow banking sector so desperately needs to be regulated.

A NATIVE OF WATERLOO, ONTARIO, Georgiou started his career in the late eighties, garnering an entry-level position at Midland

Walwyn Capital Inc. Working out of Midland's offices in neighbour-
ing Kitchener, Georgiou became one of the brokerage house's top
producers. He was a dynamo, a broker who earned $400,000 a year,
dressed to the nines, drove a Lexus and lived the high life.

One of his clients was Jack Hougassian, a self-made 32-year-old
millionaire who'd founded an executive placement firm, TechHi
Consultants Inc. in Waterloo. Now middle-aged, Hougassian is a
charming and animated man who recalls his experience with
Georgiou with bemusement, as if it all happened to someone else.
By the early nineties, Hougassian had a net worth of $5 million — $2
million of which was in the markets — and Georgiou convinced
Hougassian to let him invest the young millionaire's money. "The
first year of the relationship, I had no complaints with the guy,"
Hougassian told me when we met. But this soon changed. Midland
began receiving complaints from Georgiou's clients, including
Hougassian. Georgiou was caught making unauthorized trades with
Hougassian's money along with other reckless behaviour. Midland
was well aware of Georgiou's actions and tolerated them for years.
But this time he had gone too far and they fired him.

It was the fall of 1993, and he wasn't unemployed for very long. All
of four days, in fact. Although the investment firm Levesque Securities
Inc. knew Georgiou was a risk and that he had a track record of playing with clients' money without their permission, they hired him as a
trader anyway. A Levesque lawyer later admitted that Georgiou arrived
"with a cloud over his head," but overriding such concerns was his
talent for finding clients and making money for his employers.

Brokerages hiring investment advisers with poor reputations is
not as unusual as one might assume. Take former RBC investment
adviser Henry Cole, for example. Charged in 2011 with stealing $2
million from clients while working for the bank, RBC had hired

him years earlier knowing of Cole's involvement in a scandal in 2002 with Rampart Securities Inc., a brokerage house shut down due to numerous securities violations. Cole, a member of Rampart's executive committee, had been forced to pay $125,000 in fines and was banned from taking senior jobs in the industry for ten years, although working as an investment adviser apparently didn't violate this restriction.

Despite his own misgivings, Hougassian followed Georgiou to Levesque a few months later, a decision he soon regretted. Over the Christmas holidays in 1994, while Hougassian was away on vacation, Georgiou took the businessman's money and ploughed it into a number of unauthorized investments. Georgiou was using Hougassian's money to play the markets. If he made money, he pocketed the profits and informed Hougassian there'd been a clerical error. "What happened with these eight trades is that the stock market went down that year over the holidays," recalls Hougassian. "They all lost money and he had no money to pay it back." Hougassian was now out $400,000. When he discovered what Georgiou had done, he complained to Levesque, who tried to suggest Hougassian had in fact not lost any money and that he shouldn't complain given Hougassian was well aware of Georgiou's "methods of operation."

Waterloo veterinarian Robert Blackburn and his wife also followed Georgiou from Midland to Levesque, and ended up losing $190,000. Georgiou squandered their money by making unauthorized trades in risky investments and "churning" their accounts in order to generate more commissions for himself.

By January 1995, Levesque had no choice but to fire its rogue broker. Both Hougassian and the Blackburns sued Midland and Levesque for failing to properly manage Georgiou. "He's a classic sociopath," says Hougassian. "He once put a second mortgage on his mother's house without her knowledge to pay back a debt he owed to one of his investors. He forged the documents. She almost had a heart attack when she found out about it."

THE INVESTMENT DEALERS ASSOCIATION (IDA), one of the financial industry's regulatory bodies, opened an investigation into Georgiou and in 2000 penalized him with fines of $65,000 and banned him from trading for the next five years (he could only re-enter the profession if he rewrote some industry tests).

No matter, Georgiou had already moved into the netherworld of illegal stock promotions, and by some accounts he never stopped trading. Despite the bans, the fines and the lawsuits piling up around him, he just moved his business offshore.

But in order to continue, he needed cash. And so Georgiou set up an elaborate scam. By 2004, working out of Toronto, he and a group of Canadian co-conspirators established four publicly traded shell companies—Avicena Group, Inc., Neutron Enterprises, Inc., Hydrogen Hybrid Technologies, Inc. and Northern Ethanol, Inc.— three of which had addresses in Toronto, staff and websites, and issued press releases announcing their deals. Although it's not clear how much real business they did, they were hardly hiding from public view. Georgiou controlled a large chunk of their unrestricted stock, with only one purpose in mind: to use them as pump-and-dumps. "The essence of a pump-and-dump is a paper company," explains David Marchant, the editor of *Offshore Alert*, the Florida-based investigative newsletter that follows the offshore banking industry. "It's just a vehicle for promoters to sell shares around."

To raise money from investors, Georgiou printed up promotional mailers and sent them to millions of households across the United

States. A couple of the shell companies purported to be in the "green" energy business, and he used environmentalism to seduce investors. One mailer was headlined GAS CRISIS! and said investors could reap "500% gains" by investing in his companies and that GREEN FUEL TECHNOLOGY IS SET TO SOAR! As improbable as these claims might seem, they did attract buyers to the company's stock, which drove up share prices.

To do his trading, Georgiou used accounts in other people's names with offshore brokers in the Bahamas and Turks and Caicos. In 2006, for example, he phoned an executive at Caledonia Corporate Management Group Ltd., a broker-dealer based in the Bahamas, asking if he could open an account to trade in securities. He told Caledonia the account would be in the name of his associate Ronald Wyles, a retired Toronto broker who once worked at Richardson-Greenshields and the Bank of Nova Scotia. (Wyles was also a shareholder in one of Georgiou's shell companies, Northern Ethanol.) Georgiou said he needed a $3 million margin facility, whereby Caledonia would give him money to trade with as long as he matched it with an equal or greater sum. He would then invest the total amount. Georgiou said his collateral would be $15 million in securities in two of his shell companies, shares held by the Jitney Group Inc., a Montreal-based online broker.

The promised $15 million in securities never materialized, but after Georgiou's wife offered a personal guarantee of her own securities, Caledonia was satisfied. With Jitney on board, Caledonia opened the Wyles account and Georgiou began trading.

Georgiou took Caledonia's millions and, in essence, pocketed the cash. Technically, the money he was trading with was supplied by Jitney, but the collateral was the assets that Caledonia's investors had placed with the Bahamian brokerage. In the end, Georgiou never put up one cent of his own holdings. More astonishing still, no one at Caledonia or Jitney did a background check on him, or wondered why he insisted on using a proxy's name to carry out his trading. "It's difficult to believe that any company could allow this to happen," says David Marchant. "He was a new client, he went through this guy Wyles. This brokerage extended him a level of credit that was in the millions of dollars. It was just very bizarre. Either Caledonia was incredibly incompetent or they were part of the scheme." In fact, despite Georgiou failing to put up any money of his own, Caledonia kept on giving him credit, until he finally had access to US$26 million. Georgiou used the same ploy to similar effect with at least one other Bahamian brokerage house.

But Georgiou's luck was running out. In 2007, the FBI caught one of his collaborators, an American stock market fraud artist named Kevin Waltzer. In return for a reduced sentence, Waltzer agreed to co-operate. He introduced Georgiou to the FBI undercover agent Charlie, who went on to build a case against Georgiou for more than a year.

In early 2008, Caledonia collapsed after it became apparent the US$26 million was lost. Jitney stepped in and sold off Caledonia's assets to cover an overdrawn margin loan stemming from Georgiou's operation. Later that year, Georgiou was arrested in Philadelphia at the Ritz-Carlton. All but one of his Canadian shell companies went out of business. His Canadian collaborators walked away scot-free, however. All told, Georgiou realized at least US$21 million in ill-gotten gains, and possibly more than US$50 million.

Georgiou went on trial in Philadelphia during the summer of 2010. A jury found him guilty. He was sentenced to twenty-five years in a U.S. federal prison and ordered to return US$55 million in investors' monies. He won't be leaving prison for at least twenty years. And the liquidator in the Caledonia bankruptcy toyed with suing Jitney to get some of the Bahamian broker's money back.

Conspicuously absent from bringing Georgiou to justice was Canadian law enforcement. When I telephoned the RCMP's Integrated Market Enforcement Team Toronto office and spoke to its outgoing director, Kevin Harrison, about Georgiou and his Canadian co-conspirators, he would neither "confirm nor deny" that IMET was investigating them. When I asked why Georgiou was allowed to trade on the markets for so many years after he'd been banned by the IDA, Harrison said: "It's akin to a teacher running afoul of the regulatory bodies in British Columbia and then moving to another jurisdiction like Ontario to practise again. The systems don't necessarily talk."

The rise of an unregulated and unstable shadow banking industry, combined with an increasingly unstable traditional banking sector, reveals how the global financial system more and more resembles one big Ponzi scheme. And evidence of this disturbing reality continues to emerge.

TWELVE

PONZI SCHEMATA

"THE BANKS ARE SO fucking stupid! They are idiots!" snaps Neil Stein after a terse discussion with an RBC lawyer. I was meeting with Stein in the boardroom of his law firm, Stein & Stein Inc., on Sherbrooke Street in Montreal's west end when the call interrupted us. A small, wiry man in his sixties, Stein is one of Montreal's most highly regarded investment fraud litigators.

I'd come to see Stein because he was representing the victims of Ponzi schemer Earl Jones in a lawsuit against RBC. Working as an estate planner in Montreal, Jones ran a Ponzi scheme for nearly three decades before it collapsed in the summer of 2009, losing $51 million of 158 investors' money. A charming smooth-talker, Jones stole from anyone and everyone: kin, the kin of kin, and his closest friends, you name it. Social circles and entire family trees were plucked clean in his never-ending quest for cash to keep his fraud afloat.

Jones operated through an RBC in-trust account that he used as a carrot to persuade investors to put their life savings in his hands. He claimed the in-trust account offered interest rates of 8 to 12 percent—which it did not—and after the Ponzi scheme was exposed, his victims sued the bank for negligence, for failing to ensure the in-trust account was not abused by Jones. "Their obligation is to not cause damages to third parties," Stein said of the bank's role. "That's their obligation."

The story of Earl Jones, his Ponzi scheme and its victims received widespread media attention at the time. While not the only Ponzi scheme to unfold in Canada, it was among the most notorious because of how long it went undetected, especially in light of Jones's ties to a major bank.

Ponzi schemes take their name from the Boston-based Italian swindler Charles Ponzi, who conjured up a "fool-proof" method of defrauding investors: attract fortune seekers by promising enormous returns that were, in fact, paid out from the cash provided by new investors. In 1920, Charles Ponzi's fraud collapsed, leaving investors broke and him in jail. Brilliant in their simplicity, these schemes amounted to a classic case of robbing Peter to pay Paul.

The credit crisis and Great Recession exposed a host of previously unknown Ponzi schemes. Most infamous was that of Bernard Madoff, the New York–based investment guru whose US$65 billion investment fund imploded when too many people pulled their money from it. Like Jones, Madoff was packed off to jail, a result celebrated by investors, regulators and enforcement officials alike. But in a broader sense, the stories of Madoff and Jones stand as metaphors of what's been happening globally. Indeed, obscured in all the Sturm und Drang over the actions of such crooks is the fact that the entire financial industry has come to resemble these criminal operations writ large. Very large.

Banks and investment houses juggle vast quantities of capital that would become worthless if too many people withdrew their money from bank accounts and/or the capital markets at the same time. The subprime mortgage catastrophe serves as a parallel warning: what brought the edifice crashing down was too many bad mortgages sold to too many American homeowners who couldn't make their payments; what kept the scheme alive for years was investors continuing to buy mortgage-backed securities on capital markets, encouraged to do so by the financial industry's assurances. (After all, these securities were rated Triple-A by credit rating agencies, meaning they were never supposed to fail.) When people stopped buying mortgage-backed securities in large numbers, the global market imploded, just as a Ponzi scheme finally collapses when too little new money flows into the scam.

Your typical bank has some parallels to this structure. Canada's banks are not Ponzi operations per se. However, no bank has enough money in reserves to meet the demands of depositors if too many of them suddenly withdrew their savings or investments. For every $20 a typical bank lends out or invests, it has about $1 in cash reserves. A loss of 5 percent of asset value is all that it would take to sink a Canadian bank. This leveraging is one of the reasons Wall Street saw half of its storied investment banks (Bear Stearns, Merrill Lynch and Lehman Brothers) collapse or be sold off: they had wildly overextended themselves and when the toxic products they had been peddling began to fail, they were caught without enough cash to pay off fleeing investors and depositors. Despite the banks' reckless use of leverage, governments bailed them out with taxpayers' money. In contrast, men like Madoff or Jones were rescued by no one, despite behaving a whole lot like bankers.

WHILE THE IMAGE OF CANADA'S financial sector (inside and outside the country) is one of prudence, stability and fiscal conservatism that doesn't mean the industry won't peddle complex investment products that have Ponzi-like features. Take asset-backed commercial paper, the popular but flawed investment product sold to investors by Canada's banks and independent investment firms. ABCP was not a Ponzi scam in that the products did have legitimate assets behind them. But ABCP collapsed for the same reasons: a mismatch between the money coming in and the money going out. The income stream for ABCP originated from various forms of debt (such as commercial mortgages and credit default swaps) that mature over the long term. However, ABCP was sold to investors as a *short-term* investment, a place to park your money for a mere thirty to ninety days. The debt behind ABCP, as Canadian judge Robert Blair wrote in a 2008 judgment, "shared a common feature that proved to be the Achilles heel of the ABCP market: because of their long-term nature there was an inherent timing mismatch between the cash they generated and the cash needed to repay maturing ABCP notes. When uncertainty began to spread through the ABCP marketplace in the summer of 2007, investors stopped buying the ABCP product and existing note holders ceased to roll over their maturing notes. There was no cash to redeem those notes."

Ponzi schemes can exist for years, as long as new investors are pumping money into the pot. If investors become leery and that river of cash dries up, then the whole enterprise collapses.

BUT A MUCH CLEARER CASE of the Canadian financial industry marketing Ponzi scheme–like instruments even affected one of the nation's surest bets over the past century: the electoral fortunes of the Liberal Party of Canada.

At fault in this instance were income trusts. Developed in the

1980s, income trusts are equity-type investments traded on stock markets. Typically, the shares of a public company are sold and dividends are paid out when the business earns a profit. Income trusts, however, alter the corporate structure of a company and how money is dispensed to investors. The company converts to a trust, which is a legal designation that allows a business to function normally but offers it certain tax benefits. Investors are also promised monthly cash payments based on the cash flow the company generates.

The big flaw in income trusts comes from the frequent disconnect between what returns the company can realistically produce and what it tells investors to expect. This is how they parallel Ponzi schemes. "They purport to spew out a lot more cash than seems acceptable according to their income," explains Mark Rosen, who works as a chartered financial analyst in Toronto and has studied income trusts. "In a Ponzi scheme, a basic element is an overstatement of the return on assets. Investors pour money into it based on false results, on a figure that is made up. The parallel to income trusts is [that] the 'made-up figure' is the distributable cash, because it was such a widely manipulated, unregulated amount. So, basically, all of the trusts were making up this figure on their own."

Income trusts became popular because they allowed Canadian companies to avoid paying corporate taxes. By 2006 there were more than 250 publicly traded income trusts in Canada, with a total market capitalization of a whopping $200 billion.

As it turned out, Bay Street's enthusiasm for income trusts was as artificially manufactured as were expectations of the trusts' performance. After the tech boom went bust in 2000–2001, Canadian senior citizens and others who were relying on those sorts of investment for income were decidedly worried. Their investments were no longer producing much money and interest rates were at a historic low. The stock market was ailing too, especially after 9/11. "Seniors said, 'Get me out of the stock market,'" recalls Diane Urquhart. "So the Canadian investment industry rolls out the income trust model. They said they can get you a 10 percent yield at a time when the market yield was about 4 percent." Advertisements appeared in the business pages of newspapers touting income trusts as surefire bets.

Analyst Dr. Al Rosen, Mark Rosen's father, recognized early on that income trusts were essentially Ponzi schemes. Not known for suffering fools gladly, he once appeared before the House of Commons finance committee and said of the income trusts he'd investigated that most were scams. "My concern has been along the lines of pyramid schemes and Ponzi frauds [making up] well over half of the income trusts," Rosen told the MPs.

In 2005, Al and Mark Rosen joined forces with Diane Urquhart to study fifty of Canada's largest income trusts. They found them to be typically overvalued by as much as 28 percent, or a combined $20 billion, and that the overvaluations were due almost entirely to abuses in financial reporting and marketing. It appeared to them that income trusts claimed they could meet high returns when it would be impossible to do so, because the demands of producing so much cash would mean destroying the company itself. This created an incentive for income trusts to mislead investors about the soundness of their enterprises. In fact, 75 percent of the income trusts the Rosens and Urquhart examined had cash distributions exceeding their income and twenty-two were down 30 percent from the time of their initial public offerings. They concluded it was inevitable that many of the trusts would self-destruct, as Ponzi schemes inevitably do.

Atlas Cold Storage Holdings Inc., a Toronto-based company that employed 4,500 people and owned large storage freezers for use by the food processing industry, exemplified this. In 2000, it became an income trust and went on to raise $356 million from investors on the markets. "Atlas Cold Storage was a reasonably profitable, well-run business," says Toronto securities lawyer Joe Groia, who became involved in a lawsuit against the company, "but they took a real company and made it into something clearly it wasn't." In March 2002, Atlas announced a profit of $11.4 million for fiscal 2001. The following year, the company said its profits had climbed to $19 million and its income trust units were selling for about $12.

Then, in April 2003, an anonymous letter arrived at the OSC alleging that Atlas's financial statements for 2002 had been cooked. Atlas's board and audit committee hired forensic accountants to conduct an investigation. They soon discovered that expenditures of $3.6 million were inappropriately recorded as additions to capital assets during 2002. By the summer of 2003, Atlas's unit prices had fallen from $13 to just over $4. The company's CEO, Patrick Gouveia, and Atlas's chief financial officer and vice-president of finance resigned and were charged by the OSC for committing securities violations.

Atlas was forced to restate its finances from the previous two years. The profit of 2001 was reduced to $6.2 million and the "profit" for 2002 turned into a loss of $18.4 million. All told, the company's manipulation of its books meant investors lost nearly $500 million of the value of their Atlas units.

What happened? Both the OSC and an investors' lawsuit claimed that as the situation worsened at Atlas during 2002, some company executives conspired to cover it up. Given that executives were also unitholders in the Atlas income trust, those involved were motivated to "earn income and [make] capital gains" by manipulating the prices of the units, according to the investors' lawsuit. "The fraud was essentially inflating the sales and revenues and income," says Groia.

Between early 2001 and the summer of 2003, the Atlas accounting staff turned invoices previously showing expenses into assets, a clear violation of accounting rules. As to the charges, the company's CFO died of cancer before he got to trial. Two other senior officers settled with the commission by paying fines of $5,000 and $20,000, respectively, and accepting that they would be reprimanded under the Securities Act and may not serve as an officer of a company for five years. Finally, in 2007, after receiving new evidence from Ernst & Young and reviewing its case, the OSC requested the judge to dismiss the charges against Gouveia.

Seeking $403 million in damages, investors launched a lawsuit in 2004 against Atlas and its underwriter, BMO Nesbitt Burns, and the company's accountants, Ernst & Young. Four years later, it was settled for $40 million—the largest payout for a securities fraud in Canadian history. By then, Atlas had been bought up by an Icelandic investment firm.

DESPITE THE WARNINGS of the Rosens and Urquhart and fiascos such as Atlas (along with others, such as Spinrite, Granby Industries, Newport Partners, Heating Oil Partners and Associated Brands), Bay Street's turbo-charged hype machine blinded investors and politicians alike to the inherent Ponzi nature of income trusts. For years, the Liberal government of Jean Chrétien and his finance minister (and successor as prime minister), Paul Martin, allowed them to flourish, which would prove to be the government's undoing.

In the fall of 2005, Judy Wasylycia-Leis, the MP for Winnipeg North and finance critic for the New Democratic Party, heard there were problems with income trusts. "There was the loss of tax revenue and they were not necessarily operating under the highest ethical standards," explains Wasylycia-Leis, "and in fact, people were getting ripped off." As Christmas neared, the spectre of a federal election loomed. The Liberals, now led by Martin, had been in power for twelve years but were still reeling from the fallout of the "Ad-Scam" sponsorship scandal. Overseeing a shaky minority government, Martin was being forced to go to the polls.

Just days before the election was called, Finance Minister Ralph Goodale announced that he had no intention of imposing a tax on income trusts, despite the fact his department estimated the government lost $300 million in 2004 because so many companies were converting to trusts. Goodale was under considerable pressure from Bay Street to keep this particular golden goose alive and kicking. His statement, however, was preceded by a noticeable rise in trading volumes and share prices in income trusts, suggesting that someone in Goodale's office had leaked the news and was involved in insider trading. "I remember hearing different stories," recalls Wasylycia-Leis, "that suspected insider knowledge had led to a spike in the trading." She was not about to let such suspicions float by without being verified and quickly dashed off a letter to the RCMP asking them to investigate the possibility that a leak had occurred.

Somewhat to Wasylycia-Leis's surprise, the RCMP responded. During the Christmas holidays, RCMP Commissioner Giuliano Zaccardelli personally faxed her a letter saying that a criminal investigation was under way. This letter, arriving as it did in the middle of an election campaign, was too big a gift for Wasylycia-Leis to pass up. She held a press conference and announced the news of the RCMP's investigation. "At which point all hell broke loose," she relates. "It was certainly one factor that led to the Liberals' loss." Stephen Harper's Conservatives surged in the polls and swept to power in January 2006; the whiff of another scandal so close on the heels of the sponsorship debacle had proved too much for voters to stomach. The RCMP eventually did arrest a civil servant in the finance department who had been trading on insider information.

Income trusts would continue to roil the political landscape. Having also promised not to tax them, the Conservatives were ultimately forced to do exactly that. By November 2006, many of Canada's biggest corporations (including BCE Inc., Telus Corp. and Power Financial Corp.) were lining up to convert themselves into income trusts in order to avoid paying corporate taxes. Facing a massive loss of tax revenue—more than $1 billion according to one estimate—the new finance minister, Jim Flaherty, had little choice but to stem the income trust gusher. His decision to tax income trusts was bitterly opposed by Bay Street. The Bank of Montreal's brokerage house, BMO Nesbitt Burns, released a report arguing that they delivered higher returns than equities, failing to mention the real reason the finance industry supported income trusts: between 2001 and 2006, Canada's brokerage houses earned well in excess of $2 billion in fees by underwriting them.

THIRTEEN

NO HELP IN SIGHT

M IKE GREEN IS A jovial, gregarious engineer and the brother of comedian Rick Green, a cast member of the TV series *The Red Green Show*. Green became rich the old-fashioned way when he co-founded what would become a highly successful software services company in Toronto. In the late nineties, Green and his partners sold the business, with Green's cut being a tidy $10 million. He invested the money, a third of it with a small Etobicoke, Ontario–based wealth management firm called Affinity Financial Group Inc., part of a network of well-known investment dealers.

Green had heard of Affinity through a businessmen's group he belonged to. A fellow member was Affinity's president, David Lewis, who rhapsodized about a surefire investment plan. Lewis told Green that David Siegel, an Florida investment guru, was seeking investors to loan money based on restricted securities—a form of investment that could not be sold for a certain period of time. Investors would receive either the interest payments on the loans or proceeds from the eventual sale of the securities. Lewis convinced Green that his money would be safe, that there was no risk of losing it. So assured, Green invested $3.5 million in Siegel's brainchild.

In the spring of 2002, Green was stunned to learn that Siegel had vanished, as had all of the investors' money—US$87 million, almost half of it belonging to Canadians. "Siegel was caught on video cameras taking all of the files away from his Florida office, and all the money was gone," recalls Green. "It was a very bad day. Your blood ran cold. I remember feeling this must be a joke, this can't be happening." For three years, Affinity had given Green repeated assurances that all was well with his investment. Green and Lewis spoke frequently on the phone, continued to socialize, and Green had Affinity documents showing how his investment was flourishing. What Green didn't know, and wouldn't learn about until it was too late, was Siegel's long history of run-ins with the SEC and a track record of other problems.

Green never retrieved one cent of his money or found out what happened to it, and he still feels that investors like himself were kicked to the curb. "When this thing collapsed, you would expect the investment dealers to come forward and say, 'Hey look, you know, this is one of our guys, he's part of our network, we're sorry this thing happened, we're going to make things right,'" says Green. Instead, what Green and other victims of investment fraud discover is that after their cash vanishes into some black hole, the financial industry will not be there to bail them out or assist them in any way. The victims' only recourse is to take their chances in court, an expensive proposition, and one where they're lucky to retrieve a fraction of what they've lost, if anything at all.

———

AND THEREIN LIES ONE of the great contradictions in how Bay Street regards investors. The financial industry seduces the public with slick advertising campaigns, replete with images of Ken-and-Barbie financial advisers eager to assist you, and with Triple-A assurances from credit rating agencies slapped on investment products to assuage any fears you might harbour about their safety. But if it all turns out to be rubbish and you lose your money, then the response is a collective shrug, saying too bad, your "gamble" just didn't pan out this time.

A striking example of Bay Street's contempt for its own customer base after disaster strikes occurred in the wake of the ABCP fiasco. For most investors in third-party ABCP, the freezing of $32 billion of their money in the summer of 2007 was a catastrophe. Patrick Evans, the CEO of Vancouver-based Norsemont Mining Ltd., was looking forward to starting a mine development in Peru. By the late spring of 2007, Norsemont had raised $9 million on the markets to help realize his plan, but he needed to park his money in a secure short-term investment. Following the advice of the investment firm Canaccord Capital Inc., Norsemont put the $7 million into third-party ABCP, which they could access within thirty days. "We expected to burn through this cash pretty rapidly," Evans says. "The money was to be used for exploration and engineering studies." After the ABCP market seized up, the Peruvian mine had to be put on hold while Norsemont scrambled for funds. "We were desperate for access to this cash because we were going through a period of intense activity," recalls Evans. (The mine would eventually go ahead when more money was found a couple of years later.)

The City of Hamilton found itself in trouble too. In July 2007, the Ontario municipality had used $98 million worth of tax funds to buy third-party ABCP that was supposed to mature at the end of

September—money to be spent on city services such as fire and police. Now it was looking at a shortfall. Given that the city was one of the hardest hit in Canada by deindustrialization and recession, especially in the steel industry, this was a financial blow Hamilton could ill afford.

James Hanrahan is a retired McGill University professor whose retirement funds are invested in McGill's pension plan. When the ABCP market froze $41 million in the plan, $230,000 of which had belonged to Hanrahan, his retirement plans were thrown into limbo. "My wife and I felt as if somebody mugged us," he says. "It means that initially a third of my retirement funds was not available to me."

In September 2007, the Pan-Canadian Investors Committee for Third-Party Structured ABCP was established to sort out the mess and try to get the investors some or all of their money back. Its membership included the Caisse de dépôt et placement du Québec, ATB Financial, PSP Investments, CMHC and a mixture of credit unions and companies with large ABCP holdings. Only one of Canada's chartered banks, the National Bank, was a member. To head up the rescue operation, the committee hired Purdy Crawford, a 76-year-old securities lawyer with Osler, Hoskin & Harcourt LLP, a large Bay Street corporate law firm that does legal work for the banks.

Crawford was more than a curious choice, and one that reflects how Bay Street's elites circle the wagons to protect their own interests. He's a prominent member of the business, financial and legal establishments, an inductee of the Canadian Business Hall of Fame and the former CEO and chairman of Imasco Ltd., the Montreal-based holding company that once controlled Shoppers Drug Mart and Imperial Tobacco, Canada's largest tobacco company. He also had a sizable skeleton in his closet: in the early 1990s, during the period when Crawford was running Imasco, Imperial Tobacco set up a massive cross-border cigarette smuggling operation designed to evade paying Canadian sales taxes, a scheme that cost Canadian governments an estimated $3 billion in lost tax revenues. Crawford was never held to account for any role in the scandal (although at least one former Imasco strategic planner, Paul Finlayson, claims Crawford was fully aware of Imperial Tobacco's smuggling operation). In the summer of 2008, Imperial Tobacco and Rothmans Benson & Hedges paid out $1.15 billion in civil and criminal fines related to their involvement in cross-border smuggling—smack in the middle of the ABCP court proceedings.

Crawford's job now was to somehow find a way for ABCP investors to get their money back at a time when global markets were tanking and no one was keen on buying the paper. It's unclear whether he ever attempted to pressure the banks into fulfilling their obligations under the liquidity agreements. "What should have happened, and didn't, is the committee should have answered the fundamental question: are these liquidity agreements enforceable?" says investment consultant Colin Kilgour, who worked with firms that sold ABCP. "In all of the thousands and thousands of pages of documents I've gone through, the committee never answers that question."

While Crawford struggled for months to find the funds, investors did not sit idly by. Brian Hunter is a Calgary-based engineer who'd worked in the oil and gas industry and had $660,000 frozen in ABCP. When he discovered that none of Alberta's big law firms were willing to sue the banks for selling third-party ABCP, he began organizing the retail investors on his own. Hunter set up a Facebook page to reach out to them and garner attention. It worked. He then tried to find out what Crawford and his committee were up to. In January 2008, he spoke with Andrew Kresse, an executive at J.P. Morgan in New York, who was working with Crawford's committee. "I learned a lot," recalls Hunter. "The most important thing was that these guys wanted releases from legal responsibility. Kresse told me, 'The only thing they want is the releases.' In other words, they wanted to ensure that nobody would have the ability to sue."

Crawford's quest to find someone to bail out the third-party ABCP investors came to naught. After months of delay, in March 2008 he trotted out his "solution": a 437-page legal document that said, in essence, instead of ABCP investors getting their money back immediately, they would receive promissory notes that would mature in 2017, nine years down the road. The notes could be cashed in earlier, but investors would take a bath if they were. Furthermore, this plan said ABCP investors could not sue the banks and investment firms who'd sold them the product in the first place. Not surprisingly, as they learned of the details, investors became enraged (and panic-stricken), and when Crawford went on a road trip that same month to sell the plan, the meetings were testy, heated affairs.

"I'm here because I want my money. I don't want coupons," one elderly woman shouted at him in Vancouver.

"I have had to go back to work at age sixty-five," said another furiously and in tears. "Just give it back."

"That was a great session, Mr. Crawford," someone snorted sarcastically, "but I didn't understand anything you said."

Crawford's sales job floundered and he responded by painting a doomsday scenario: if retail investors didn't sign on to his plan, they would get "damn little," he told *The Financial Post*. "That's not a threat. It's a reality."

Crawford had made a major miscalculation. The entire process was being conducted under the Companies' Creditors Arrangement Act (CCAA), the Canadian equivalent of the American Chapter 11 law that allows ailing companies to reorganize themselves instead of declaring bankruptcy. But CCAA decrees that every investor holds just one vote, no matter how many shares he or she owns; that is, a senior citizen with one share has the same clout as a huge company with millions of shares. Given that there were about 400 corporate holders of ABCP and 1,800 retail investors, the voting power to approve any plan lay with the retail investors. And once they understood this, en masse the retail investors rejected Crawford's solution (and thinly veiled threats) and told him, in essence, to shove his nine-year notes. He had run into citizen activism and, largely, a grey revolt.

Many then signed on with the class action lawsuit Henry Juroviesky was putting together, and soon the Toronto securities lawyer found himself sparring with Crawford's committee. "In a passive-aggressive manner, they started to deal with us," remembers Juroviesky. "First they made us a lowball offer and we said no. I said to them, 'You cannot tell me that my people should be taking any haircut,' and 'You know what? We are all of the view that if this thing crashes and burns, we will take our chances in court.'"

And Crawford had other problems. The corporate community was hardly thrilled with his plan either. Gold mining giant Barrick Gold Corp., in particular, was outraged. After the company discovered it couldn't access the $66 million it had invested in ABCP, it wanted to sue CIBC World Markets for misleading it about the soundness of the product (and because the bank refused to return the company's money). Crawford's committee initially persuaded Barrick to hold off on launching the suit, but the company wisely kept the option open in the event they were dissatisfied with the committee's proposed remedy. After examining Crawford's report in March 2008, Barrick's senior executives had seen enough. They realized it was uncertain they would ever get their money back, *and* the plan would bar Barrick from taking CIBC to court. Barrick moved ahead with its plan to sue CIBC World Markets for the return of its money, putting Crawford's entire restructuring plan in jeopardy.

ONLY AT THIS JUNCTURE, facing calamity, did Crawford's committee come up with a simple but cunning resolution: pay off as many of the malcontents needed to achieve a yes vote on their deal. First, they proposed that investors holding less than $1 million in ABCP would get all of their money back at the time of a successful restructuring of the frozen ABCP: in other words, quite soon. This meant that most of the 1,800 retail investors would be looked after. The cost of paying them came to a mere $187 million (out of $32 billion owed). "Yup, they bought the votes," says Brian Hunter. "They really needed the releases at the end of the day. That was the key." In return for getting their money back, the deal said retail investors could not sue Bay Street for selling the flawed ABCP. Desperate to get their assets back, the retail investors voted overwhelmingly to approve this Faustian pact.

Refusing to buckle under pressure to drop its lawsuit against CIBC, Barrick Gold also got its money. Federal finance minister Jim Flaherty had stepped in and telephoned senior executives at the bank, pressing them to return Barrick's cash. CIBC reluctantly handed over $49 million to settle the matter.

The remainder of the ABCP investors got stuck with the nine-year notes whether they liked it or not. More troublingly, thirty-six families who owned more than $1 million of ABCP, companies and governments were also permanently barred from seeking recourse against Bay Street through the courts for selling them what was basically a toxic investment product. Patrick Evans, for one, was deeply upset by this turn of events. Norsemont was short $7 million (with no real way of retrieving any of it for nine years). He went on Business News Network in April 2008 and blasted the banking community. "You have to ask yourself why [are] Canaccord and the other banks involved insisting on immunity from prosecution?" he asked. "It's because they're concerned about being prosecuted by companies like ourselves . . . They misrepresented themselves, there was a conflict of interest, they were receiving commissions on the sale of ABCP to us, so of course they are concerned about legal liability in this regard." Norsemont launched a suit against Canaccord in British Columbia that was dismissed after Canada's Supreme Court ruled that Crawford's plan, with its immunity-from-prosecution clause, was constitutional. "This [decision by the court] amounts to the expropriation of private property rights," fumes Evans. "This establishes a very very serious precedent. Essentially what they have allowed is they have opened the door for financial institutions in Canada to take away the savings and investments of Canadian citizens with impunity."

In fact, not only did Bay Street not have to immediately repay such investors, it also dodged a bullet for what amounted to fraudulent conduct, says Juroviesky. He points out that the classic definition of fraud is selling something with the intention of ripping someone else off. "The key variable for fraud is knowledge," he explains. "Did the perpetrator know beforehand? Does he have knowledge that what he is doing is a lie and will cause damage?" But reckless indifference to the truth—knowing that your behaviour might cause someone to lose their money—he insists, is also fraud. And this applies to third-party ABCP, he argues, because the industry knew there was a good chance it would blow up yet sold it to investors anyway. In the end, it would appear that the third-party ABCP saga demonstrates how Bay Street can mislead the public about the safety of an investment and receive a mere slap on the wrist. "It was an absolute travesty that the justice system would allow something like this to occur," says Brian Hunter. "But that's the way it happens. The laws are only enforced against little guys."

The financial industry did not emerge from the debacle entirely unscathed. The OSC, the Investment Industry Regulatory Organization of Canada (IIROC) and Quebec's securities commission, the Autorité des marchés financiers (AMF), levied nearly $140 million in fines against seven investment dealers for "failing to respond to emerging issues" in the ABCP market while they continued to sell the paper. In 2010, the OSC held a series of hearings into the role Coventree Inc. and its owners played in the fiasco, trying to determine if the investment firm pushed ABCP it knew to be toxic. It was a questionable inquiry given that the commission overlooked the role played by Bay Street's bigger players. "It's a witch hunt," says former Coventree banker Daryl Ching. "They were not about to nail anyone specifically from the banks. If you want blood, Coventree is the easiest target."

Still, the OSC's hearings into Coventree unearthed damning evidence. They found internal emails showing that senior Coventree executives knew the market for third-party ABCP was likely to freeze in August 2007 but decided against telling shareholders. The OSC also discovered that Coventree and other dealers who distributed ABCP notes during that month "had knowledge of liquidity-related events and developments in the ABCP market that were important to investors considering the purchase of ABCP. It is unlikely that any investor would have purchased Coventree-sponsored ABCP, or any other ABCP, if they had been aware of those market events and developments." Internal documents portrayed executives in states of high distress behind the scenes—while publicly calming the market. In

September 2011, the OSC ruled that Coventree and its two top executives were guilty of securities violations and levied penalties and costs totalling $2 million on them. And what did investors lose? No one will know for certain until 2017, when the notes finally mature. Diane Urquhart has crunched the numbers and estimates at least $7 billion of the $32 billion frozen in 2007 is gone for good. Not one Bay Street executive was criminally charged. "I would've been pleased to see these people taken before a criminal court," says Toronto lawyer Brian Iler, who had $229,000 of his savings frozen in ABCP. "This kind of stuff shouldn't be happening in the Canadian financial industry. But this seemed to be business as usual for the Bay Street boys."

THE ABCP MESS is hardly the only instance of Canada's disregard for victims of corporate fraud. The aftermath of Nortel's collapse saw such callousness plumb even greater depths.

In June 2009, Mike Zafirovski sat before the finance committee of the House of Commons in Ottawa, giving an account of himself. A tall man with a pinched face, Zafirovski was the last CEO of Nortel, the telecommunications giant having filed for CCAA protection five months earlier. All of Nortel's assets were being sold off to its competitors. "Before we get into the details, let me say that not a day goes by that I don't think about the implications of our difficult decisions which have hit both former and current employees," Zafirovski said in his opening remarks to MPs. What he failed to mention was that as a creditor, he was in line for a payout of $12.2 million, even though he had already taken home nearly $43 million while failing miserably in his efforts to turn the company around (his compensation for his last year amounted to $2.3 million). He is also promised a pension of nearly $366,000 a year.

Zafirovski was not the only person going to profit handsomely from the demise of Nortel. Like many companies that choose CCAA protection, Nortel paid so-called "retention bonuses" to the remaining managers still running the company. Under the Key Executive Incentive Plan (KEIP) and Key Executive Retention Plan (KERP) — extra payments above and beyond salaries to encourage managers to stay around while the company is wound down — two months after the corporation went bust, US$45 million in such outlays were paid to almost a thousand senior Nortel managers and employees (eight executives would share US$7.3 million). The logic behind these bonuses is clearly flawed, says former Nortel president Robert Ferchat. "They got a bonus although they lost money and the company was dead in the water and they were selling it off to the scrap heap?" he asks. "What on earth for?" Others cashed in too. In August 2009, Nortel's new three-person board increased their payments from $175,000 to $225,000. The newly appointed chairman, David Richardson — a former chairman of Ernst & Young Inc. (Canada), the accounting firm that landed the lucrative job of bankruptcy monitor in the Nortel case — got a $100,000 raise, from $225,000 to $325,000.

In the fall of 2009, Nortel decided to award more bonuses to its seventy-two top managers, totalling US$7.5 million. The top benefactor was John Doolittle, the company's acting president, who received a compensation increase of 60 percent, to nearly $1.7 million for his annual salary. Prior to the company's collapse, Doolittle had a base salary of $354,000 in his job as CFO; he was now guaranteed more than $3.3 million before he would leave his new post.

In total, through the court-approved incentive and retention bonus plans, executives and managers pocketed $138 million during 2009–2010. On top of this were the annual inventive plan bonuses,

THIEVES OF BAY STREET

totalling $305 million, paid after Nortel filed for bankruptcy. The lawyers, accountants and consultants involved in selling off the company took home an additional $130 million in Canada and $230 million in the United States. George Riedel, Nortel's former chief strategy officer, was paid nearly $3 million in 2010, almost 80 percent more than a year earlier. Former chief financial officer Pavi Binning got $3 million before he left the company in April 2010, a salary boost of 55 percent over the previous year. Richard Lowe, the head of Nortel's carrier networks, left in the fall of 2009 having pocketed $2.4 million that year.

Meanwhile, Nortel's investors had lost $375 billion from when the stock peaked in 2000 and the company's former employees and pensioners were stripped of $2 billion in pensions, medical allowances, long-term disability insurance payments and severance pay. At the finance committee hearing, Donald Sproule, chair of a Nortel retirees' committee and representing 17,500 Nortel pensioners, said that Nortel's pension plan had been underfunded by $1 billion, and Nortel's plan for its 400 long-term disability employees had been gutted of $75 million and was soon to run dry. The pensioners were unlikely to get much of anything from the sale of Nortel's assets, and many faced a future of subsisting on welfare.

Indeed, in the summer of 2011, Nortel pensioners received a letter from their pension administrator announcing a cut in benefits. The cuts were as high as 31 percent for employees outside of Ontario. The Ontario Pension Benefit Guarantee Fund, which tops up the first $1,000 of monthly income, softens the blow for pensioners in that province; the Ontario government estimates the average non-unionized Nortel employee will experience an 18 percent reduction in benefits. For some pensioners, this meant a loss of $600 a month on top of a $52 reduction to cover a previous benefits overpayment.

The average age of Nortel pensioners was 74, with more than 350 over the age of 85.

IN THE SPRING OF 2011, Peter Burns passed away. He was out fishing with some friends when he took ill and died shortly thereafter. From Ottawa, Burns joined Nortel's performance engineering department in 1997. He had master's degrees in electrical engineering and astrophysics and had previously worked at Atomic Energy of Canada Ltd., General Electric and Petro-Canada. Burns made $90,000 a year at Nortel, and his biggest triumph occurred shortly after Nortel promised a German telephone company a piece of technology that could route one million calls an hour. Unfortunately the company couldn't make its equipment handle more than 100,000 calls an hour, and if Nortel failed to meet the promised level of performance, it would be slapped with nearly $1 billion in penalties. Burns fixed the glitch by writing an innovative mathematical algorithm. "The manager came to me and said I literally saved the company $900 million," he recalled. "The equation I produced solved this problem."

But then Burns's health began to decline, he believes due to the long hours he put in at the office. "Nortel did encourage working too hard," he claimed. He rarely saw his wife and three children and developed serious back pain by 2000. Soon his limbs were going numb, and an MRI found a tumour on his spine. He was immediately rushed into surgery, where the surgeon nicked an artery during the operation. Burns had a post-operative stroke leading to a neurological condition that prevented him from holding down a job. In 2007, his marriage ended and he hit rock bottom, living alone in a rooming house where his neighbours were drug addicts.

Burns was eligible for Nortel's disability insurance, which combined with his CPP disability income paid him $5,000 a month for living and medical expenses. But in the aftermath of the company's 2009 bankruptcy, he discovered that Nortel's health and welfare trust had been pillaged, reducing it by over $100 million. It now had only enough money to pay about 30 percent of his disability insurance. Finally, at the end of 2010, Nortel's disabled workers had their disability income cut off entirely.

When he passed away, Burns was subsisting on only his CPP disability cheques of $1,000 a month. He was particularly enraged about all of the Nortel executives and employees who pocketed $440 million in bonuses after the company's bankruptcy while the disabled employees were being impoverished. "Why would you give the executives who broke the company bonuses and incentives?" he asked. "To tell the disabled that it's really important to give these executives this money when they steal [millions] from our trust fund—it boggles my imagination to understand what's going on in these people's minds."

Banks, brokerages and corporations are not alone in their indifference to the plight of investors and employees who lose everything to white-collar crime. The corporate lawyers, credit rating agencies and underwriters who service the industry, along with the analysts and regulators who are supposed to watch over it, demonstrate similar disregard. All too often, they are the enablers of fraud.

— FOURTEEN —

THE ENABLERS

P AUL STERN WAS CLEARLY annoyed. In a spacious room at
Osgoode Hall in downtown Toronto, where lawyers sit in judgment of each other, he vented, his protestations echoing off the walls
as he requested yet another adjournment. It was May 2010 and Stern
was working as a prosecutor for the Law Society of Upper Canada,
the regulatory body for Ontario's forty-one thousand lawyers, explaining to a panel of his peers how he'd *just* discovered new evidence in
the case he was about to prosecute. A lean, normally contained man,
Stern was diplomatic yet couldn't hide his frustration about news of
168 boxes of documents that had suddenly materialized at Torys
LLP, one of Canada's most powerful corporate law firms—boxes
filled with material that could be germane to his case, and that he
would now have to review.

The discovery of these boxes was just another hurdle in the ongoing attempt by the Law Society to prosecute two of its own. Darren
Sukonick, a pale forty-year-old with a friendly face, pecked away at his

laptop as he listened to Stern. Beside Sukonick sat Beth DeMerchant, a woman in her mid-fifties wearing a navy blue dress, a pearl necklace and a stony expression. Stern's protests were being heard by three lawyers assigned to determine the fates of DeMerchant and Sukonick. DeMerchant had already quit her lucrative partnership at Torys and was no longer practising law; Sukonick was still at the law firm but had been shunted into the corporate career purgatory of pro bono cases.

It had been a dismal few years for them both. The pair were once considered legal stars on Bay Street, so well regarded that they'd been assigned the high-profile task of helping Conrad Black sell off his considerable newspaper holdings. From 2000 to 2003, DeMerchant and Sukonick counselled Black and Hollinger's senior executives over numerous deals—sales that became the focus of charges laid in the United States against Black and his lieutenants for stealing from shareholders. Both lawyers testified during Black's trial in 2007—and it had not gone well. Two years later, the Law Society finally charged Sukonick and DeMerchant with breaking conflict-of-interest rules with respect to their reporting of executive compensation to regulatory authorities. They faced a heavy slate of allegations.

DeMerchant and Sukonick's role in the events that led to Black's calamitous fall from grace is more than just a footnote. Their story reflects how white-collar criminals use lawyers, credit rating agencies, analysts and underwriters to aid them in their schemes. Sometimes these "enablers" consciously assist the criminals and are intricately involved in frauds; sometimes they simply turn a blind eye in order to make a lot of money; and sometimes they screw up. Either way, their behaviour is part and parcel of the investment world's culture, one that suggests declining morals and a dearth of concern for investors' interests.

———

CREDIT RATING AGENCIES stand out among the chief enablers of securities fraud. In fact, one of the revelations that emerged from the 2007–2009 global economic meltdown was the pernicious role played by these benighted institutions.

The power of credit rating agencies—of which over a hundred exist worldwide—is staggering. In the summer of 2011, as the U.S. government wrestled over raising its national debt limit, what alarmed President Barack Obama's White House the most about the possibility of default was the threat of credit rating agencies imposing their first-ever U.S. government downgrade. If they did so, it would cost American taxpayers hundreds of billions of dollars in extra interest payments on their debt. And such fears were realized: days after the debt limit was finally raised, Standard & Poor's (S&P) downgraded the U.S.A. from Triple-A to AA+. It seemed an odd, symbolic, perhaps even ideological thing to do, given that the United States had never defaulted on its debt and would not do so any time soon. But all three major U.S. credit rating agencies had already downgraded Greece's sovereign debt to such a low level that default for that country was assured.

Standard & Poor's was soon being pilloried—and not surprisingly, given that American credit rating agencies have little credibility. In the early 2000s, Moody's, Fitch and Standard & Poor's slapped Triple-A ratings on investment products so rickety they set off the worst recession in eighty-five years. (In 2011, the SEC opened an investigation into S&P because four years earlier the agency had assigned its highest rating, Triple-A, to a CDO that had "dummy" or hypothetical assets in it. Moreover, even after bankers replaced the dummy assets with low-quality mortgage assets, the Triple-A rating remained in place.)

As the credit crisis gathered strength in 2008, the SEC investigated the agencies and found them to be an unholy mess. The commission said the agencies were clearly overwhelmed by the complexity and volume of the mortgage-backed products they were assessing, there was a lack of rating criteria, the monitoring was poor once products were on the markets and conflicts of interest clouded their judgment: after all, they are paid by the very financial institutions whose products they're assessing. Nonetheless, investors continue to rely on credit rating agencies to decide how much risk they will face when buying an investment product.

Credit rating is a $5 billion-a-year business in the U.S.A. How these agencies make their money is simple: corporations and governments pay them a fee to assess the soundness of their debt. Moreover, the agencies can also earn a percentage from the sale of those same products; in other words, the more sold, the more the agencies themselves pocket. All of this creates an incentive *not* to carry out due diligence. Investment bankers will even play one agency off against another in hopes of encouraging one or the other to lower its standards in order to get the business. The SEC found internal emails in which senior managers of credit rating agencies worried that if they refused to okay certain products, they would lose business. They fretted when a competitor approved products, and did indeed suggest their own agency lower its standards so as not to lose Wall Street clients.

Dominion Bond Rating Service Ltd. is the only wholly Canadian-owned credit rating agency. Founded in 1976 by former Bay Street bond expert Walter Schroeder (who still controls it), DBRS's role in the 2007 third-party ABCP meltdown is an example of how deeply compromised it is. DBRS gave third-party ABCP a Triple-A rating, even though the two biggest American credit rating agencies refused to rate this product at all, believing it to be too dangerous. Like all other credit rating agencies, DBRS is in a conflict of interest as it earns fees from every investment product it grades and for the amount sold. The agency justifies this arrangement by saying that investors know about the "issuer-pay model," as it's called, and that their ratings should be seen as a tool and not the deciding factor when buying a product. It's safe to assume, however, that few investors knew about DBRS's cozy relationship with the financial institutions that were peddling ABCP. "They became part-time investment bankers, working hand in glove with the major banks and dealers as to how the products should be structured," Anthony Fell, former chairman of RBC Dominion Securities, said in a 2007 speech. "They were, in effect, rating their own product, which is a clear conflict."

"DBRS was central to the ABCP fiasco in Canada," adds Diane Urquhart. "They sat within the rooms of the people who designed the product and the marketing of it." In fact, DBRS knew there were issues with ABCP before the third-party ABCP market froze. A few months earlier, the agency had announced it would no longer give third-party ABCP a Triple-A rating. Nevertheless, DBRS decided against removing the Triple-A rating on the tens of billions of dollars' worth of third-party ABCP they had already approved based on criteria it now admitted were shaky.

BUT IT'S NOT JUST CREDIT RATING agencies that are in the assessment business. So are underwriters, who are also tasked to carry out due diligence. Underwriters are generally major brokerage houses that raise money for companies seeking capital from investors. And like credit rating agencies, the reputation of the underwriter helps investors determine whether they should buy an investment or not. Underwriting new companies' stock is lucrative work for the brokerage business. In the case of income trusts, for example, Bay Street brokers made at least $1.9 billion in underwriting fees between 2001 and 2006 alone, earning fees averaging 5.3 percent.

FMF Capital, the Michigan-based subprime mortgage lender that bilked Canadian investors of $200 million in 2005, provides a particularly blatant case of underwriters abandoning due diligence. To help it sell shares, the company hired BMO Nesbitt Burns as its premier underwriter, along with TD Securities, National Bank Financial, Sprott Securities, Canaccord Capital and Blackmont Capital. In an investors' lawsuit launched against FMF Capital, the Bay Street underwriters were accused of conducting a merely superficial examination of FMF's underlying business and of being "unduly credulous and recklessly indifferent to the truth, or, at a minimum, grossly negligent." The OSC, when it investigated BMO Nesbitt Burns in 2010, also found that the brokerage firm failed to carry out proper due diligence. "If they'd actually scrutinized and spoken to the people on the ground and conducted a detailed investigation on the lending patterns of the company, they would have known it inevitably would have blown up," observes Dimitri Lascaris, a lawyer involved in suing FMF Capital and the underwriters. In fact, the OSC discovered that BMO Nesbitt Burns allowed FMF Capital to select which of its mortgages would be reviewed as part of BMO's due diligence and then approved the prospectus even after FMF Capital failed to produce crucial information the underwriter had demanded.

YET THE REAL BLIND cheerleaders of the investment industry are financial analysts. Like credit rating agencies and underwriters, analysts give investors their opinions on whether they should buy or (theoretically) sell investment products. Generally, however, most analysts do a poor job. "Analysts don't read financial statements," insists Ross Healy, himself a stock analyst who runs his own independent firm, Strategic Analysis Corporation in Toronto. "That's just a true story."

Healy contends that studies have shows that as few as 5 percent of analysts ever consult a company's balance sheet before making a recommendation. Moreover, he says a diligent analyst can detect signs of fraud in a company or investment product simply by scrutinizing their financial statements. "If you want to find out something about a company, just read the damn financials," he says. And in all of the major financial scandals that have plagued Canada in recent years, from Nortel, YBM, Bre-X and income trusts to ABCP and FMF Capital and Sino-Forest, analysts have invariably been gung-ho boosters of the companies' stock or investment products right up until the bitter end.

In the Sino-Forest Corp. case, the Chinese forestry company was listed on the Toronto Stock Exchange, and had a market capitalization of $6 billion and public debt of $1.7 billion. In the spring of 2011, Muddy Waters Research, an investment firm, issued a report claiming Sino-Forest "massively exaggerates its assets" and was little more than a Ponzi scheme. Investors were soon worrying they might have lost as much as $7 billion, an amount that would dwarf Bre-X in scale if their fears were realized. Yet analysts had trumpeted Sino-Forest to the heavens. Richard Kelertas, a financial analyst at Dundee Securities Corp., for example, insisted Sino-Forest was a "class act in timberland management in China" and called the fraud allegations a "pile of crap." After the OSC opened an investigation into Sino-Forest because of its suspicious financial statements, Kelertas stopped talking to the press.

This sort of overconfidence is commonplace. In 1996, Egizio Bianchini, a mining analyst at Nesbitt Burns, told investors he'd been to the exploration site and labs of Bre-X Minerals Ltd. and could vouch for their work. The rumours of it being a $6 billion scam, he said, were "so preposterous, I am not even going to address the possibility," and he insisted, "The gold is there." Bianchini kept his job, and in 2011 was promoted to vice-chair at BMO Capital Markets (Nesbitt Burns had been bought by BMO in the interim).

Analysts get it wrong for a number of reasons. One is the fact that they are often employed by the very same brokerage firms that are trying to woo investors to new issues of stocks, bonds and other investment products. In fact, analysts typically get paid from bonus pools that share the firm's investment banking, proprietary trading and secondary market commissions, so it's in their interest to persuade investors to buy the firms' investment offerings.

The easiest way to get fired as an analyst is to recommend to clients that they sell their stocks or bonds. Any such recommendation is considered sacrilegious. Analysts recommend either "Buy" or "Hold" but almost never "Sell," even in the face of impending disaster. After all, the name of the game is keeping investors' assets in play in the markets no matter what, because that's the only way the industry can make money for itself. And those brave souls who are too critical? John Olson was a veteran Houston-based analyst working for Merrill Lynch & Co. in 1998, when Enron was at its peak. Olson refused to recommend to investors they buy Enron stock due his suspicions over the energy company's soundness. Enron retaliated by not including Merrill Lynch in a lucrative stock underwriting deal. When his bosses at Merrill realized why they'd lost the deal, they fired Olson. "They decided that doing more business with Enron was more important than having me around, so I was wiped," Olson later told the media.

Studies show that analysts are usually far too optimistic about how companies will perform, and are subject to herd mentality. In 2010, the consulting firm McKinsey & Co. looked at a quarter-century of analysts' earnings forecasts and compared them to the actual earnings companies eventually reported. The study examined analysts employed by brokerage firms that help bring new companies to the stock market. McKinsey found that they were "typically over-optimistic, slow to revise their forecasts to reflect new economic conditions, and prone to making increasingly inaccurate forecasts when economic growth declined." And a 2011 paper written for the *Journal of Economic Behavior & Organization*, by John Beshears, an assistant professor of finance at Stanford University, and Katherine Milkman, a professor at the Wharton School of the University of Pennsylvania, found that in cases where their forecasts were proving to be wrong, analysts were reluctant to adjust their estimates to reflect new data. If anything, they would stubbornly cling to them.

AND THEN THERE ARE THE LAWYERS. Whether it's servicing financial institutions, influencing the regulatory environment or defending white-collar criminals, lawyers are critical actors in capital markets. The power of the so-called "Seven Sisters," the corporate law firms that dominate Bay Street—Blake, Cassels & Graydon, Davies Ward Phillips & Vineberg, Goodmans, McCarthy Tétrault, Osler, Hoskin & Harcourt, Stikeman Elliott, and Torys—is reflected in the fact that their offices take up floor after floor of the most expensive commercial real estate in the country, the banking towers that crowd the skylines of Canada's largest cities. These firms regularly represent several related parties in the same corporate family, and the environment is clubby to say the least.

Bay Street's top lawyers pull in high six-figure salaries and live in the leafy downtown Toronto neighbourhoods where Canada's captains of industry and bankers habitually congregate. They send their children to the same schools, socialize at the same clubs and sit on the same charity boards. And they see their firms first and foremost as businesses, as opposed to shining beacons of justice. "The concerns of professionalism are shoved aside and what counts is bringing in business, keeping business and making it as profitable as possible," says Philip Slayton, formerly a Bay Street corporate lawyer for seventeen years. "Your success at a law firm depends on your ability to do that. So things like scrupulous professionalism are not particularly valued, and indeed in some cases [are] regarded as an impediment."

This legal cartel profits handsomely from its ties to the financial sector. Whenever a company makes a public offering to sell shares to investors, for instance, law firms advise it and draft the necessary documents to be submitted to regulators. And when things blow up, the lawyers cash in as well, garnering whatever money is left over in bankrupt estates, charging astronomical legal fees over the course of CCAA court proceedings. After the $32 billion third-party ABCP market froze in 2007, more than 120 lawyers worked to sort out the mess, including barristers from Goodmans, Torys, Blake, Cassels & Graydon, Borden Ladner Gervais, McCarthy Tétrault, Miller Thomson, Davies Ward Phillips & Vineberg and Stikeman Elliott, and they billed more than $130 million for the job. The Stelco CCAA restructuring generated over $100 million in legal fees. In the dismantling of Nortel, more than a dozen law firms and hundreds of lawyers around the world were involved in selling off the company's assets. They were paid more than $360 million over the first two years of CCAA court proceedings, even as 400 disabled Nortel employees were losing their income and medical benefits.

Lawyers who work for the financial industry also dominate the boards of Canada's thirteen provincial and territorial securities commissions. The OSC's former chairs include David Brown, a long-time corporate lawyer at Davies Ward Phillips & Vineberg in Toronto, Edward J. Waitzer (Stikeman Elliott), Peter Dey (Osler, Hoskin & Harcourt), James C. Baillie, a senior partner at Torys LLP, and former Osgoode Hall Law School dean Stanley Beck, who sat on many corporate boards, including Scotiabank's Utility Corp., GMP Securities Inc., Canadian Tire Bank Inc. and Hollinger Inc.

THE STORY OF DEMERCHANT AND SUKONICK AND TORYS LLP reveals how incestuous ties to the establishment can lead a law firm to disaster should members of the business elite be hell-bent on committing fraud. Torys paid a hefty price for its entanglement in the Conrad Black saga: it was investigated by the SEC, denounced by Hollinger International's independent trustees, forced to hand over US$30 million to the company to settle a threatened malpractice suit, and was named as a defendant in three Canadian shareholder class actions. And it all stemmed from the fact that the law firm represented both Black's privately held companies, Ravelston Corporation Ltd. and Hollinger Inc., and his publicly traded U.S.-based company, Hollinger International.

Torys began representing Black and his companies in the 1980s, but its real problems started as Black began selling his newspaper assets to pay down corporate debt in 2000. The biggest sale of newspapers was to Izzy Asper's CanWest Global Communications Corp. Torys was the lead mergers and acquisitions counsel on the $3.5 billion deal, and DeMerchant, a senior partner, and Sukonick, a fifth-year associate, worked the file.

What ultimately proved to be their Waterloo was the US$53 million in non-compete payments shelled out by CanWest to Black, David Radler and two other executives as a result of the CanWest deal (the amount alleged to have been paid out in the non competes in total varied over the course of the proceedings, from as low as US$52 million to as much as US$84 million). For the Torys lawyers, questions immediately arose about how this cash should be characterized, how the recipients should be paid, and what should be reported to regulators and shareholders. For one thing, so Black and his executives would not be taxed, Sukonick suggested that this money be characterized as non-competes as opposed to bonuses, and CanWest shouldn't know who received what. For Hollinger International's board, Sukonick described the payments as "consistent with prior transactions," even though Hollinger International had never previously paid Ravelston officers anything over similar sales.

In January 2001, two months after the CanWest deal closed, DeMerchant and Sukonick were asked by Hollinger's executives whether they should inform the SEC about the non-compete agreements. Sukonick reported back to them that disclosure was unnecessary because the payments went directly to Ravelston executives from CanWest, not through the publicly listed company of Hollinger International, and that the money did not represent executive compensation anyway. But in the agreement that Sukonick drafted, the money *did* flow through Hollinger International. In the end, the payments were not mentioned in either the Hollinger proxy statement or the company's April 2001 annual 10-K financial report to the SEC, and they were referred to as "bonuses" in board minutes.

Sukonick initially told Hollinger's senior executives that the New York law firm of Cravath, Swaine & Moore LLP supported his opinion that it wasn't necessary to report the payments to the SEC. But

Cravath had offered no such view and outlined in a letter to the executives the potential pitfalls of failing to report the non-competes, such as being charged by the SEC (Cravath also said that Sukonick was incorrect in saying their firm supported his opinion that the payments didn't need to be disclosed). DeMerchant and Sukonick backtracked, and in May 2001, Hollinger finally disclosed the CanWest non-compete payments in an SEC quarterly filing.

Two years later, Hollinger International's board hired former SEC chairman Richard C. Breeden to conduct an internal investigation of questionable payments made to Black. Breeden discovered the existence of the non-compete payments dating from 1999 through 2001—money he felt clearly should have gone to shareholders. His 513-page report, issued in 2004, explored the role that Torys played in assisting Black and his top lieutenants. Breeden criticized the CanWest deal, alleging that Torys had failed to operate at arm's length from Black in representing Hollinger. "Torys, which represented not only Hollinger, but also Ravelston, [advised] that these inconvenient [disclosure] rules did not apply to large portions of the cash transferred to Black and Radler through Ravelston," says the Breeden report. "The result was to obscure the magnitude of what Black, Radler and their associates were taking at the expense of Hollinger's shareholders."

When Hollinger International threatened to file a malpractice suit against Torys for violating its duty as the company's counsel, Torys settled, paying $30 million, the largest-ever civil settlement by a Canadian law firm at that point in time. The firm did not admit to any wrongdoing and said Breeden was mistaken in accusing it of a conflict of interest.

When Black went on trial for fraud in 2007 in Chicago, both Sukonick and DeMerchant made video depositions. For U.S.

prosecutors, the work carried out by the Torys attorneys was further evidence that Black and other defendants had tried to obscure the nature of the payments. Black's defence team, however, argued that the Torys lawyers could be blamed for the entire cock-up, claiming it was their poor legal advice that caused the problem, not Black's ethical shortcomings.

When he testified in 2007, Sukonick said he had based his advice on his knowledge at the time and the advice of other, more senior Torys partners. Under cross-examination he admitted that he had actually suggested several times that Hollinger pay non-compete fees to executives as a way of avoiding paying taxes. Several emails suggested that Sukonick was an architect of the payment scheme, and he testified that he urged all the payments go to Black's private holding company, Ravelston, because "that way, CanWest need not know how much has been allocated to each individual." Sukonick further testified that he didn't see anything wrong with CanWest not knowing the amounts of the personal payments and he believed it was Hollinger's management who would decide how to distribute them.

Sukonick appeared to be suggesting ways to be less transparent about the existence of the payments—methods his clients had not come to on their own. When Peter Atkinson, Hollinger's general counsel, argued that CanWest should write separate cheques to all the executives "so it would have all been out in the open," Sukonick replied, "I wonder if for privacy reasons you might prefer to have one cheque written to Ravelston."

DeMerchant, who earned $600,000 to $900,000 a year at Torys, admitted during Black's trial that the firm's lawyers had committed a serious disclosure error by initially informing Hollinger that the non-compete payments didn't have to be reported to the SEC. She left the firm in 2006. When the two lawyers were charged by the Law Society, it was for breaching conflict-of-interest rules over the non-compete payments, and for their characterization of tax writeoffs in the Hollinger–CanWest deal. The Law Society case against the lawyers was still ongoing by 2012.

CRIMINALS WHO LAUNDER MONEY through the capital markets are no strangers to legal representation. One particularly helpful thing lawyers can offer is assistance in setting up opaque trust accounts for clients, accounts where criminals can park their ill-gotten gains, ostensibly to pay legal fees. Regulations introduced in 2000 by the federal government to close this loophole were met with lawsuits from the legal profession, which argued that the changes would undermine the principle of solicitor–client privilege. The B.C. Supreme Court ruled in the lawyers' favour.

Not surprisingly, a 2004 study by criminologist Stephen Schneider of York University looked at the 149 major money-laundering and proceeds-of-crime cases the RCMP solved in a five-year period during the 1990s and found that lawyers played a role in half of them (sometimes unwittingly). It's perhaps no accident that one of Montreal crime boss Vito Rizzuto's closest associates and relatives was Joe Lagana, an attorney who laundered drug profits for the Rizzutos in the 1990s.

In 2002, Bermuda Short, a joint RCMP–FBI sting operation, arrested fifty-eight stock market fraudsters, mostly operating pump-and-dumps. About one-third of the suspects arrested were Canadians. One of them was attorney Simon Rosenfeld, a sole practitioner with an office in a handsome old brownstone in downtown Toronto. Rosenfeld has a colourful past, having been convicted and fined

US$2.8 million in 2001 by the SEC for operating a company called Synpro Environmental Services, Inc. as a pump-and-dump. Rosenfeld was a wealthy man, although his property and art collection were, very presciently, in his wife's name.

Rosenfeld was nabbed after an undercover RCMP officer visited him in 2002, pretending to be a money launderer for a Colombian drug cartel who needed to wash $1 million to $3 million a month. In one conversation, Rosenfeld offered to set up a meeting between the officer and Vito Rizzuto, with whom the lawyer claimed to have done business (Rosenfeld also said he had relationships with the Hells Angels and Colombian drug dealers). The officer later returned to Rosenfeld's office carrying a bag with $250,000 to be laundered. "I'll tell you this . . . this is all coke money," explained the Mountie, to which Rosenfeld didn't bat an eye. Instead, Rosenfeld said he would put the money into a local bank and wire it to an offshore account, where his client could collect it within a week. The Mountie handed Rosenfeld a piece of paper with the account number of a bank in Miami. Rosenfeld then made four wire transfers to shift the money from Canada to the Florida-based bank though a foreign exchange company in Montreal called Denarius Financial Group, and two from a Richmond Hill, Ontario, company called Connectix Inc.

Rosenfeld was arrested soon afterwards, convicted in 2005, sentenced to three years in prison and fined $43,000 (in 2009, the Ontario Court of Appeal increased Rosenfeld's sentence to five years, saying his crimes deserved a harsher punishment). To this day, he has not been disbarred by the Law Society of Upper Canada.

AND THEN THERE ARE LAWYERS who simply take advantage of their position within the corporate world to steal for themselves, often with the help of the big brokerage houses. Stanko Grmovsek and Gil Cornblum met during their first week attending Osgoode Hall Law School in 1990 and became fast friends. In 1993, while Grmovsek was a summer student at the Bay Street law firm Osler, Hoskin & Harcourt, he overheard another student explain that he was wearing spiffy new driving shoes because he'd just bought a car "with the money he made from a deal he was working on." It dawned on Grmovsek that some of Osler's articling students were trading stock based on inside information they gleaned from the law firm's corporate files.

Cornblum was articling at Fraser Milner at the time, and the two would-be barristers decided to set up their own insider trading scheme to exploit information from their law firms. Cornblum found out all he could about pending transactions, going to work very early in the morning, wandering the halls, looking at other lawyers' work or documents left in fax or photocopy rooms, on their desks and elsewhere, accessing electronic files, seeking clues about mergers. All information gleaned was passed on to Grmovsek, who, working out of an office in his northern Toronto home, used it to buy and sell stock. The insider trading scheme they operated stretched over two separate periods, 1994 to 1999 and 2004 to 2008.

In 1996, when Grmovsek was working as a junior lawyer for the law firm Johnstone & Company, he met an attorney who specialized in setting up offshore accounts for Canadians wishing to execute trades in the Bahamas or Turks and Caicos. This lawyer helped Grmovsek establish his first offshore company, from which he could execute trades. Accounts were disguised with names such as "I Need Money" or "Through God All Things Are Possible," and the transactions included trading on Office Depot Inc.'s proposed takeover of Staples Inc., Onex Corp.'s takeover of Labatt Brewing Co. Ltd., and

Norwest Corp.'s buyout of Wells Fargo & Co. By the late 1990s, Grmovsek and Cornblum had amassed more than US$6 million from their illicit trading.

In 1999, Grmovsek met a broker, Sandy Bortolin, at BMO Nesbitt Burns in Toronto and hired him to assist with his offshore transactions. For the next nine years, he used Bortolin's services. The broker demanded that Grmovsek move his offshore accounts over to his management. Bortolin would move the trading account more than once, including to Switzerland, before settling on the Bahamas offices of Swiss private bank Clariden Leu.

After making money from insider trading, Grmovsek and Cornblum needed to transfer it from the Bahamas to Canada and hide its origins as a precautionary measure. Bortolin suggested a solution to this problem. He had clients with cash in Toronto. Using a wire transfer, he could move money from Grmovsek and Cornblum's offshore account to his client's offshore account. When the monies arrived in Toronto, Grmovsek would go to Bortolin's office and leave with an envelope of cash. Grmovsek agreed to this proposal. The Clariden Leu records show ten wire transfers of $49,000 each. Bortolin was making good money out of this arrangement, both by collecting fees from the transfers and by charging $3,000 every three months for managing the account. In total he pocketed $78,000.

Meanwhile, Cornblum pursued his legal career. In the mid-nineties, he moved to New York to work for the powerhouse Wall Street firm Sullivan & Cromwell, but he returned to Toronto in 1998, the stress related to his illegal activities having become "painful and debilitating," he would later testify. He joined a Toronto law firm to be closer to his future wife, and stopped feeding information to Grmovsek, despite his friend's "pestering questions."

In 2001, Cornblum was hired by a large Minneapolis-based

corporate law firm, Dorsey & Whitney. He worked out of its Toronto office and eventually became an equity partner. Three years after joining the firm, however, he found his "life cracking open," he would later claim. After some career setbacks, his wife's breast cancer diagnosis and what he claimed was Grmovsek's pressure to start making money again through insider trading, he relented. Once again they began their illicit trading, made millions and, as it turned out, got sloppy. "In the early time period, I don't believe there was any substantial likelihood they would have been caught by market surveillance or a regulator," explains Joe Groia, Grmovsek's lawyer. "They were very sophisticated in how they did it, in small tranches and engaged in a myriad of associated trading. In the later stages, however, they took leave of their senses and began to trade in significant volumes and thinly traded stocks. It was almost inevitable they were going to get caught."

By 2008, Grmovsek's trading had become, by his own admission, "moronic," and sure enough, the U.S. Financial Industry Regulatory Authority caught wind of it. The evidence led to Cornblum, who was confronted by Dorsey & Whitney personnel. He denied the allegations but was fired anyway. Soon afterwards, on two separate occasions, he tried to kill himself. Investigations by the RCMP and OSC, the SEC and U.S. Department of Justice ensued, with the two men agreeing to co-operate.

All told, Grmovsek and Cornblum raked in nearly $10 million, by far the biggest case of insider trading in Canadian history and one of the most significant in North America. "If you look at Martha Stewart—hers was only a $45,000 insider trading case," points out Kevin Harrison, the superintendent in charge of the RCMP's Integrated Market Enforcement Team in Toronto, who investigated Cornblum and Grmovsek.

In October 2009, just days before the two men were to be sentenced, the 39-year-old Cornblum threw himself off a Toronto overpass. His wife, Marilyn, told *The Globe and Mail* that her husband's suicide was the "culmination of a lifelong battle with severe depression." Grmovsek called it a "tragedy," and it was, especially given that Cornblum would have spent mere months behind bars.

Grmovsek was sentenced to thirty-nine months in jail and ordered to pay $1.1 million in penalties to the OSC. He was out of prison in 2011. Bortolin was fired from BMO Nesbitt Burns in 2009 and then went to work for another investment dealer, which he left in the late summer of 2011, shortly before IIROC laid charges against him for his involvement in the Grmovsek and Cornblum scandal.

GRMOVSEK AND CORNBLUM were not alone in embracing this particular method of fraud. Mitchell Finkelstein was a 41-year-old partner with the powerhouse Toronto law firm Davies Ward Phillips & Vineberg LLP. In 2011, he was charged by the OSC for insider trading when he was accused of feeding information about pending corporate takeovers to a group of traders working for some of the biggest brokerage houses on Bay Street. Finkelstein was no punter: he handled some of his law firm's biggest files. Raised among Montreal's English-speaking elite before moving to Toronto, he had a stellar pedigree and a mansion in Forest Hill, a $500,000 annual salary and a healthy network of wealthy and influential friends.

According to the OSC, in 2004, Finkelstein started passing on information about upcoming mergers to an old university chum of his, Paul Azeff, who worked as a trader at CIBC World Markets. In turn, Azeff passed on the details to others, including two traders at TD Waterhouse. They accumulated shares in the target companies worth $16.5 million before the public announcements of the take-over deals. The OSC said Finkelstein and Azeff spoke several times just before each deal was announced publicly and Finkelstein made cash deposits in a bank account afterwards.

Finkelstein acquired material by scouring through his law firm's documents management system. The insider trading involved deals with such big-name companies as Kohlberg Kravis Roberts & Co., Barrick Gold, Placer Dome, Sherritt International and Dynatec. Profits from the entire scam were some $3 million. The brokers were forced to resign and Finkelstein left his law firm. None of them were criminally charged. Finkelstein has denied allegations of insider trading and as of early 2012 he is awaiting a decision in his case with the OSC.

As bad as the lawyers, credit rating agencies, underwriters and analysts might be, in many respects the worst enablers of all are the market regulators and police, who repeatedly prove themselves pow-erless, or unwilling, to rein the fraudsters in.

— FIFTEEN —

KISSING COUSINS: THE REGULATORS

WHILE CONRAD BLACK BOUNDED from success to success during the 1990s, building his media empire, Paul Winkler experienced Hollinger's seamier side. Back then, he was briefly the publisher of one of Black's papers, the *Capital News*, in Kelowna, British Columbia, a small city of 106,000 people in the Okanagan Valley. "Working for Hollinger was like being in the Mafia," Winkler once told me.

A tall, rusty-haired man in his mid fifties with ruddy cheeks, old-school charm and an air of incorruptibility, Winkler bears a striking resemblance to Jimmy Stewart in *Mr. Smith Goes to Washington*. He's spent most of his working life in the newspaper industry, primarily at small-city weeklies in southern Ontario, and then on the west coast in 1996 after accepting a job as general manager of the thrice-weekly *Capital News*, owned by Lower Mainland Publishing Ltd. (LMPL). His task was to turn the paper around and cripple the local competition, the Kelowna *Daily Courier*. And he did. Winkler rapidly improved the *Capital*'s readership and profitability, driving its advertising market share from 32 to 51 percent, gains that came most certainly at the *Daily*'s expense. He also made the small paper a lot of money—a profit of $2 million, up from merely breaking even only three years earlier—and did so without laying off any staff.

In the fall of 1998, Hollinger International acquired LMPL and Winkler had a new boss, David Radler, and soon his career began to unravel. A few months later his competitor, the *Daily*, was sold to a mysterious company called Horizon Publications Inc., run by Todd Vogt, who was believed to be close to Radler. "This had a bad smell to it. This guy was thirty-two years old and had no financial resources behind him," explains Winkler. "We all knew Todd was an appendage of David Radler."

If, in fact, Horizon was owned by Hollinger, Winkler realized this could pose a serious problem with the Competition Bureau, which forbade two papers being owned by one company in the same city. "I knew we had a common owner," he says. "I was told that Horizon was an arm of Hollinger, that it was owned by Conrad Black and David Radler." After Winkler began voicing his concerns, on November 18, 1999, he heard on a local radio station that he'd been fired. A day later, the company said it would "accept" his resignation. Winkler fought back, suing LMPL for breach of his contract and constructive dismissal.

Unemployed, he and his wife and four children lived on savings for two years before the case went to trial in January 2002. The lawsuit clearly alarmed Hollinger, with Radler flying in to testify. Trying to determine who controlled the *Daily*, Winkler's lawyer asked Radler on the stand about the ownership of Horizon Publications. "Combined, [Black and I] had 48 percent," replied Radler, meaning a minority stake.

This was a lie, although Winkler didn't know it at the time. Seven months later, the judge rendered her verdict: Winkler won his wrongful dismissal suit and she awarded him $160,000. By then, he had moved back to Ontario, convinced that Black and Radler had misrepresented the extent of their ownership of Horizon, which struck him as suspicious behaviour for a publicly run company. He was now determined to press the Canadian regulatory authorities to look into the matter. In January 2003, Winkler emailed copies of his court judgment to the B.C. and Ontario securities commissions. In his cover letter, he wrote: "I believe Hollinger's top two executives, Conrad Black and David Radler, were involved in a conflict of interest and breached their fiduciary responsibilities." He pointed out that the pair had hidden their ownership position in Horizon.

Winkler received a swift response from the OSC. "It was brief and to the point and said they saw no reason to investigate," he recalls. That is, six months before Hollinger International hired former SEC chairman Richard Breeden to investigate how Black and his executives managed the company, and ten months before US$32 million in unauthorized payments to Black and Radler was revealed, the OSC turned down an opportunity to investigate corporate executives engaged in potentially illegal business practices.

Had the OSC and BCSC launched an inquiry, they would have uncovered one of the most cynical of Black and Radler's schemes. As the two men began unloading Hollinger's newspapers to pay off corporate debt, they devised a plan to sell the publicly traded company's small community newspapers, which were highly profitable, to themselves. The two men sold Hollinger's newspapers to Horizon—in which they controlled a large majority stake, 73 percent (not the 48 percent Radler had stated in the Kelowna courtroom)— at huge discounts all the while demanding non-compete payments as part of the deals (some of the Hollinger papers were sold to Horizon for as low as one dollar a piece). In effect, they paid themselves not to compete with themselves, while snagging Hollinger's profitable papers for dirt cheap. Not only were they ripping off shareholders in the form of the non compete payments, they were also lying about the true value of the small papers they were moving from the publicly traded company to Horizon, their own private company. (Black denies that he knew Radler owned more than 24 percent of Horizon.)

Winkler was not alone in warning the OSC about Black's activities long before U.S. authorities began investigating the media mogul. Stephen Jarislowsky built one of the most successful investment management firms in Canada, Jarislowsky Fraser Ltd., eventually overseeing assets of more than $45 billion (in 2011, Jarislowsky was the twenty-fourth richest man in Canada). Jarislowsky is a shareholders' activist who, going back in time, was both a business ally and an enemy of Black, someone Jarislowsky describes as "brilliant" as well as a "delightful scoundrel" who has a history "of going to the edge of the law and sometimes over it." Black invited Jarislowsky on to the board of newspaper companies Southam Inc. and later to the Telegraph plc (owner of *The Daily Telegraph*) in the U.K. At first, everything seemed to be in order, but Jarislowsky soon became alarmed at Black's habit of pocketing non-compete payments when assets were being sold. "That whole thing was absolutely wrong—he had no right to that money," says Jarislowsky. "It belonged to shareholders."

In 2001, Jarislowsky wrote to the OSC and spoke to them on the phone about Black's actions. "The Securities Commission knew about [the non-compete payments] and the Securities Commission did nothing," he told me from his Montreal offices. "They didn't seem overly concerned."

———

THAT THE OSC AND OTHER Canadian regulators had good cause to investigate Black but didn't bother doing so suggests that they have little appetite for prosecuting white-collar fraud, especially when the highest levels of the country's corporate establishment might be involved. It also explains why the country is such a haven for investment fraud.

Canada has a fractured, crazy-quilt regulatory apparatus overseeing its capital markets. At the top are thirteen provincial and territorial securities commissions, and, not incidentally, of the more than one hundred countries belonging to the International Organization of Securities Commissions (IOSCO), only Canada and Bosnia-Herzegovina don't have a national-level securities regulator. James C. Baillie, a former OSC chair and a senior partner at Torys LLP, once told me that "it's deeply embarrassing to go to the IOSCO meetings and see representatives of the regulatory commissions for France, the United Kingdom and the U.S., and then you see one from Ontario, Quebec, B.C., Alberta and all of the other provinces. It suggests we can't get our act together."

Beneath the securities commissions are a bevy of self-regulatory bodies, or SROs—effectively industry-run agencies of mostly bankers and brokers who investigate themselves. The most prominent is the Investment Industry Regulatory Organization of Canada. There is also, of course, law enforcement, specifically the RCMP and its Integrated Market Enforcement Teams.

Calls to reform the regulatory system have been heard for years. In 2003, for example, the Wise Persons' Committee to Review the Structure of Securities Regulation in Canada, chaired by investment banker Michael Phelps, produced a large report for the federal finance minister recommending the creation of a national securities regulator. *It's Time*, read the blunt title in case anyone missed the point. "Canada suffers from inadequate enforcement and inconsistent investor protection," says the document. "The system is too costly, duplicative and inefficient . . . Canada's international competitiveness is undermined by regulatory complexity." It was a damning indictment of a "system" that remains stubbornly in place to this day.

A year later, Bank of Canada governor David Dodge mused that whenever he visited New York, Boston or London, he kept hearing that Canada is "a bit like a Wild West in terms of the degree to which rules and regulations are enforced, and that perception doesn't really help us when we go to try and raise money on foreign markets." In 2007, Jim Flaherty, the new finance minister of the Conservative federal government, said that "for many outside of Canada, our system is seen as cumbersome, fragmented, slow, repetitive and lacking the proper tools of enforcement." That same year, Claude Lamoureux, the just-retired CEO of the powerful Ontario Teachers' Pension Plan, accused regulators of just "pretending to oversee" securities rules, and he lambasted them for their light-handed treatment of white-collar crime.

And yet Howell Jackson, a law professor at Harvard Law School, published a study in 2006 comparing the resources spent on Canada's securities regulatory agencies with those of the United States and found that "in terms of budgets and staffing levels, the Canadian regulatory system is comparable to the overall regulatory system in the United States." But he then observed, "The level of public enforcement activity in Canada was much lower than that of the United States and the differences are so huge that they swamp any possible scaling adjustment." In other words, money was being spent on trying to catch the bad guys, but few crooks were actually being apprehended.

Finally, in 2009, in the wake of the credit crisis, the Harper government took steps to set up a national securities regulator, even establishing an agency to coordinate the task. They won't have an easy time of it. Essentially, Canada is a country run by dynastic families clustered in city strongholds who can, quite easily, influence local regulatory bodies, and this arrangement suits them just fine. "If you have a country run by very few people, it leads often to stability," says Utpal Bhattacharya, a professor of finance at Indiana University who has studied Canada's enforcement system. "So there's not a confrontational approach. But that also leads to bad equilibrium in the sense that if you scratch my back, I'll scratch yours . . . [Canada's] financial system is too much of an old boys' network."

There's more. The habit of not questioning economic elites has led to Canada becoming a go-to country for fraud. In 2007, the Canadian Securities Administrators released a report saying that over one million Canadians had been victims of investment fraud. Another report, by Port Hope–based Measuredmarkets Inc., said that thirty-three of fifty-two large Canadian mergers in 2006 showed signs of aberrant trading just before the mergers were publicly announced, a rate of 63 percent (as compared to 41 percent in the States). In 2009, PricewaterhouseCoopers published a global economic crime survey that found Canada was number four in the world among countries reporting the highest levels of fraud. And there is no shortage of fiascos to point to. As a *New York Times* columnist once observed, "It seems like Canada produces more stock market fraud, at least per capita, than do other countries." Wild West indeed.

This poor oversight costs us, too. John Coffee, a law professor at Columbia University and a member of a 2006 task force that examined Canada's securities laws, says that due to our weak regulatory regime, issuers have to sell more securities in Canadian markets to raise the same amount of money as an issuer would, say, in the United States. In short, weak oversight devalues Canadian securities.

THE CHIEF ROLE OF CANADA'S thirteen securities commissions is to oversee $3.3 trillion of capital in the markets, all publicly traded companies and more than two hundred investment firms. Together, they employ just over 1,000 staff, and every year spend about $140 million on enforcement, average 124 actions and lay fines totalling around $230 million. Exactly how well they perform is difficult to gauge, particularly because the commissions themselves are so secretive.

In 2005, the Task Force to Modernize Securities Legislation in Canada asked Utpal Bhattacharya to compare the provincial securities commissions' track record with that of the American SEC. An internationally recognized expert on market regulation, Bhattacharya started off by asking the commissions for data. None replied. He did find enforcement statistics on the OSC's website, however, and the following year produced a report that said between 1997 and 2005 (with the size of the stock markets taken into consideration), the OSC prosecuted ten times fewer cases overall than the SEC, and twenty times fewer cases of insider trading. Moreover, the SEC resolved cases faster than the OSC and levied fines seventeen times higher per insider trading case than the OSC. From 1997 to 2000, the OSC didn't launch a single case or lay a single charge for insider trading (and launched only two during the following two years), while the SEC launched 137 cases. In 2005, while the SEC initiated 500 cases of securities violations among 6,407 firms, the OSC opened only 24 among 3,610 companies. "Enforcement in Canada is pathetic," says Bhattacharya. "Canada is a first-world country with second-world capital markets and third-world enforcement."

Bhattacharya points to serious economic repercussions from having such a poor regulatory regime. "If Canadian companies have to pay a higher cost for raising capital [because of slipshod enforcement], they won't raise money, they won't have investments, and you won't have growth and jobs. No one is going to give you money unless you trust them. Enforcement is critical to trust."

It's difficult to see if the OSC's track record has improved much since Bhattacharya's study was published. In 2010, the commission took only four cases to court, compared to two the year before and none in 2008. All told, the OSC launched 24 proceedings dealing with securities violations in 2010, compared with 681 by the SEC; and the OSC levied $36 million in penalties and disgorgements, compared to US$2.8 billion by the SEC.

The OSC's record for obtaining convictions is also dreadful. In the example of Bre-X Minerals Ltd., it lost its case against John Felderhof, the vice-chairman of the mining company, after an expensive trial that dragged on for seven years. It never laid a finger on Conrad Black. In the case of Nortel, the SEC obtained US$35 million in a settlement over accounting manipulations compared with just $1 million negotiated by the OSC, and this figure only covered the commission's investigation costs. (The OSC did lay civil fraud charges against three Nortel executives for securities violations in 2007, although those cases have since languished.) On third-party ABCP, the OSC levied fines against seven investment dealers and pursued the small investment firm Coventree Inc. (although the OSC fined Coventree $2 million, its enforcement branch was demanding $16.5 million). However the commission did not examine the role played in the fiasco by the big banks. And then there's property developer Mascan Corp. In 1986, the OSC began a case against the company's owner for allegedly using shareholders' money to pay off personal debts. The matter was dropped twenty-four years later. Moreover, the OSC regularly stands aside and allows American authorities to prosecute Canadian corporate criminals, again such as Conrad Black. "They have really abdicated the territory to the Americans," says Joel Rochon, a Toronto securities lawyer.

There's little reason to believe Canada's other securities commissions have a better track record. Admittedly, there are few studies examining their effectiveness. For years, however, scandal has dogged the Alberta Securities Commission (ASC). In January 2004, Wayne Alford, the ASC's former director of enforcement, sent a letter to Alberta's revenue minister alleging that ASC chair Stephen Sibold and executive director David Linder treated the regulator "as their own private domain" and used "their unchecked power to benefit those that please them." They had, he wrote, created a "two-tier regulatory regime" with two sets of rules, one for "normal" market participants and another for the "powerful." The ASC oversees Canada's second-largest capital market.

In 2004 and 2005, five probes investigated Alford's and other allegations. The results from at least two of the investigations were sealed and never made public. When Alberta's provincial auditor general launched a probe, the ASC went to court to stop the audit from proceeding. That audit went ahead anyway and in 2005 discovered that ASC enforcement director John Petch traded shares in a company while it was under investigation by his own staff. Examining eighty-two cases, the auditor found myriad examples of poor documentation and haphazard enforcement procedures.

Interviews of ASC employees conducted for an investigative exposé by *Western Standard* magazine in 2005 were replete with complaints that political interference was common at the ASC. "We would have an enforcement file and would want to proceed

with enforcement action, and it would be killed," one former ASC
employee told the magazine. Cases involving powerful people would
mysteriously vanish, they said, and sometimes the orders came
straight from the Alberta government. "I saw them meddling in
enforcement," said an ex-manager.

REFLECTING ON A CASE I explored in a previous chapter, it appears
there is also a tendency by the securities commissions to ignore or
reject decisions made by other regulatory bodies. This is true in no
province more so than British Columbia, generally considered the
most corrupt capital market in the country. In 2003, the Investment
Dealers Association of Canada (IDA) found Victoria broker Carolann
Steinhoff guilty of making an unauthorized trade. She appealed to
the B.C. Securities Commission (BCSC), who overturned the IDA's
ruling. A few years later, the IDA's successor agency, IIROC, charged
Steinhoff again, finding her guilty of instructing her staff to paste
signatures onto clients' documents. The BCSC threw out that ruling,
too. IIROC charged her yet again and found Steinhoff guilty for misleading clients, although she continues to work in the industry.

In 2004, IIROC also banned Kianosh Rahmani from working in
the securities industry after it was discovered he'd failed to mention
being convicted for sexual assault while working at CIBC World
Markets. Rahmani lied twice on official forms that he had never
been criminally convicted. In 2009, the BCSC overturned the lifetime ban and gave him a five-year suspension instead, saying his
misconduct would not call into question his ability to perform his
duties honestly.

Why does this culture of indifference persist? "I think a significant part of the problem is a lack of political will," says Dimitri

Lascaris, a lawyer with Siskinds LLP, a London, Ontario, law firm that keeps a close watch over the investment industry. "It's easy to go after people in the boiler room who are ripping off retirees, but they don't have real power. To go after people who have real power and influence requires a significant amount of political will. Many senior officials from the OSC return to the private sector after they leave the commission, and it's realistic to expect that their career prospects would suffer if they aggressively pursued senior officers of large public corporations while they were at the OSC. These things are going to come back and have an impact on their prospects, and that's just reality. And who is not going to be influenced by that unless you're a saint?"

The very idea of putting a CEO or member of the establishment in jail for stealing other people's money seems, well, just too un-Canadian for the regulators. As Michael Watson, then the head of enforcement at the OSC, told the *Toronto Star* in 2007, jail sentences of ten years or more for white-collar criminals are "just not going to happen here. It's not part of the Canadian justice system. Other than vindictiveness, I'm not sure why people are saying jail sentences are not long enough."

This mindset benefits those who commit fraud. "We have a securities regulation system in Canada that works with the investment industry to cover up its bad behaviour and fraudulent conduct," says Diane Urquhart. "If they were to take on a case like Conrad Black, it would be an admission that members of the establishment have committed fraud that had an impact on ordinary Canadians. They would rather not do such a case."

For a sense of the incestuousness of the relationship between regulators and the financial sector, one need only examine who fills the positions of chairs and boards of directors at the securities commissions. Overwhelmingly, they are people who work in the financial sector itself or are corporate lawyers whose clients include banks and brokerages. For instance, before David Wilson became chairman of the OSC (2005 to 2010), he was vice-chairman of the Bank of Nova Scotia and CEO of its brokerage house, Scotia Capital. By 2011, the OSC's board included vice-chair James Turner, a securities lawyer and senior partner at Torys LLP, a law firm for all the big banks; Sinan Akdeniz, the former vice-chair of TD Securities, the Toronto-Dominion Bank's brokerage house; Margot Howard, a financial analyst who's worked at top brokerage houses such as McLeod Young Weir and with the money management firm AMI Partners Inc.; and Kevin Kelly, the former president and co-CEO of the investment house Wellington West Capital Inc. Other members include lawyers from McCarthy Tétrault, Borden Ladner Gervais and Osler, Hoskin & Harcourt, all of whom service the financial industry. "It's a problem when you have the commission too closely connected to the financial industry," agrees lawyer Ermanno Pascutto, a former head of staff at the OSC who heads up the Foundation for Advancement of Investor Rights (FAIR), an independent investors' advocacy group. "You need professional regulators . . . But right now they're basically all from Bay Street. Even if they're well intentioned, if you're all from the same club, it makes it very difficult."

While the OSC is keen to hear from corporate lawyers and bankers, it's less interested in the views of ordinary investors. OSC chair David Brown (1998–2005) set up an investors' advisory committee as he was leaving the job; after David Wilson took over, the committee was eventually disbanded.

———

CHRIS MORGIS IS A WEALTHY LANDLORD, the owner and president of Morgis Properties Ltd., which owns rental apartment buildings in Toronto. A pale, self-effacing man with slicked-back hair, he works out of a dingy office in one of his buildings in North York, part of Toronto's north end.

In the late 1990s, Morgis decided to invest $3 million of his savings with an investment firm called Thomson Kernaghan & Co. Ltd., a well-regarded presence on Bay Street since 1949. Thomson Kernaghan was managed by Mark Valentine, a whiz kid in his late twenties. Tall, athletic and soft-spoken, Valentine was, for a brief shining moment, the Justin Bieber of Bay Street—rich beyond his wildest dreams, the owner of a sprawling home in Forest Hill, a cottage on Lake Simcoe and a Falcon jet to shuttle his family about, including to his beach house in Florida's tony Key Biscayne community. He is the private school–educated son of diplomat Douglas Valentine, a former Canadian ambassador to Saudi Arabia. He once bought himself a Ferrari with a license plate with the word "giddyup," which is what he would tell his traders to motivate them.

Not long after Morgis invested with Thomson Kernaghan, he began seeing alarming transactions in his account, including unauthorized trades, his money being invested in risky stocks, cash going missing and a forged signature on a US$20,000 cheque. "At that point I stepped in," he says.

First, he withdrew all of his cash because, by 2001, he'd lost $800,000 of his $3 million investment. Incensed, Morgis approached the IDA. Created in 1916, the IDA eventually morphed into the investment industry's self-regulating watchdog and lobbyist. In 2008 the IDA became the Investment Industry Regulatory Organization of Canada, which is run by the brokerage industry itself. And the problem with that, as Morgis observes, is "you are taking your complaint to the very people whom you have issue with." One indicator of IIROC's regulatory weakness was revealed in 2011, when it imposed a $1 million fine on a former TD Waterhouse broker, Mark Allen Dennis, who worked in Hamilton, Ontario. The problem with that was he was accused of stealing $1.4 million from a widow's brokerage account. IIROC staff had even recommended a fine of $1.45 million, but the IIROC panel overseeing the case said their existing rules did not allow for "disgorgement" of ill-gotten gains in cases where money had actually been pilfered from a client.

In the case of Morgis, in March 2001 he made a formal complaint to the IDA about Thomson Kernaghan. And then he waited for something to happen. Feeling that no one was taking his complaint seriously, he hired McCarthy Tétrault, paying them $50,000 to write a lengthy brief documenting how Thomson Kernaghan had mishandled his money. He submitted the document (and wrote six letters) to the IDA. "A year after my complaint, they got back to me," he says. Finally, Morgis got his meeting with the IDA.

IDA responded—and claims it did so earlier than Morgis says—and it did open a file and assign an investigator to Morgis's case, but the watchdog dragged its heels, unwilling, it would seem, to intervene and prevent a disaster. By 2002, Mark Valentine was being accused of engaging in "death spiral" financing, a form of trading that artificially drives down the value of companies' stock to their detriment, but which is profitable for traders. That summer, Valentine was arrested by American law enforcement for engaging in stock market fraud, and Thomson Kernaghan went bust. In 2004, Valentine pled guilty to one charge of securities fraud and received a four-year sentence of probation and nine months of house arrest.

Angry that IDA had shown so little interest in his warnings, Morgis sued both Thomson Kernaghan and the association for not moving promptly against the company. "Had the IDA acted in 2001 when I arrived at their offices, what played out in 2002 at Thomson Kernaghan could have been avoided," he says. "There were a lot of people harmed in that meltdown." Morgis's lawyer argued that the IDA owed her client a "duty of care" given that its primary role is to protect investors. The courts dismissed this argument and blocked Morgis from suing the IDA, citing a 2001 Supreme Court of Canada ruling that says regulators cannot be found negligent for doing a poor job. "I spent $250,000 to $300,000 in legal fees to make the point that this system is broken, it does not work," explains Morgis, "[and] the position of the regulators is that they owe you nothing, not even a duty of care, and to me that is appalling."

ROBERT KYLE SPENT TWENTY YEARS on Bay Street working as a derivatives trader before becoming an investors' activist in the late nineties. In 2007, while poking about on the IDA's website, he came across a list of more than 2,800 brokers whom the public had lodged complaints against between 2002 and 2005—complaints, nearly all of them, the IDA had failed to investigate or act on. Not realizing that the IDA had intended this information to be inaccessible to the public, Kyle downloaded the list and posted it on his own website. Soon afterwards, he received a letter from the IDA's lawyers demanding that he "immediately remove from your website the information relating to IDA members and brokers." The IDA hinted they might sue Kyle. Interestingly, complaints about brokers are made publicly available in the U.S.A.

Kyle refused to take down the list and it remains on his website.

One broker on the list, Hugh Bagnell, used to work at RBC Dominion Securities and had twenty-five complaints and one lawsuit against him. One of his clients was Donald Kennedy, a Nova Scotia dairy farmer who'd inherited $155,000 and invested it through RBC Dominion Securities. Bagnell took over managing Kennedy's money and lost all of it except for $1,800. "It just kept disappearing and disappearing," Kennedy told CTV. Bagnell quit the industry in 2003 as the complaints against him piled up, and the IDA, after the fact, fined him $61,700 and barred him from working in the business again—although by then he'd done his damage. Another broker listed was Bertrand Trudel, who worked for the securites firm Lévesque Beaubien Inc. in Joliette, Quebec. Trudel had attracted a whopping fifty-nine complaints and lawsuits and yet the IDA had taken no action against him. Immediately after Kyle put the list of brokers online, the Association opened an investigation into Trudel, eventually fining him $51,400 for a variety of infractions, including making unauthorized trades with his clients' money. Yet the IDA refused to chuck him out of the industry and Trudel kept his job. "What the IDA found embarrassing was that there were 2,800 brokers who had complaints lodged against them," says Kyle. "They were only interested in protecting the 'good name' of their industry when I released that information."

IN 2003, WITH THE URGING of then RCMP commissioner Giuliano Zaccardelli, the RCMP opened the offices of its Integrated Market Enforcement Teams, a dedicated group of RCMP investigators with capital markets fraud experience. They were deployed in Montreal, Toronto, Calgary and Vancouver.

Former undercover RCMP officer Bill Majcher was promoted to run the IMET office in Vancouver, and he proceeded to assemble a crack team of commercial crime investigators, steering them towards

some promising cases. One was the Pay Pop pump-and-dump scam
that one of his officers, Bud Cramm, had come across in the late
nineties. When Cramm asked that charges be laid against Pay Pop,
both the Department of Justice lawyer assigned to the IMET squad
and the provincial Crown Attorney's Office refused. Cramm ended
up taking the case instead to the SEC in the United States, which
prosecuted the company.

The case of Getty Copper was all too similar. A copper mining
company, Getty has been described by Majcher as a "Baby Bre-X"
because it made exaggerated claims about its copper holdings. The
company was accused of misleading investors, who had given $18
million to Getty over the years. The IMET team put three investigators on the case and raided the company's offices, as well as those of
its lawyer and accountant. Again, the same Department of Justice
lawyer refused to take the case to the Crown to lay charges.

IMET had no more success elsewhere. In perhaps the most celebrated instance, Bay Street lawyer and investors' advocate Wesley
Voorheis approached and urged IMET to investigate Conrad Black
and the hedge fund Norshield. IMET said no. Years later, when I
asked why, they cited a lack of resources to take on such complicated
cases. Their inaction led *Vancouver Sun* business columnist and
investigative journalist David Baines to begin deriding the teams as
"impotent" and a "disaster-in-progress," and his criticisms were well
founded: by the end of 2007, IMET had spent $80 million but had
laid only one charge in Vancouver and four in Toronto; its Montreal
and Calgary teams had charged no one. "I think it is just incompetence and indifference," says Majcher, who was pushed out of IMET
in 2005 and quit the RCMP altogether two years later. "As an organization, we strived for mediocrity and often achieved it." Despite
having a 170 full-time staff and spending $19 million a year, by the

end of 2009 IMET could boast only five convictions, of which at least two required little investigation.·

Why had IMET performed so miserably? The reasons were numerous, including legal hurdles making it difficult to gather evidence and bring white-collar fraud cases to court. One problem is that IMET often initiates criminal investigations only after they've been signed off by a consultation committee made up of representatives of the provincial securities commissions and self-regulatory organizations like IIROC. Senior IMET officers complain about management interference to stop high-profile investigations against investment bank executives. And there's constant reassignment of investment fraud investigators to other policing activities, like security for the 2010 Vancouver Olympics or Toronto G20 Summit. Many former IMET officers also blame the RCMP's balkanized internal culture. "We were like the bastard child in the family," says Majcher. "We were undermined from within."

IN 2009, THE HARPER GOVERNMENT set up the Canadian Securities Transition Office and appointed Douglas Hyndman, the long-standing chair of the BCSC, to lead the charge in getting a national securities regulator established (the government introduced legislation to see it happen as well). Hyndman was a peculiar choice. He had presided over the most scandal-plagued stock market in the country for twenty-two years and played a hand in overturning a ban levelled by the TSX against convicted cop killer Bill Nichols, who wanted to conduct investor relations for listed companies. Nichols had misled the exchange about his criminal record (omitting to mention the person he murdered was a police officer and nineteen other convictions for criminal activity, including armed robbery and kidnapping), but the BCSC and Hyndman insisted that Nichols was a changed man. "This was ludicrous," wrote David Baines in *The Vancouver Sun*. "[Nichols] was not so changed that he wouldn't lie about his past."

Hyndman's executive vice-president was Lawrence Ritchie, on secondment from his job as vice-chair of the OSC and a partner at the corporate law firm Osler, Hoskin & Harcourt. Ritchie is pure corporate legal establishment, married to the daughter of Purdy Crawford, the former chairman of Imasco Ltd. who headed up the committee that was put in charge of trying to sort out the third-party ABCP fiasco and ultimately allowed the big banks off the hook for peddling this asset. Whether such men will be able to conjure up a national securities regulator that actually has some teeth and is not as captive to Bay Street as its provincial predecessors remains to be seen.

SIXTEEN

NOT TO BE TRUSTED

O N A FRIGID EVENING in February 2009, two cars filled with men in their thirties cruised the manicured boulevards of north Toronto's Ledbury Park, a middle-to-upper-class neighbourhood that's home to a large number of Orthodox Jews. They drove past faux châteaux with spotless front lawns, perfectly spaced elm trees and luxury sedans in the driveways. The young professionals and businessmen in the cars were looking for someone they had once considered a personal friend, a first-rate concert pianist who played Chopin and Bach like a seraph, usually on a 1912 Bösendorfer grand piano.

On this night, however, the men had no interest in their friend's musical prowess. Instead, they were in a panic, wanting to know exactly what had happened to millions of dollars of their money, and to money belonging to their friends and relatives — $27 million owed to seventy-six creditors, nearly all of whom were members of this tightly knit community and most of whom now faced financial ruin.

They all feared that their savings had vanished down the rabbit hole of an investment fraud. And so a modern-day posse was on the prowl.

Being hunted was one Tzvi Erez, a 41-year-old businessman from a wealthy and cultured family, and the owner of the printing company Erez Graphix Inc. "We went to his house and then to his parents' house to find out where he was," recalls Akiva Aronson, one of the young men searching for Erez. "When we drove by his sister's house, we saw Tzvi's car in the driveway. And so we blocked his car."

Earlier that day, the men had received news from Erez's lawyer that his company was finished and that all of the creditors' money was gone, and they were determined to make him come clean. After they pounded on the door of his sister's house, a nervous-looking Erez finally emerged. "Where's our money?" one of them demanded.

"I can't talk about it. You'll find out soon," Erez replied before returning inside.

The men grew alarmed that Erez might bolt the country, and when Erez's sister came out to ask them to leave, they called the police. A cruiser showed up and the officers agreed to watch the house while the men drove to the local division house to file their complaint. In the end, Erez did not flee, although this proved little solace to his victims.

THE STORY OF TZVI EREZ is one of misplaced trust. It also stands as a metaphor for the entire financial industry. The investment business operates on the notion that you can place your faith in its professionals to take care of your wealth and make it grow. "It's a confidence game," says Utpal Bhattacharya, "and if investors lose your trust, the whole thing crumbles like a house of cards."

Indeed, the mantra of countless advertisements churned out by banks and investment firms every year is: We will look after you, you're in good hands, you can trust us. And investors *do* trust the industry. And yet: Ian Thow managed to separate $32 million from ordinary people without handing over a single piece of paper showing them where their money had gone or whether it was actually generating any returns (even fake ones). Taking advantage of their shared Armenian heritage, Harry Migirdic convinced Haroutioun Markarian to sign guarantees covering the losses on perfect strangers' accounts, not once but on numerous occasions. And although Jack Hougassian had been burned by broker George Georgiou when Georgiou worked for Midland Walwyn, Hougassian allowed Georgiou to continue to handle his money even after Georgiou was fired for unethical behaviour. And then Georgiou burned Hougassian all over again.

The gullibility of investors and their willingness to trust is a central reason the industry is rarely held to account. After all, the almost universal response from bankers, brokers and their apologists when an investment blows up or a fraud is uncovered is to blame investors for not doing *their* due diligence. Furthermore, the investment industry points to the consistent rise in the stock market—albeit with some significant "corrections"—since World War II as evidence of its acumen, failing to mention that this was largely due to the facts of inflation, that the economy quadrupled in size over those decades and, more importantly, that markets were heavily regulated during most of this period. The dismantling of the regulatory regimes over the past twenty years is what led to the credit crisis of 2007–2009 and is why most advanced economies and global markets are now inherently unstable.

In fact, the evidence is overwhelming: you can't trust the financial industry to look after your money. So whom can you trust?

Many people place their financial affairs in the hands of friends and family and members of their own community. Yet I've lost count of the investors I've spoken to over the years who recall being introduced to crooked financial advisers or toxic investments through those very same friends or relatives or pillars of the community. My own parents sank money into the fraudulent Principal Trust in the 1980s on the advice of a family friend. The story of Tzvi Erez and others reveals this folly in the starkest of terms.

There are exceptions, of course—ethical investment advisers and gurus who've demonstrated great talent in making investors' portfolios grow. Warren Buffett in the United States and Stephen Jarislowsky in Canada come foremost to mind. And there are many talented independent advisers who put investors' interests first. But on the whole, the system, gladly perpetuated by the people who work in it, is engineered to milk investors, not make them rich.

DANNY EDELL AND I meet at a bustling coffee shop near Bathurst and Lawrence in Toronto. Edell's face looks fatigued and puffy, with half-moon circles under the eyes. I initially put his exhaustion down to his being a young father, but it soon becomes apparent that his sickly look has more to do with Tzvi Erez. "I hate talking about this," Edell tells me. And it's no wonder: he unwittingly drew ten of his closest friends and family members into Erez's scam—people he had the utmost respect for, and most of whom took a deep financial hit. "Tzvi played everyone, from very rich people to poor people who mortgaged their houses," Edell says. "He owes me and my family about half a million dollars."

Erez's fraud is remarkable partly because it was concocted and executed by such an unlikely person. Erez was born in Israel, and his stepfather, Yehuda, is a prominent real estate developer who lives in a large multi-million-dollar home in Thornhill, Ontario. The Erez family is well known among Toronto's observant Jewish community, and they garnered widespread sympathy after Tzvi's younger brother, Niv, was fatally shot in 2000 during a botched robbery attempt at the Richmond Hill jewellery outlet where he worked. "The name is everything, right?" says Edell. "Why would Donald Trump's son or daughter run such a scheme? They lacked for nothing. Tzvi drove a $100,000 BMW and wore a $30,000 watch. He had everything he wanted. He didn't have to work."

Erez was cultured and well educated, a superb pianist with an MBA from York University's Schulich School of Business. He had created his own label, NiV Music, in memory of his brother (many of whose friends became his victims). Erez founded a small printing business in North York in the late nineties and initiated his investment fraud in 2003. He told investors his business was based on "factoring"—basically, borrowing money against the value of your accounts receivable—and that he had printing jobs from blue-chip companies such as Tommy Hilfiger, Subway, Loblaws and Movado. He approached investors asking them for bridge financing, money used to prepay suppliers, which would allow him to negotiate steep discounts for paper, other supplies and production costs. The profits, he said, would amount to 20 percent or more, and would be passed back to anyone who lent him money.

Unfortunately, none of this was true. Instead, Erez had immaculately forged his paperwork, including contracts and invoices from phony corporate clients. "As the scheme became more sophisticated, everything from company financials, purchase orders, invoices, his suppliers' invoices, orders to suppliers, bank statements, tax returns, a three-year financial history, the entire documentation for three or four orders, was produced," recalls Edell. Some investors checked this paperwork, found it to be in order and gave Erez money. Others didn't even bother.

At first, it all seemed to work. Like the architect of a Ponzi scheme, he paid out redemptions to old investors with the money handed over by new ones, and soon more and more people in this Jewish enclave wanted part of the action. Erez recruited a handful of his friends and acquaintances to solicit new clients through their own networks. "Everyone from bubbies to doctors, lawyers, accountants, professionals, sophisticated investors and unsophisticated investors," says Edell. "Ultimately, he played everyone." If problems arose, if cheques bounced or there were delays in paying back investors, Erez was adept at forging credible-looking letters from bank managers who apologized and took full responsibility.

Erez had other secrets too, the most troubling being a gambling addiction. He began making covert trips to casinos and playing high-stakes poker online under an alias. From 2007 until his scam was disclosed in 2009, he lost more than $3.6 million, primarily to European gambling websites. (In 2006, he was charged with issuing false cheques to an Ontario casino and forced to cough up $700,000.) "I have never seen a worse poker player in my life," wrote a player on a poker discussion board. "Just giving away money playing 200/400 [a form of online poker] like the most clueless fish ever. It was surreal."

Things began to fall apart in late 2008 after Erez swindled Willy Tencer, the owner of Timberlane Wood Products in North York. The two had been talking about Tencer investing in Erez's business for weeks, and at one point Tencer asked if he could talk to Erez's suppliers. Erez demurred, telling him, "We do not feel comfortable with contacting suppliers, as it raises questions and it is just not worth it for us." Erez had asked Tencer for nearly $400,000 to finance a printing job for the Swiss watchmaker Movado, and sent him a steady stream of carefully forged documents to secure his agreement. Tencer eventually handed over the money and continued to increase his investment through the fall of 2008, shelling out more than $1.1 million in the process.

But then Tencer wanted to redeem his investment. To his alarm, he found he couldn't. By late January 2009, Erez was dodging him, and Tencer grew desperate. "Can you call me. I would like to contain the situation," he begged in one email. "You owe me way over a million dollars. Need to talk to you as to how this will be proceeding. Please!!!!!" Finally, Erez admitted that his company was short of funds and his bankers and (alleged) corporate clients were being hard-nosed. In fact, his lawyer had already sent a letter to investors saying that Erez was winding down the company.

Looking woebegone, Erez met with a group of anxious investors at a coffee shop to discuss what was happening. "We agreed to meet again the next day," recalls Edell. But Erez didn't show up for the second meeting, and "at that point we knew we were fucked," laments Edell. "We just didn't know how badly."

Tencer went to his lawyers, who in turn contacted Erez's supposed corporate clients, sending them copies of the contracts Erez had shown Tencer. Loblaws and Tommy Hilfiger said they had no record of deals with Erez Graphix and that the letters were forgeries. The police were called and a receiver was appointed to find out what had happened to the money. Erez had gone into hiding.

WHILE EREZ'S INVESTORS may have been hoodwinked, his own bank could have and should have spotted the fraud in midstream. Erez conducted his company's banking at a small North York CIBC branch—where he'd been a customer since the early 1990s—even though in 2004 the branch had caught him engaging in unusual activity such as kiting cheques. (Kiting involves withdrawing money from an account with a cheque after you have deposited into the same account another cheque that turns out to be worthless. Before the cheque being deposited bounces, you are able to withdraw real cash with the second cheque.) In late 2007, with Erez's scam well under way, the CIBC branch staff noticed something terribly amiss. They drew up a seven-page "Suspicious Transaction" form about Erez's accounts and sent it to the Financial Transactions and Reports Analysis Centre of Canada (FINTRAC), the federal government agency tasked with uncovering money-laundering operations.

By then, Erez was juggling huge sums of money every month. Over two years, $38.9 million went through eight different bank accounts he controlled. In November 2007, for instance, he had nearly $5 million in his CIBC accounts, and bank officials noted that "the client made several deposits near the $10,000 Large Cash Transaction reporting limit into this account." Under federal law, any cash deposit over $10,000 is investigated to see if money is being laundered, and Erez had frequently deposited $9,900, an amount so close to the cut-off that an investigation was triggered. "It appears that the customer may have structured his deposits in order to avoid the Large Cash Transaction Report," the CIBC report said. FINTRAC received the report, but neither the agency nor CIBC did much about it. In fact, Danny Edell recalls accompanying Erez into this very same CIBC branch, with Erez carrying $50,000 in cash in a bag. "He handed it to them and they wrote a money order," he told me.

The role of CIBC and what it should have done in regards to Erez remains a contentious issue. "This is a guy that could once barely float a $50,000 loan from the bank because his business was a scant quarter of a million bucks, he'd defaulted on a loan, never paid it back and was put in the bad debts department," explains Lou Brzezinski, a Toronto-based commercial litigator with Blaney McMurtry LLP, a Bay Street law firm that represented Willy Tencer. "And then, within three years, millions of dollars are going into his accounts and the bank doesn't blink once, even though he was thrown out of a number of banks for not paying back loans." Brzezinski insists that CIBC enabled Erez, a view shared by Jerry Henechowicz, the receiver hired to investigate the scam. "[CIBC] filed that suspicious transactions report and all these issues were going on. Surprisingly, in the middle of it all, in June of 2008, they gave Erez a $1.3 million mortgage on his house," he told me.

Erez was charged with fraud in June 2009. Earlier, his stepfather negotiated with his son's investors to reimburse some of their losses — that is, until one morning in March 2009 when Erez's brother-in-law, David Meisels, awoke to the sound of gunfire. His glass front door was shattered, the wooden frame pockmarked by bullets. On a nearby lawn, police discovered the weapon. "A rifle that was left conveniently on the front lawn and five or six rifle-shot shells," says Brzezinski. "There was an investigation, but nobody could find out who did this." Threatening emails were received by the school that Erez's children attended, forcing him to remove them. The Erez family terminated the negotiations for a settlement with investors.

In the fall of 2010, the charges against Erez were dropped because Ontario's attorney general's office said they didn't have the resources to prosecute him — an indication of how seriously they view white-collar crime. However, Erez was charged again in the fall of 2011. By then, none of the stolen money had been recovered. Meanwhile, Edell was grappling with a full-blown depression — understandable given that he'd encouraged his own father to invest his life savings with Erez. "How do you tell your 65-year-old father who is looking after your brother who has multiple sclerosis that his savings are all gone?" he asks. There was little indication that Erez (or CIBC) felt any remorse for his actions.

THE EREZ STORY is not as extraordinary as you might think. Weizhen Tang, an irrepressible huckster who billed himself as the "Chinese Warren Buffett" and "The King of 1% Weekly Returns," and who preyed on the more insular quarters of Toronto's Chinese community, claimed he could get investors a 1 percent weekly increase in their investments. By 2009, however, with suspicions rising over whether his fund was legitimate, Tang foolishly agreed to hold a special five-day event at his Toronto offices where he would demonstrate his special method of garnering this return for all to see.

Drawn by the spectacle, investors and journalists gathered to watch him trade. The event was even filmed for an online feed. By the end of the week, Tang was ruined, having made only a minuscule return. At an investors' meeting held a month later in a Holiday Inn in Markham, 120 angry investors confronted Tang, who conceded that all of their money was gone, and even signed a statement admitting the investment statements he'd been issuing for years were "falsified and forged" and that his conduct "amounts to fraud." Tang was arrested in 2010 and charged. He had bilked two hundred investors in Canada, the United States and Asia out of at least $30 million.

WHEN IT COMES TO betraying people's trust, few have topped Earl Jones. "It's unbelievable what he did to people," Bevan Jones, Earl's older brother, told me, shaking his head in disgust. "You've got to be sick—this person is really sick. I don't believe he gives a damn about anybody. He robbed his two brothers, robbed my daughter, my son-in-law, his best friends. This man—I don't believe has any heart at all."

I sat in the living room of the rustic wood-shingled home of Bevan Jones and his wife, Frances Gordon, a warm, cozy cottage perched on the edge of Lac Rond in Montcalm, Quebec, two hours north of Montreal. In their seventies, Jones and Gordon are a study in contrasts: him stoic, she bubbly and outgoing. Together, they've enjoyed a mostly prosperous and pleasurable life. Today, however, their retirement savings are short $250,000, stolen by Earl through the Ponzi scheme he ran for nearly thirty years, robbing $50 million from 158 of his clients.

Jones was a genius at fleecing people and had no end of clever ways to do so. Sometimes he'd tell his clients he was going to use their money to "lend" to other clients at a good rate of interest. "Earl would say, 'Mr. So-and-so died and there is a million-dollar estate, but it will take a year to settle,'" recalls Frances Gordon. "'So if you lend this person $50,000, you will get a return when the estate is resolved,' he'd say. So you give him $50,000 and he would spend it."

Margaret Davis was exactly the kind of person Jones targeted—a middle-aged woman unsophisticated about the world of high finance. She lost about $200,000 of her savings in the fraud. "He went after the vulnerable—women who were divorced or elderly," said Joey Davis, Margaret's son, when I met them at the apartment they share in Montreal. "They were very trusting types. Easily charmed. He had a very easy way and sense of authority about him, that he knew what he was talking about."

At other times, Jones would divide families to get access to their wealth. Kevin Curran is a Montrealer who lives in Los Angeles. An architect in his early fifties, he has a laid-back California sensibility. His mother, Karlene, met Jones in 1982 at a Montreal golf course. When her husband died in 2002, he left behind a $1.3 million estate to be divided between his wife and children. "But that didn't work out," says Curran bitterly, "because Earl Jones fucked everything up. He got in the middle, as he did with every estate. He would pit the stepson against Karlene. It became a dog's breakfast . . . It was acrimonious, unbelievably acrimonious. I don't speak to my stepbrother anymore." After the estate was divided up, Jones stole Karlene's $500,000 share by pretending to invest it, when in fact he just pocketed the money. A condo she bought will now be lost because she can't afford the expensive mortgage that Jones pressed her to take. "Every single activity he did was to feed the hole," says Curran.

As Jones's thievery grew, so did his appetite for luxurious living. He had four condominiums—in Dorval, Mont Tremblant, Florida and Massachusetts, the latter for his handicapped daughter. Despite declaring an annual income of only $40,000, he lived in a well-appointed upscale home in the West Island of Montreal and drove a steel-grey 3 Series BMW. He was a member of the Royal Montreal and two other golf clubs, travelled extensively and ate at the best restaurants. But after thirty years of robbing people to fund his own extravagances, Jones got cocky and careless.

LIKE TZVI EREZ, Jones could have been stopped if his bank had been more diligent. Jones, an estate planner, used an RBC branch in a suburb of Montreal, where he opened an in-trust account that he told his clients offered interest rates as high as 8 to 12 percent— the carrot to woo them to give him money to invest. It was all a lie, however, and the bank overlooked two glaring clues that Jones was running a scam. One was that they were aware he was managing the money of strangers, for which he should have been using a formal trust account. Instead, Jones was using his in-trust account as his own personal account, which is forbidden if he's managing other people's money. In 2001, about twenty years after his fraud began, the bank realized this was not appropriate and told Jones to cease and desist. He said he would and then carried on as usual. RBC did no follow-up.

Secondly, Jones got hold of clients' cheques made out to other people and forged signatures to indicate that the cheques had been endorsed to him, allowing him to deposit the money into his RBC account. Banks usually don't accept endorsed cheques because they can't validate the signatures. But in the case of Earl Jones, they did.

THINGS CAME TO A HEAD in June 2009 when cheques Jones sent to his investors began to bounce. Soon his office was shuttered, with only his answering machine to deal with his clients' desperate pleas. Jones had disappeared. His investors got organized and called the police to find out what had happened. Three weeks later, Earl Jones gave himself up.

Jones did express remorse at his sentencing hearing in January 2010, at which he received an eleven-year sentence. He admitted to pocketing $13 million of the $51 million that had gone missing. Nonetheless, he spent only twenty-two months in prison and was released at the end of 2011. "I don't think someone who robs the lives of 150 people should get just twenty-two months in a minimum-security prison," says his brother Bevan. "It's insane." Perhaps most alarmingly, Jones had left more than a hundred female senior citizens without any life savings, old women like Kevin Curran's mother who, he says, now feel utterly adrift. "These women are alone now," Curran observes. "Their world is quite small, their senses deteriorating. Now they're isolated. These souls are adrift in the world, and in the ocean of currency they don't have a paddle. They are fucked. I see depression and, in the aftermath, I see addiction."

— AFTERWORD —

INVESTMENT FRAUD IS EPIDEMIC in Canada, but it's a uniquely hidden crime. Given the billions stolen every year and the number of people driven into poverty after they lose what they've spent a lifetime accruing, you would think there would be more public outcry over the crisis, especially considering that fewer than twenty Canadians have gone to jail in the last twenty-five years for committing this type of felony.

Shame is the reason so many victims of investment fraud don't make a greater fuss about their losses. Many victims are professionals, intelligent and educated, and therefore feel they somehow should have prevented it all from happening. Clayton Wilson stands as a good example—a middle-class, middle-aged engineer and father of two daughters who lives in the bedroom community of Bedford, Nova Scotia, a suburb of Halifax. I reached him in the summer of 2010, and his despondency was pronounced even over the phone.

By December 2005, Wilson and his wife had put aside $700,000 to invest in something safe and conservative for their retirement. Wilson didn't have much faith in the big banks, so he visited a broker at Canaccord Financial Inc., an independent investment dealer. The broker put most of the Wilsons' money into income trusts. "I have no idea what an income trust is," Wilson admitted to me. "I was told it was safe and it would generate a monthly income." It didn't. Indeed, much to his horror, over the ensuing months Wilson watched his money dissipate like sand in an hourglass. "We met with the broker and he was so reassuring," Wilson recalls. The broker told him and his wife they needn't worry about their investment. But the nightmare continued, and by the summer of 2008 their portfolio was down to less than $60,000. The broker, meanwhile, had left Canaccord after being diagnosed with cancer. When Wilson confronted Canaccord's managers, he discovered the broker had secretly altered their investment wishes from "conservative" to "high risk." Wilson says Canaccord blew him off. In the fall of 2009, Wilson had a stress attack so severe he was forced to take a leave of absence from his job. "I was so ashamed of letting my wife and daughters down," he told me.

Such embarrassment is a boon to the investment industry, helping to keep its crimes hushed up. Also working to its benefit is the fact that while we treat violent crime seriously, white-collar finance crimes get a pass, an injustice mostly related to class. Many of those committing investment fraud are among the wealthiest people in society, politically well connected, and they have the money to hire the best lawyers and benefit from weak laws and securities enforcement regimes that work in their favour. "It's considered a 'gentlemen's crime,'" says Utpal Bhattacharya, "but in my opinion it does as much damage to society as blue-collar crime, if not more."

Stan Buell agrees. A retired engineer who was once defrauded by his broker, in 1998 Buell founded the Small Investors Protection Association (SIPA), a non-profit lobby group for retail investors. "The consequences of white-collar crime for small retail investors are probably greater than the consequences of a violent attack against them," he argues. "In many cases, it destroys their lives and livelihoods and leaves them in their senior years destitute, whereas if they are mugged on the street their injuries could heal. There is simply not enough attention paid to victims of white-collar crime."

This is what gets lost in the mix in scandals such as Bre-X, Nortel, Livent, Norshield, Portus, Cinar, Earl Jones or any of the countless other scams or disasters that have befallen the Canadian public. The damage from such criminal behaviour lingers for years, and yet the victims are rendered invisible.

In the summer of 2008, I interviewed James Markis for a TV story about investment fraud. Markis is a computer consultant in his late forties living in Bolton, Ontario, a tall, mild-mannered and private individual who had taken a severance package a few years earlier and tried to earn a living by investing online. He set himself up in his basement, computer at the ready, and began playing the markets. In April 2004, he sank $104,000 of his savings into Nortel stock, then selling at about $10 a share. (Nortel's shares had been rising in value since 2002 after bottoming out at 47 cents.) Markis found Nortel appealing, he told me, because "the financial statements indicated an enormous turnaround. A lot of good orders were coming in, they were on their way back. It looked to me like a blue-chip stock headed on the way up."

As it turned out, Markis invested in Nortel at pretty much the worst possible time. Two weeks later, Nortel fired its CEO, Frank Dunn, and a handful of top executives for manipulating the company's books, and then announced that its glowing sales and profit numbers and predictions were fictitious. The stock plunged to $5 and Markis's investment spiralled down to about $30,000 in value. "I went from building a nest egg and multiplying it to a debt situation," Markis explained. He sold his Nortel stock before it hit rock bottom, and had he not done so, "they would have come to collect the keys to my house."

What struck me the most about Markis was his sense of his own failure, even though what had happened to him was not remotely his fault. He believed what a reputable company said about its finances and prospects, and could never have known that Nortel's executives were cooking the books. Markis was trying to raise a teenaged son and recover from a bad divorce, which was exacerbated by him losing most of his money. His home had a sad, funereal air about it, as if a member of the family had recently passed away. "I think we are underestimating the impact of white-collar crime," Markis said at one point. "Divorces, suicides, health problems—it has an impact on a massive scale and is really understated in this country."

CANADA'S FINANCIAL INDUSTRY is a behemoth, a titan that generally escapes scrutiny, employs armies of lobbyists, lawyers and advertising mercenaries to do its bidding, and, with rare exception, benefits from a media that doesn't examine its structural failings. It has acquired a strutting arrogance as a result of weathering the credit crisis better than its American counterpart, but what gets overlooked—as the industry bamboozles the public about its virtues— are the people it runs over in the dead of night.

Take Harry Migirdic, the broker employed by CIBC Wood Gundy who went on a thieving tear during the 1990s, losing his clients' money with reckless abandon and hiding their losses by tricking some of his other clients into signing guarantees to cover those debts. One of his victims was Kiganouchi Papazian, a member of the Armenian community in Montreal, who held a low-paying job in a retail store. This is what a 2006 court judgment against CIBC Wood Gundy in the Migirdic affair said about what happened to Ms. Papazian:

> Her assets were meagre. They consisted of her home and her life savings, which she entrusted to Migirdic. He had her sign a guarantee in June 1993 in favour of perfect strangers, without her knowing and without her ever being informed. She was sixty-four years of age at the time. She was also treated to Migirdic's "medicine": [knowing she was] unaware of the guarantee, he made changes in her client profiles many times without her knowing and without her authorization; increases in the risk related to her account up to "High Risk 100%", a change in the value of the assets indicated in the client profile, unauthorized transactions and so on. In her case, Migirdic even allowed himself to engage in very speculative transactions using her account, transactions that were obviously not authorized and were extremely risky (especially for a person of her age). CIBC Wood Gundy's Compliance Department also intervened in regard to her account several times as it was concerned about such transactions for a woman her age, the incongruity of the guarantee and her awareness of it. The intervention yielded no results. In 2001, she ended up losing everything she had. She was then seventy-six years of age and never got over it. She died a few years later, completely broken-hearted . . .

To add insult to injury, CIBC seized $300,000 of Ms. Papazian's hard-earned savings by enacting the fraudulently obtained guarantees.

WHAT CAN BE DONE?

Creating a national securities regulator free of political influence by the financial industry, streamlining our securities laws to make it easier to prosecute white-collar criminals and increasing penalties for this sort of crime are reforms long overdue. Ensuring that white collar criminals are criminally charged, as opposed to just being hit with securities act violations, would also help enormously as a disincentive. Ironically, even some elements within Bay Street are champions of reform as they recognize that clean and accountable capital markets are good for business and the Canadian economy. The Harper government, spurred on by the 2007–2009 meltdown, also seems to recognize that Canada has to stop being a First World country saddled with a Third World regulatory system, although it's been slow to do much about it. By 2012, after six years in power, the Conservatives still hadn't managed to create a national securities regulator (the law they'd crafted spent almost two years languishing at the Supreme Court of Canada, which ruled late in 2011 that the proposed legislation was unconstitutional).

Given how deeply entrenched the Canadian establishment is and their desire not to put their own friends and neighbours in jail, don't expect the road to reform to come easily. In fact, as the credit crisis fades into the twilight, a moment seems to have passed, with the balkanized structure having regrouped and remaining very much untouched.

More alarmingly, the investment frauds continue to show up. In 2011, Sino-Forest Corp. (SFC) hit the news as a potential rerun of the

Bre-X scandal. Domiciled in Canada with an office in Mississauga, Ontario, but run out of Hong Kong with assets of timberland in China, SFC is one of about two hundred firms, mostly Chinese, exploiting a North American flag of convenience. Since their operations are primarily in Asia, it's almost impossible for investors and regulators to determine if these businesses are legitimate or not. Throughout 2011, these firms managed to lose $10 billion of shareholder value due to suspicions about their real worth.

In short, Canada's capital markets, and Canadians' investments, are now part and parcel of a global financial system that has become almost permanently destabilized. The credit crisis of 2007-2009, says hedge fund manager and philanthropist George Soros, led to the destabilization of Europe's economy in 2011 and the crisis over the euro and eurozone's viability, with repercussions that pushed the global economy back into recession (although it still hadn't climbed out of the original recession). Now, talk of depression is becoming commonplace. And the dark times ahead seem never-ending, with individual governments unable or unwilling to do much to address the structural problems of a financial industry that transcends borders. At its heart, global finance is really little more than a handful of people moving numbers around computer screens. As inconceivable as it seems, their decisions, be they in pursuit of prosperity, profit or outright theft, or the results of simple incompetence, change the fortunes of nations. And until someone finds a way to curb their power over us, we are all, it seems, hostages of a system that can only lead to ruin.

INTRODUCTION

In the summer of 2009, I was leaked an internal Nortel compensation document detailing a set of new bonuses. Dated September 22, 2009, it listed all proposed salaries for remaining Nortel staff, including bonuses totalling US$7.5 million. This chart became the focus of a lead story I produced for CBC TV's *The National*. Nortel threatened the CBC with legal action in an effort to have the document removed from the broadcaster's website and pursued an internal investigation to uncover the source of the leak.

The sum estimating the size of Canada's financial sector was derived from information contained in a report produced by the Investment Industry Regulatory Organization of Canada (IIROC) in October 2008 on the asset-backed commercial paper (ABCP) fiasco, entitled *Regulatory Study, Review and Recommendations concerning the manufacture and distribution by IIROC member firms of Third-Party Asset-Backed Commercial Paper in Canada*.

Paul Krugman's column on Canada's banking sector was published in *The New York Times* on January 31, 2010.

To estimate the number of white-collar criminals jailed, I scoured newspaper and magazine articles over the past twenty-five years.

The dollar amounts sought in class action lawsuits and the number of court actions are listed in reports produced by the consulting firm NERA Economic Consulting dated January 2009; January 2010; and June 4, 2010.

Estimates of the amount of wealth flowing toward the wealthiest segment of Canada's population comes from a December 2010 study written by Armine Yalnizyan for the Canadian Centre for Policy Alternatives entitled *The Rise of Canada's Richest 1%*. In December 2011 the OECD published a study called *Divided We Stand: Why Inequality Keeps Rising*, which discusses Canada's income gap.

Bank bonuses for 2010 are cited in an article published in *The Financial Post*, December 8, 2010, by John Greenwood, entitled "Big Six set aside $8.9B, up from $8.8B."

Figures on the median family income come from a *Maclean's* magazine story entitled "The New Middle Class Reality," published on February 4, 2009.

The total Canadian consumer debt figure of $1.5 trillion was compiled by the Certified General Accountants Association of Canada and published in a report entitled *A Driving Force No More: Have Canadian Consumers Reached Their Limits?* in June 2011.

The figure of one million Canadians who lost money to investment fraud came from a study produced by the Innovative Research Group for the Canadian Securities Administrators (CSA), published in October 2007. The CSA is the lobby for Canada's provincial and territorial securities commissions.

CHAPTER 1

On June 24, 2010, the U.S. Supreme Court produced a ruling on "honest services" in *Black et al. v. United States*. This decision followed the same logic made in the case of former Enron CEO Jeffrey Skilling, who argued the "honest services" provisions were being misapplied in the case of his defrauding his former employer. In the Skilling case, the court noted that fraudulent deprivation of "the intangible right of honest services" is properly confined to cover only bribery and kickback schemes. Because Skilling's alleged misconduct entailed no bribe or kickback, it did not fall within the legal definition. In fact, courts had ruled for decades that "honest services" could be applied to private companies and their employees who commit fraud. The U.S. Supreme Court struck down the statute as they applied to corporate fraud, finding that lower courts and prosecutors had strayed too far from its original intent.

This quote from John Fraser appears in an article entitled "Judgment Day" in *Men's Vogue* published on November 1, 2007, written by Canadian investigative journalist Nicholas Stein.

The lists of billionaires were published in *Forbes* magazine on March 9, 2011, and March 17, 2003.

The sums on fixed income securities were cited in "The Giant Pool of Money," which aired on *This American Life*, June 9, 2008, on National Public Radio (NPR).

Rebounding CEO salaries and corporate profits are documented in a *New York Times* business article, "The Drought Is Over (at Least for C.E.O.'s)" published April 10, 2011.

Figures on the unofficial unemployment rate in the U.S. can be found in an msn.com article by Mary Engel, "The real unemployment rate? 16.6%," published June 4, 2010.

Figures on the size of the Canadian financial industry are available on the Government of Canada website www.investincanada.gc.ca under "Financial Services."

Background on Black stems from books *Wrong Way: The Fall of Conrad Black* by Jacquie McNish and Sinclair Stewart, Viking Canada, 2004; *Shades of Black* by Richard Siklos, McLelland & Stewart, 2004; *Lord Black:*

The Biography by George Tombs, Hushion House, 2004; and *Conrad and Lady Black* by Tom Bower, Harper Collins, 2006.

Figures on the number of newspapers in Black's empire and their annual revenues are derived from the *Report of Investigation by the Special Committee of the Board of Directors of Hollinger International Inc.*, published on August 30, 2004. The report became known as the Breeden report, named for Richard C. Breeden, who led the committee and submitted it to the SEC.

The most compelling description of Black's wealth was published in *Here Be Dragons: Telling Tales of People, Passion and Power* by Peter C. Newman, published by McClelland & Stewart in 2005.

A description of the structure of Black's empire is contained in the Breeden report.

Hollinger International 10-K forms submitted to the SEC report the company's losses in 2002 and 2003. Figures detailing the company's executive compensation can be found in the Breeden report.

A 1984 report by analyst David Ramsay at Wood Gundy cited a "Black Factor" that depressed the stock value of some of Black's companies by an estimated 10 percent. The "Black Factor" has come up repeatedly since then, including in an article in *Fortune* from October 13, 2003, published with the headline "Black & Blue Shareholders are beating up Hollinger CEO Conrad Black over his huge, tricky pay packages. He calls them 'governance terrorists.'"

Black's email on the cheap use of other people's capital appears in the Breeden report on page 98.

The quote from Black in *Vanity Fair* about his disdain for regulators, etc., comes from an article by Bryan Burroughs entitled "The Convictions of Conrad Black," published in the October 2011 issue.

Two articles, "Black Mischief" by Maureen Orth in *Vanity Fair*, February 2007, and "The Black Watch," by Duff McDonald in the July 2004 issue of

The Financial Post Magazine, capture the early stages of shareholders' investigations into the manner in which Black and his fellow executives were spending Hollinger International's money.

All figures used to contrast compensation for Hollinger International versus *The New York Times* and *The Washington Post* companies are cited in the Breeden report, as a description of Hollinger's stock performance.

Barbara Amiel Black's annual US$1.1 million compensation is documented on page 143 of the Breeden report, which noted that for this sum "she performed no meaningful work in return."

An affidavit by Candace L. Preston was submitted as evidence for *Howard Green and Anne Bell v. CIBC, Gerald McCaughey, Tom Woods, Brian G. Shaw and Ken Gilgour,* dated January 14, 2010.

All figures of CIBC executive salaries and Special Incentive Plan (SIP) are from a report written by Diane A. Urquhart entitled *CIBC Executives Always Win, But Is It Legal?* published on February 4, 2008.

Verdun found first mention of the SIP in the CIBC proxy statement *Report on Executive Compensation,* dated March 1, 2001. It states, "Under SIP, participants share in net gains from certain CIBC merchant banking investments." What those investments are is not made clear.

CHAPTER 2

Algoma's turnaround from failure into the world's most efficient steelmaker is analyzed in a profile of CEO Denis Turcotte in *Canadian Business,* October 9, 2006.

CAW economist Jim Stanford wrote *Having Their Cake and Eating It Too,* a paper that examines tax policies and their effect on Canada's economy for the Canadian Centre for Policy Alternatives (CCPA) in April, 2011. It charts the shift in the Canadian economy over the past twenty years from a well-rounded capitalist power to one that is more dependent on natural resources.

Job losses in manufacturing recorded by Statistics Canada can be found at www.statcan.gc.ca in "Manufacturing" under the subheading "Shrinking Employment."

The Globe and Mail editorial "Potash and the misbegotten fear of recolonization" published on November 2, 2010, argues against the Harper government's intervention in the sale of Potash Corp. "Just as Canadian corporations can and do buy firms in other countries, foreign corporations, such as BHP Billiton Ltd., should be welcome to make offers to buy Canadian ones, such as Potash Corp. of Saskatchewan Inc., and government intervention should be the exception."

A European Parliament report on hedge funds, *Hedge Funds and Private Equity—A Critical Analysis*, was produced by the Socialist Group in the European Parliament and presented by Poul Nyrup Rasmussen and Ieke van den Burg in April 2007.

A *New York Times* September 11, 2011 article, "Is Manufacturing Falling Off the Radar?", by Louis Uchitelle noted that while the American manufacturing sector continues to produce goods, its percentage of the GDP has declined steadily since the 1950s. A paper by Statistics Canada in July 2009, *The Canadian Manufacturing Sector: Adapting to Challenges*, found the same trends in Canada.

William Lazonick's paper on the problems of the U.S. economy, *Marketization, Globalization, Financialization: The Fragility of the U.S. Economy in an Era of Global Change*, was published as part of the National Adjustments to a Changing Global Economy project funded by the Alfred P. Sloan Foundation in March 2010.

Background on John Paulson is discussed in "Algoma, Paulson head toward showdown" by Shawn McCarthy in *The Globe and Mail* on January 9, 2006. In his attempt to alter the makeup of Algoma's board, Paulson tried to have himself, Desjardins Securities International Inc. president Ronald Mayers, Senator J. Trevor Eyton, the former chairman and director of

Brascan Corp., Farokh Hakimi, the executive vice-president and former chief financial officer of Inco Ltd., and Nicholas Tolerico, the president of ThyssenKrupp Steel Services, added to the board.

Gregory Zuckerman's January 15, 2008, *Wall Street Journal* profile of John Paulson, "Trader Made Billions on Subprime," talked about Paulson's subprime winnings.

Allegations about the nature of the scheme conceived by Paulson and Goldman Sachs are described in the charges laid out in *SEC v. Goldman Sachs & Co. and Fabrice Tourre* dated April 16, 2010.

Paulson's 2011 results and his involvement in Sino-Forest Corp. are described in Kelly Bit's September 15, 2011 *Globe and Mail* article, "Has John Paulson Lost His Touch?"

CHAPTER 3

By 2005, according to Statistics Canada, Hamilton actually had the highest rate of poverty in Ontario, tied with Toronto, with 90,000 of its 500,000 citizens living below the low income cut-off line (which is $34,000 for a family of four). Since then, due to the concerted efforts of community groups, this level has been slightly reduced by 2011 to allow the city to rank second after Toronto.

According to a March 29, 2004 article by Greg Keenan in *The Globe and Mail*, Stelco stopped fully topping up its employees' pension plan in 1996. The move was in compliance with Ontario's *Pension Benefits Act*, passed in 1990, and allowed the steel company's pension liability to grow.

Figures on Stelco's losses prior to going into CCAA protection and the company's subsequent rebound can be found in "What a mess: Stelco's CCAA fiasco" in the January 30, 2006 issue of *Canadian Business*, written by Thomas Watson. The abuse of CCAA by corporations to dispose of pension problems, wipe out original shareholders and reward executives with bonuses is commonplace. For example, in December 2008 CanWest Global

Communications went into CCAA protection in order to deal with the media conglomerate's $4 billion debt load. Three directors, four top executives and thirteen other senior members of management received hefty cash payments. The total cost was $9.8 million. Meanwhile, CanWest employees who were laid off received no severance or vacation pay.

Brookfield Asset Management's transformation from the old Brascan empire into its current incarnation is detailed by Joanna Pachner in "A Perfect Predator," published in *Canadian Business* on August 16, 2010. She claims, "At its peak, the conglomerate that [Jack] Cockwell forged with Edward and Peter Bronfman's money represented a third of the Toronto Stock Exchange's value and owned parts of more than 200 companies—including John Labatt Ltd., MacMillan Bloedel, Royal LePage and Royal Trust—connected in a web of holding companies. One analyst said the organizational chart from that period 'looked like someone threw a plate of spaghetti on the floor.'"

A good article detailing Tricap Partners Ltd.'s work as a distress investment fund, written by Karen Mazurkewich, was published in *Financial Post Magazine* on December 1, 2008. "Tricap is a type of private-equity investor that buys the cheap debt of struggling companies or offers loans directly to the firms, drawing on capital from investors in its 'distress' or 'restructuring' funds," it says. In one case, a company called Birch Mountain, after being bought by Tricap, "is now likely to be liquidated and its shareholders' stakes obliterated. The only likely winner is Tricap, which in addition to its lending fees, hopes to recoup its initial investment—and more—by selling the company or its assets."

Navigant Consulting was hired by a group of Stelco's original shareholders, including AGF Management Ltd. and Pollitt & Co. Navigant concluded that Stelco's shareholder equity should be worth between $1.1 billion and $1.3 billion, but later revised that estimate down to $750 million.

As of 2011, *Forbes* magazine estimates David Tepper's net worth at US$5 billion and ranks him as the 66th wealthiest American and 208th wealthiest person in the world.

According to data from the Canadian Steel Producers Association (CPSA), as of 2010 the Canadian steel industry was producing annually 13 million tons of steel, valued at $14 billion. Domestic consumption was 15.5 million tons. Imports were 8.5 million tons. And exports were worth $6.8 billion. "Over one-third of global steel production is traded internationally, and in Canada, over half of the steel consumed domestically is imported," the CPSA says. "On balance, Canada is a net importer of steel."

Chapter 4

The travails of Research In Motion (RIM) through 2010 and 2011 were regular fodder for the business media: everything from interruptions in customer service, to a tablet device that was seen as a dud, to loss of market share to its competitors, to an uninspired product line, layoffs and plunging stock. By the fall of 2011, analysts were regularly denigrating RIM and openly speculating that it would be swallowed whole by one of its competitors. "RIM is down 77% since its highs of February this year," Bernstein Research analyst Pierre Ferragu wrote in a research note in November 2011. "The company's current challenges are now well understood by investors and we believe a failure of the current strategy is now well priced-in and we see upside risks making a short position unwise today. In the medium term, as the failure of RIM's current strategy becomes more obvious, we see shareholder activism leading to a change in management and a takeover—or at least the anticipation of it, as potential upsides making the risk-reward of a short position not attractive anymore."

Inside Agency: The Rise and Fall of Nortel was written by Timothy Fogarty, Professor and Associate Dean of Weatherhead School of Management, Case Western Reserve University in Cleveland, Ohio; Michel Magnan, Professor and Associate Dean of John Molson School of Business, Concordia

University, Montreal, Quebec; Garen Markarian, Assistant Professor, Instituto de Empresa, Madrid, Spain; and Serge Bohdjalian, John Molson School of Business, Concordia University, Montreal, Quebec, and was published in August 2007.

In June and August 2000, Ross Healy went on Canadian television and made his deep discount re-evaluations of Nortel's stock price. "The company officially never responded to me," Healy told me when I spoke to him in 2010. "I was just a little fish working with my own company. They could ignore me and they did."

In May 2000, writing in *Canadian Business*, Al Rosen castigated analysts for embracing Nortel's financial calculations that deliberately excluded acquisition costs and failed to report the fact that the company was losing money. He criticized Roth for his purchases of dot-com companies that appeared to bolster its revenue. In the *National Post*, Rosen also condemned Nortel's use of "earnings from operations" numbers. Roth responded by criticizing Rosen for undermining the ability of Canadian high-tech companies to raise money.

On October 24, 2000, Nortel issued a press release for its third quarter results in which CEO John Roth was quoted liberally, giving a rosy picture of the company's situation. "Carriers and service providers around the world continued the drive to provide a broad range of wireless, internet and e-Business services to their customers," he said.

On October 15, 2007, the SEC laid charges against Nortel Networks Corp. for a revenue fraud scheme and an earnings management scheme. The SEC revealed how, under Roth's management, Nortel manipulated its figures to give investors a fraudulent picture of the company's overall well being. "The first scheme accelerated material amounts of revenues into 2000 and created the false appearance that Nortel was weathering an economic downturn better than its competitors," reads the statement of allegations. "The second scheme reduced or increased Nortel's earnings as necessary to create the false appearance that Nortel had stabilized its operations and returned to profitability."

On September 12, 2007, the SEC laid charges of fraud against former Nortel executives Frank Dunn, Douglas Beatty, Michael Gollogly, Mary Anne E. Pahapill, Douglas Hamilton, Craig Johnson, James Kinney and Kenneth Taylor for their involvement in the revenue fraud scheme and an earnings management scheme that enabled Nortel "to meet the unrealistic revenue and earnings guidance that its top executives had provided to Wall Street in 2000 and again in 2002 and 2003."

In a front-page article in *The Wall Street Journal* on July 2, 2004, Ken Brown and Mark Heinzl document Nortel's practice of using excess reserves to manipulate the numbers. "The practice of holding extra reserves was so common that Nortel executives gave it a name: 'hardness,'" reads the article. "In Nortel parlance, having hardness meant having reserves on hand that could be released at some later date to help the company meet Wall Street's profit targets."

Investor lawsuits against CIBC included *Rick Hong Chi Law and Leslie Frohlinger v. Nortel Networks Corp., John Andrew Roth, Frank Dunn, F. William Conner, Chahram Bolouri, William R. Hawe and Deloitte & Touche LLP*; and *Peter Gallardi v. Nortel Networks Corp., Frank A. Dunn, Douglas Beatty, Michael Gollogly, John Edward Cleghorn, Robert Ellis Brown, Robert Alexander Ingram, Guylaine Saucier, Sherwood Hubbard Smith, Jr. and Deloitte & Touche*. These lawsuits detail the misuse of press releases and other duplicitous practices calculated to mislead investors about the soundness of the company.

CBC News conducted an interview with John Foster in November of 2004.

Frank Dunn purchased land in Oakville in 2002, ten months after he took over as CEO of Nortel. He paid $4.3 million cash for the waterfront property at a time when the company was downsizing on a massive scale.

When Dunn was fired in 2004, he was building a 10,800 square foot, six-bedroom mansion on the land. "The home, on 1.6 acres with 56 metres of lakefront, was designed in a French-chateau style with a separate three-car garage," claimed the *Toronto Star* on June 20, 2008. "It also included a boat slip, dock and boathouse. The asking price was originally $10.7 million for a house that had only been completed to the drywall. Millions more would be needed to finish the interior . . . He later dropped the price to $9.5 million. The unfinished home was eventually purchased in 2005 for $8,881,000, according to property records. The sale went to a Royal Bank of Canada executive."

In the fall of 2008 and spring and summer of 2009, the Harper government refused to intervene in Nortel's descent into bankruptcy or in the sale of its assets to foreign buyers. On August 7, 2009, RIM co-CEO Mike Lazaridis testified at the Standing Committee on Industry, Science and Technology about the sale of Nortel. RIM had been negotiating with Nortel before it declared bankruptcy in the hopes of buying some of its divisions. Lazaridis said to the committee, "How our discussions with Nortel failed to produce a good outcome for RIM and for Canada is another sorry story in the debacle that is Nortel. Suffice it to say that Nortel failed to bargain in good faith and failed to honour promises made to RIM on many occasions. Without regard for these promises, Nortel made deals with Nokia Siemens Networks and then with Ericsson that rendered Nortel's assets in LTE of limited value to RIM or to any other firm. When we later tried to enter the auction for the entire wireless division in an effort to preserve the value of these assets, Nortel delayed and demanded a condition that would have prevented RIM from offering to acquire the important LTE assets. This condition was irrelevant to the other bidders but not to RIM. I simply could not agree to it. Those of you who have visited me in Waterloo will remember the model Avro Arrow that always sits on my desk. By sheer coincidence, this year is the fiftieth anniversary of the cancellation of the Arrow program.

Whatever anyone may think, good or bad, about the decision to cancel, one fact is clear. The failure to salvage the valuable intellectual property and to maintain the workforce from the abandoned project was a strategic error. By discarding the intellectual property and dismissing the workforce, Canada threw away a significant beachhead in the future of aviation that could have benefited our citizens for many generations to come. Fifty years later, we consider the disposition of another beachhead built by Canadian ingenuity. Let us learn from our history and not make the same mistake again. The current government fully understands what happened."

CHAPTER 5

The figure listing 750,000 Canadians employed in the financial services sector comes from the Government of Canada and can be found on www. investincanada.gc.ca under "Financial Services."

Information on the estimated 300,000 people working for the financial sector in Toronto—along with the designs of the Ontario government to turn the city into a global financial servicing hub—can be found in Philip Preville's article "The Good News About the Bad Times," published in *Toronto Life*, February 2009.

The lawsuit against the CBC for the story I produced about brokers was launched by Caldwell Securities Ltd., even though Caldwell's name never appeared in the piece. I had found film footage in the CBC archives of two men speaking on phones and used it in the broker story to generically illustrate brokers. As it turned out, the footage had been shot years earlier at Caldwell's offices. Using this footage as background, the narrator stated that one of the causes of the credit crisis is the fact that brokers don't always understand the complexity of the investment products they sell—a demonstrably true statement. Caldwell decided it was being libelled by the suggestion that their brokers in particular sold products they didn't fully comprehend. Caldwell had obtained private emails I had sent to the Investment Industry

Association of Canada, the financial sector's lobby group, in which I had remarked upon the arrogance and lack of accountability of the financial industry. The CBC paid out a small sum to cover Caldwell's legal expenses. The offending footage was removed, but the story remained online.

In August 1996, the FBI produced a 121-page report (with supporting documentation) on Semion Mogilevich and his global organization detailing all of his companies, his criminal activities and his associates in the underworld. YBM Magnex is mentioned prominently in this document.

Robert I. Friedman's groundbreaking article on Semion Mogilevich appeared in the May 20-26 issue of *The Village Voice* entitled "The Most Dangerous Mobster in the World" which discusses his crimes in great detail. This article prompted Mogilevich to put a $100,000 contract on Friedman's life.

The story about Mogilevich laundering money in the U.K. through Blakes Solicitors is reported in *The Sunday Times*, September 5, 1999, in an article entitled "Hunt for the Red Don."

The story of Pratecs Technologies Inc. on the Alberta Stock Exchange was first documented by Adrian du Plessis, a freelance reporter in B.C. writing about Howe Street scandals. Du Plessis teamed up with *Vancouver Sun* business reporter David Baines for a series of stories about YBM and its origins as Pratecs and the reluctance of ASE officials to closely examine the company. This series won a National Newspaper Award in 1999.

The Fairfax briefing notes that formed the basis of their presentation to YBM's special committee were obtained and reported on by *Financial Post* reporter Sandra Rubin. Rubin did the most thorough reporting on the YBM scandal and, in November 1999, met and interviewed Mogilevich in a Moscow hotel.

The Fairfax investigators testified at the OSC hearings into YBM and gave their account of the special committee's reaction to their report, as well as their reaction to the report produced by Mitchell and Wilder for the board.

TSE chief investigator Michael Haddad wrote his letter to the OSC on June 5, 1997, addressed to Heidi Franken, manager of the Commission's continuous disclosure division. It contained a memo about his conversation with the French banking officials plus a document detailing the strange facts about YBM.

Kathy Soden, who was the OSC's manager of market operations at the time, wrote a "Strictly Confidential" memo on November 20, 1997, about the YBM prospectus. This memo laid out the OSC's investigations into YBM, including a phone conversation with Charlie McDermott of the TSE's enforcement division, who relayed information from the RCMP about a potential witness. What that witness said was redacted from the memo because his information was given in confidence. This memo also indicated that other OSC staff felt the receipt for the prospectus should be issued, although it was ultimately Soden's decision.

David R. Peterson v. Ontario Securities Commission and Kathryn Soden was launched in May 2000 and further amended in 2001. The lawsuit claimed that because the OSC knew YBM was a front for organized crime and failed to pass that information on to YBM, it did not have the grounds to pursue YBM's directors after the company collapsed. In its factum in response, the OSC noted that YBM withheld information from the commission, including the existence of the Fairfax investigation.

The OSC's 120-page ruling on YBM Magnex and its directors came down on June 27, 2003. Interestingly enough, the decision says in its third paragraph, "Despite a hearing which took over 124 hearing days to complete, this case is not about organized crime, money laundering or whether the respondents believed YBM was not a real company. It is about the disclosure of risk."

Eric Reguly's *Globe and Mail* piece about David Peterson and YBM appeared on July 3, 2003. He writes, "This could be called the Peterson defence: Don't blame me, dear shareholders, because I didn't know enough to protect you fully. And you thought all directors of all companies work together. Companies' directors, of course, are not expected to have equal degrees of competence. But the OSC is apparently saying it's acceptable to exercise extremely unequal degrees of diligence."

In April 2001, court-appointed receiver Ernst & Young filed a lawsuit seeking $475 million in damages for breach of fiduciary responsibility, fraud and breach of contract against, among others, Griffiths McBurney & Partners; National Bank Financial Corp.; Owen Mitchell, a director of National Bank Financial and a YBM director; Cassels Brock & Blackwell; and David Peterson. In this lawsuit, Ernst & Young accused Griffiths McBurney of trading in YBM stock months after it had been halted from trading by the OSC on the TSE.

The U.S. indictment against Mogilevich was filed in the U.S. District Court for the Eastern District of Pennsylvania on April 24, 2003. It laid out extensive allegations of the mobster and his associates' myriad crimes.

The Rizzutos' investments in Penway Explorers, Financement Malts and in the Montreal City and District Savings Bank (now Laurentian Bank of Canada) is documented in *Mafia Inc.*, a book written by Montreal journalists André Cédilot and André Noël, published in English by Random House Canada in 2011, and in *The Sixth Family* by Lee Lamothe and Adrian Humphreys, published by Wiley in 2006.

The story of the Hells Angels' investments in B.C. is discussed in *The Road to Hell: How the Biker Gangs Are Conquering Canada*, written by Julian Sher and William Marsden and published by Knopf Canada in 2004. Martin Chambers, a Vancouver lawyer, has been linked by the CBC program *Disclosure* and other researchers with helping B.C.'s biker gangs set up holding companies.

CHAPTER 6

Larry Elford's *Lethbridge Herald* column appeared on October 8, 2000, under the headline "Two fee or not two fee? That's the question." In it, he claims that you can't be certain whether investment advisers are giving you advice or just trying to sell you investment products. In regards to mutual funds, he wrote, "So why is it that some still pay a sales commission for the privilege of owning this type of investment, while others do not? It seems to revolve around whether your investment representative practices as an adviser or a salesperson."

In July 2009, the Canadian Securities Administrators published new rules for firms and individuals who deal in securities or provide investment advice. In their release, they said that Canada had 2,000 firms and 130,000 individuals registered to deal in or advise on securities.

On August 23, 2011, *The Globe and Mail* published a story headlined "Banks move to bump up mortgage rates" by Tara Perkins and Steve Ladurantaye. They quoted an RBC official saying, "Our long-term funding costs have gone up considerably due to global economic concerns, and while we have held off in passing on these rate changes to our clients, it is now necessary for us to increase this mortgage rate." The reporters also spoke to Alyssa Richards, CEO of RateHub.ca, who said banks tend to move their variable rates higher as they near the end of their fiscal years to help pad their profits and meet targets.

To pass the Canadian Securities Course you need to complete two 100-question multiple-choice tests with a two-hour time limit for each part. If you pass, you can become a certified mutual fund representative.

The *Daily Telegraph* article about the £7.3 billion that is skimmed off by British bankers and fund managers was published on July 30, 2010, under the headline "£7 billion a year skimmed off our savings" and was written by Holly Watt, Jon Swaine and Elizabeth Colman. "Customers have no way of claiming back their lost savings because fund managers are not doing anything illegal or beyond the rules," said the piece.

"Losing Ground: Do Canadian mutual funds produce fair value for their customers?" by Keith Ambachtsheer and Rob Bauer appeared in the Spring

2007 issue of *Canadian Investment Review*. Ambachtsheer is director of the Rotman International Centre for Pension Management at the University of Toronto. Bauer is professor of finance at the University of Maastricht in the Netherlands.

Morningstar Inc.'s May 2009 research report on the experiences of global fund investors was written by John Rekenthaler, Michelle Swartzentruber and Cindy Sin-Yi. It examines the ways mutual fund shareholders are treated in various countries. Overall, Canada received a "B" rating from the study's authors.

On May 15, 2007, the lawyers for KPMG Inc., the receiver in the case of Portus Alternative Asset Management Inc., produced a special report detailing the findings of their investigation into the collapse of the hedge fund two years previously. They found that of the more than $800 million raised, an estimated $110 million was diverted by the fund's managers for "other purposes" and an additional US$53 million was hidden in offshore accounts.

Chapter 7

The most thorough description of Ian Thow's crime spree appeared in the *Report on Business Magazine* in August 2007. "Hiding in Plain Sight" was written by Lyle Jenish.

Details of Ian Thow's crimes and actions against his victims appear in the Agreed Statement of Facts in *Regina v. Ian Gregory Thow* produced on February 23, 2010. The BCSC's October 16, 2007, ruling on Thow's case describes his misdemeanors as well.

The Carolann Steinhoff case is most thoroughly documented by the decisions of the Investment Dealers Association of Canada (IDA) and its predecessor organization, the Investment Industry Regulatory Organization of Canada (IIROC). The IDA's decision on whether Steinhoff engaged in unauthorized trading appeared on April 16, 2003; IIROC's decision on the pasting of clients' signatures onto documents was released on March 5,

2010; and IIROC's decision on the young couple's investments was released on October 6, 2011.

Media coverage of the Steinhoff case appeared in *The Vancouver Sun*, among other papers, as well as *Canadian Business* magazine on June 6, 2005, in an article by Matthew McClearn, "Broker wars: Whose clients are they, anyway?"

The Harry Migirdic case is laid out in great detail in *Markarian v. CIBC World Markets Inc.*, a decision rendered by Quebec Superior Court justice Jean-Pierre Senécal on June 14, 2006. Other supporting documents include the court transcripts, in particular the testimony of Thomas Monahan given on February 14 and 15, 2005. The IDA's decision on Migirdic was released on April 16, 2004. Paul Delean of *The Gazette* covered the case and trial extensively.

CHAPTER 8

A story that documents the rise of Canada's banks in the midst of the credit crisis is "Our So-Called Genius Banks" by Andrew Coyne, from *Maclean's*, April 13, 2009.

The CMHC program was called the Insured Mortgage Purchase Program and was introduced in the fall of 2008. The best summation of how this program worked and the monies made available to Canada's banks is an article published by Scott Blythe in the November 11, 2011 issue of *Canadian Investment Review*. It links to other articles on the matter and can be seen at http://www.investmentreview.com/expert-opinion/did-the-cmhc-bail-out-banks-in-2008-5592.

The case against RBC is laid out in a lawsuit between the Wisconsin school boards and Stifel Nicolaous, Stifel Financial Corp., James M. Zemlyak, Royal Bank of Canada Europe Ltd., RBC Capital Markets Corp. and RBC Capital Markets Holdings (USA) Inc. and launched on February 5, 2010. As well, the webpage www.schoollawsuitfacts.com documented the case. The SEC announced, in a press release on September 27, 2011, its US$30.4 million settlement with RBC.

On July 20, 2011, the Massachusetts Office of the Secretary of the Commonwealth, Securities Division, sued RBC Capital Markets, LCC and Michael D. Zukowski over exchanged traded funds (ETFs).

The biggest investors' lawsuit launched against Enron Corp., its executives, accountants and its banks was by the University of California on May 14, 2003, and contains allegations about the CIBC's involvement in the company's fraud. Moreover, on June 30, 2003, the third interim report of Neal Batson, the court-appointed examiner in the Enron bankruptcy, produced a 79-page appendix detailing CIBC's involvement with Enron. Finally, on December 22, 2003, the director of the U.S. Department of Justice's Enron Task Force, Leslie R. Caldwell, wrote a letter laying out the agreement between the department and CIBC regarding the bank's involvement in Enron's fraud.

The details of the Global Crossing scandal are explained in a series of lawsuits and articles. In a lawsuit launched by the Global Crossing estate representative and liquidating trustee Andrew J. Entwistle on June 20, 2006, against CIBC and other investment companies involved in Global Crossing, the bank is accused of distorting the company's financial situation to investors. On March 22, 2004, a class action lawsuit was launched in the Southern District of New York by Global Crossing investors that discusses CIBC's involvement and accuses the bank of making false and misleading statements about the company's health. Probably the most damning media investigation into Global Crossing was the *Fortune* magazine article "The Emperor of Greed" by Julie Creswell and Nomi Prins, June 24, 2002.

The best description of the Pay Pop scandal is laid out in the lawsuit launched on September 25, 2003, by the SEC against the company's executives, including CIBC Mellon Trust manager Alnoor Jiwan (*SEC v. Daryl G. Desjardins, Robert S. Zaba, Alnoor Jiwan, Ronald D. Brouiliette, Jr. and*

Brian A. Koehn). As well, articles in the *Vancouver Sun* by Kim Bolan examine the criminal career of Daryl Desjardins.

CHAPTER 9

The $7 billion in estimated losses incurred from the third-party ABCP debacle was calculated for me by former Bay Street analyst Diane Urquhart.

In 2011, the Certified General Accountants Association of Canada published *A Driving Force No More: Have Canadian Consumers Reached Their Limits?*, which examined the debt situation of Canadian consumers. They compared the debt-to-income ratio of Canadians compared to other OECD countries. The Canadian ratio reached a new record high of 146.9% in the first quarter of 2011.

Important books on the origins and history of the credit crisis include Charles R. Morris's book *The Trillion Dollar Meltdown: Easy Money, High Rollers and the Great Credit Crash* published by PublicAffairs in 2008 and Michael Lewis's book *The Big Short: Inside the Doomsday Machine* published by W. W. Norton & Company, Inc. in 2010.

A story about the fate of Xceed Mortgage Corp. by Greg McArthur and Jacquie McNish was published in *The Globe and Mail* on December 6, 2009, entitled "'Orphaned homeowners face foreclosure.'"

The Neighborhood Assistance Corporation of America (NACA), located on the outskirts of Boston, is a remarkable mortgage lender. Not only do they create mortgages for working-class Americans at low interest rates but also engage in pitched battles with Wall Street and the mainstream mortgage-lending industry and its CEOs (whose homes they picket). Bruce Marks, its CEO, is a former Federal Reserve Bank of New York official who formed NACA in 1988 and was named Bostonian of the year by *The Boston Globe* in 2007 for his work on behalf of low-income homeowners.

The two main class action lawsuits launched over the FMF Capital scandal were by Siskinds LLP in January 2006 in Ontario Superior Court, and by

Juroviesky & Ricci LLP and Frank, Haron, Weiner & Navarro in the Michigan courts in 2005. These suits were combined and resulted in one settlement.

On November 8, 2010, the OSC issued its settlement agreement with BMO Nesbitt Burns Inc. over the FMF Capital scandal. In *The Financial Post*, columnist Barry Critchley wrote on November 13, 2010, under the headline "OSC slaps BMO with a feather," that one investor asked, "If the role of lead underwriter is to perform proper due diligence and BMO failed to do so, why was the penalty so light?"

NERA Economic Consulting published a report in 2007 on FMF Capital entitled *The Canary in the Coal Mine* that examined the settlement in this case.

After examining their financial statements, Diane Urquhart estimated that Canada's banks lost $12 billion on U.S. subprime mortgage-related investments.

The shareholders' lawsuit against CIBC over subprime losses is *Howard Green and Anne Bell v. CIBC, Gerald McCaughey, Tom Woods, Brian G. Shaw, and Ken Kilgour* and was launched in Ontario Superior Court in January 2010, by Rochon Genova LLP.

Gordon Richardson's report on CIBC's accounting is described in a *Financial Post* article by Jim Middlemiss entitled "Subprime suit challenges CIBC accounting," from August 10, 2010.

CIBC's market capitalization figures are derived from the bank's annual reports.

The most in-depth media coverage of the ABCP fiasco was conducted by *The Globe and Mail*, in particular a piece on November 17, 2007, entitled "The ABCP black box explodes" by Boyd Erman, Jacquie McNish, Tara Perkins and Heather Scoffield, which won a National Newspaper Award in 2008.

In October, 2008, IIROC produced an extensive report on the third-party ABCP meltdown entitled *Regulatory Study, Review and Recommendations concerning the manufacture and distribution by IIROC member firms of Third-Party Asset-Backed Commercial Paper in Canada.*

On August 1, 2002, Standard & Poor's (S&P) published an analysis of third-party ABCP entitled *Leap of Faith: Canadian Asset-Backed Commercial Paper Often Lacks Liquidity Backup*. S&P famously refused to rate third-party ABCP and this report explained why—a good five years before the product blew up. "A peculiar feature of the Canadian ABCP market is that the conduit structures do not typically incorporate widely available backup liquidity facilities," it notes, referring to the lack of bank support for ABCP. Furthermore it points out that "widespread market disruption" is so vaguely defined, no commercial paper can be issued at any price in the Canadian market. Hence the conditions under which the bank liquidity lines ought to be drawn from are "narrow to the point of being almost meaningless."

The sponsors of the American Securitization Forum in 2007 at which Elizabeth McCaul was keynote speaker included RBC Capital Markets, BMO Capital Markets and Canada's only credit rating agency, Dominion Bond Rating Service.

The allegations of fraud levelled against Deutsche Bank Securities Ltd. over the sale of third-party ABCP are laid out in the IIROC notice of hearing, dated December 7, 2009, as well as in a lawsuit launched by the City of Hamilton, dated September 25, 2009.

The allegations made by Barrick Gold Corp. against CIBC World Markets over the sale of third-party ABCP in the Ironstone trust are laid out in an affidavit by James W. Mavor, the treasurer of Barrick, in April 17, 2008, as well as a "Notice of Motion" and "Factum," both dated April 22, 2008. These documents were in support of Barrick's lawsuit against the brokerage house.

CHAPTER 10

Details of the assault of John Xanthoudakis can be found in the RCMP's 2007 *Projet Colisée* report, "Projet Colisée, Têtes Dirigeantes—Aperçu de la

Preuve." *Death Spiral: The Collapse of Cinar, Norshield and Mount Real* by William Urseth, a book published by ECW Press in 2008 about the Norshield collapse, describes the assault as well.

Francesco Del Balso's career within the Rizzuto crime family is described in *Mafia Inc.*, by André Cédilot and André Noël, published by Random House Canada in 2011.

The size and importance of the shadow banking industry is highlighted in an October 8, 2008, *TIME* magazine story entitled "Are Paulson and Bernanke Running Out of Options?" by Massimo Calabres.

The use of credit default swaps by a small group of speculators to bet against subprime mortgage debt is best described in Michael Lewis's *The Big Short: Inside the Doomsday Machine*, published by W. W. Norton & Company, Inc. in 2010.

The use of offshore havens to hide tax monies and the cash of the very wealthy is laid out in *Treasure Islands: Tax Havens and the Men Who Stole the World* by Nicholas Shaxson, published by Palgrave MacMillan in 2011.

Diane Francis's column on tax havens was published in *The Financial Post*, May 1, 2008, with the headline "Loophole big enough to sink a yacht."

An account of David Smith's crimes are laid out in the sentencing memorandum in *United States of America v. David A. Smith* in August 2011.

A description of Hallmark Bank & Trust's Mastercard tax-dodging operation and Brian Trowbridge's controversial track record is described in an April 1, 2010, *Bloomberg Businessweek* article by Jessica Silver-Greenberg entitled "Mastercard, Visa and the Card Sharks."

One of the more interesting accounts of the Canada Revenue Agency's many efforts to go after tax dodgers is "Taxing pursuit: While the U.S. extracts billions of tax dollars from around the globe, Canada's CRA takes a more relaxed approach" by John Greenwood and David Pett in *The Financial Post*, Oct 1, 2011.

The story of Paul Eustace and his career in high finance is described in a series of U.S. court documents, specifically in *Commodity Futures Trading Commission v. Paul M. Eustace and Philadelphia Alternative Asset Management Company, LLC*; the Statement of Allegations, dated June 28, 2005; and the court's decision in this case, issued on January 26, 2009. As well, the criminal indictment is captured in *United States of America v. Paul M. Eustace* filed on May 6, 2010, and in an October 18, 2007, *Globe and Mail* article, "The fund manager, the stripper and the missing millions" by Paul Waldie.

Estimates on the number of hedge funds that exist in the world are unreliable, although 8,300 is the figure most commonly cited. The amount of assets they have under management also varies wildly: US$2 trillion is a conservative estimate.

Canadian hedge funds are described in "Hedge Funds Canada," an online report produced by Richard C. Wilson at HedgeFundBlogger.com.

Poul Nyrup Rasmussen wrote a scathing indictment of hedge funds in an article for Project Syndicate called "Taming the Private Equity 'Locusts,'" published on April 4, 2008.

The story of John Xanthoudakis, Norshield and its demise is laid out in a variety of sources, including *Death Spiral: The Collapse of Cinar, Norshield and Mount Real* by William Urseth, a book published by ECW Press in 2008, and by the numerous reports of the court-appointed receiver, Raymond Massi, of RSM Richter Inc., in the Norshield bankruptcy. I have also drawn upon information from two investors' lawsuits aimed at the Royal Bank of Canada and its brokerage houses, including *Shelia Calder vs. Royal Bank of Canada*, filed on May 14, 2008 in the Quebec courts, and *Balanced Return Fund Limited; Mendot a Capital Inc., Commax Investors Services, Ltd; and Comprehensive Investors Services Ltd. vs. Royal Bank of Canada (et al)*, filed in New York's Supreme Court on March 27, 2009. I found the OSC's statement of allegations in the Norshield case, dated October 11, 2006, helpful, as well as its reason for the decision delivered on March 8, 2010. Finally, several articles in the Montreal *Gazette* were useful, in particular a June 10, 2006, profile of John Xanthoudakis, "In the eye of the storm" by Don MacDonald.

References about Robert Daviault's testimony regarding his work for Norshield and its funds were gleaned from *Gazette* articles published in 2006.

CHAPTER 11

The material on George Georgiou was drawn from a variety of sources. They include the decisions in two lawsuits launched by his clients when he worked as a broker in Kitchener: *Gale Blackburn and Robert H. Blackburn v. Midland Walwyn Capital Inc., Levesque Securities Inc. and George Georgiou*, which was issued on January 22, 2003; and *Techhi Holdings Ltd. v. Merrill Lynch Securities Inc., Levesque Securities Inc. and George Georgiou* on May 18, 2004. The IDA decision on Georgiou came down on November 27, 2000. His U.S. criminal indictment is *United States of America v. George Georgiou*, dated February 12, 2009. The SEC complaint against Georgiou, *Securities and Exchange Commission v. George Georgiou* is dated February 12, 2009. Also, the criminal indictment of Georgiou's co-conspirator and later, FBI informant, Kevin Waltzer, was useful — *United States of America v. Kevin Waltzer*, on September 11, 2008.

CHAPTER 12

Judge Robert Blair's Ontario Court of Appeal observations are found in *Metcalfe & Mansfield Alternative Investments II Corp., (Re), 2008 ONCA 587.*

Dr. L.S. (Al) Rosen, Mark Rosen and Diane Urquhart produced their report on income trusts, *The Worst Is Yet to Come: The $20 Billion Deception that Dwarfs the Tax Debate*, on November 16, 2005, for the Accountability Research Corporation. Urquhart also wrote her own report, *Income Trusts: Heads I Win, Tails You Lose: Retail Investors and Pension Funds Take Note of the Flawed Structure*, which was produced on October 12, 2006.

Dr. Al Rosen testified about income trusts at the Standing Committee on Finance on February 13, 2007. At one point he told the MPs, "We sat through the Nortel fiasco; we're now sitting through the income trusts. If you look at my track record, I've called many of these over the last twenty or thirty years. So I'm saying we have a crisis in Canada—the worst I have ever seen. It absolutely shocks me that we're foot-dragging on what is clearly the cause of the problems of the gentlemen here and many others."

The main lawsuit against Atlas Cold Storage was *Paul Lawrence, Anne Eagles and Charles Simon, Evelyn Simon and Erica Prussky v. Atlas Cold Storage Holdings Inc. et al.* that was initially issued on February 25, 2004.

The OSC's statement of allegations against Patrick Gouveia, Andrew Peters, Ronald Perryman and Paul Vickery was issued on June 2, 2004.

An academic paper on Atlas Cold Storage by J.E. Boritz and L.A. Robinson was published in October 2004, for the Centre for Accounting Ethics, School of Accounting and Finance, University of Waterloo, Ontario.

CHAPTER 13

The details of the David Siegel scam can be found in SEC rulings and allegations, specifically *Securities and Exchange Commission v. American Financial Group of Aventura, Inc., and David H. Siegel and American Wealth Management of Aventura, Inc.*, dated July 24, 2002, and the complaint for injunctive relief.

It has been claimed by the City of Hamilton, in its lawsuit, and by IIROC that Deutsche Bank Securities Ltd. sold third-party ABCP in the summer of 2007 when they must have known the instrument would become toxic. Allegations against Deutsche were laid out in an IIROC case launched against the brokerage house on December 7, 2009, which says, "During the period between July 25 and August 13, 2007, the Respondent failed to observe high standards of ethics and conduct in the transaction of their business." The City of Hamilton also sued Deutsche, CIBC Mellon Trust, Barclays

Bank, DBRS and others in a statement of claim filed on September 25, 2009, in the Ontario courts over third-party ABCP.

Imperial Tobacco's smuggling operation is detailed in an RCMP affidavit for a warrant to search the premises of Imperial Tobacco Canada Ltd.'s Montreal offices in 2004 (the RCMP raided the offices on November 26, 2004). This 200-page document, which can be found on the website of Physicians for a Smoke-Free Canada, contains a paper trail of Imperial internal documents, court documents and documents from other industry sources obtained by the RCMP that discuss the duration and structure of Imperial's smuggling operation during the early nineties. Purdy Crawford's name is listed in the documents as an executive in charge of Imasco at the time the smuggling was occuring. *Gazette* investigative journalist William Marsden also wrote a paper on Imperial's smuggling operation for the Center for Public Integrity, produced on October 20, 2008, entitled "How to Get Away With Smuggling." Paul Finlayson, a former Imasco strategic planner, was interviewed in January 2009 by Carole MacNeil for a *CBC News: Sunday* story I produced about Imperial's smuggling operation. This story was broadcast across Canada. Finlayson said he was asked by Imasco to draw up plans for the smuggling operation and its costs. Estimates of how much tax monies Imperial dodged as a result of its smuggling operation was made by Physicians for a Smoke-Free Canada, extrapolated from internal tobacco industry projections.

The Pan-Canadian Investors Committee for Third-Party Structured ABCP's proposal to investors was entitled *Proposed Restructuring of Canadian Third-Party Structure Asset-Backed Commercial Paper* and dated March 20, 2008.

Barrick Gold launched its suit to get its money back from its investment in third-party ABCP on April 22, 2008. It claimed, "CIBC breached its obligation to Ironstone Trust under the Liquidity Agreement when it refused to repay the maturing notes under the Liquidity Agreement."

Patrick Evans, CEO of Norsemont Mining, appeared on Business News Network on April 30, 2008.

On December 21, 2009, the OSC, AMF and IIROC jointly announced that seven investment dealers—National Bank Financial, Scotia Capital, CIBC and CIBC World Markets, HSBC Bank Canada, Laurentian Bank Securities, Canaccord Financial and Credential Securities—agreed to pay a total of $138.8 million in administrative penalties and investigation costs. The press release said, "Five of the institutions involved are alleged to have failed to adequately respond to issues in the third party ABCP market, as they continued to buy and/or sell without engaging compliance and other appropriate processes for assessing such issues. Particularly, they did not disclose to all their clients the July 24th email from Coventree providing the subprime exposure of each Coventree ABCP conduit."

The OSC's reasons for its decision on Coventree's involvement with ABCP came down on September 28, 2011: *In the Matter of The Securities Act, R.S.O. 1990, c. S.5, as amended and In the Matter of Coventree Inc., Geoffrey Cornish and Dean Tai.*

Former Nortel CEO Mike S. Zafirovski appeared in front of the House of Commons' Standing Committee on Finance on June 18, 2009.

Nortel's executives describe and justify the KEIP and KERP bonuses in a debtors' motion filed in the U.S. bankruptcy court in Delaware seeking Chapter 11 protection. The file is entitled "Debtors' Motion for an Order Seeking Approval of Key Employee Retention Plan and Key Executive Incentive Plan And Certain Other Related Relief" and dated February 27, 2009.

Dated September 22, 2009, an internal Nortel document listed the proposed salaries after an additional US$7.5 million bonus was awarded to senior executives, including a pay hike for acting president John Doolittle.

The June 2011 issue of *Report on Business Magazine* contained a story entitled "Nortel cheques out" detailing the final salaries of Nortel's top executives postbankruptcy.

The cutbacks forced upon Nortel pensioners in 2011 are discussed in a July 15, 2011 front-page article by Michael Lewis in the *Toronto Star*, "Deep cuts, clawbacks hit Nortel pensioners."

CHAPTER 14

Charges against Beth DeMerchant and Darren Sukonick were filed by the Law Society of Upper Canada on May 4, 2009, and encompass their role on the sale of Hollinger International's assets to CanWest Global Communications, Osprey Media Holdings Inc., the sale of NP Holdings Company, the loans to 504468 N.B. Inc., offsetting debt transactions and Conrad Black's renunciation of his Canadian citizenship.

Among the many voices condemning Standard & Poor's over its downgrading of U.S. government debt was *New York Times* veteran business writer and op-ed columnist Joe Nocera. On August 8, 2011, under the headline "While the Markets Swoon . . ." he wrote, "It's hard not to feel a certain contempt for Standard & Poor's in the wake of its downgrade of American debt. Its sole job as a credit-rating agency is to gauge the creditworthiness of bonds, yet like its competitors, Moody's and Fitch, it has consistently fallen short. It downgraded Enron days before the company went bankrupt. Its willingness to slap a AAA rating on securitized subprime junk was the foundation upon which the entire financial crisis was built. And now, to show that it's got some spine, S&P decided to downgrade the United States? From a purely economic standpoint, the likelihood of a U.S. default is nil."

The SEC's investigation of Standard & Poor's for approving "dummy assets" is described in a September 27, 2011, *Wall Street Journal* article by Jeannette Neumann and Jean Eaglesham, "SEC Eyes Ratings from S&P."

Dated July 2008, the SEC's report on credit rating agencies is titled "Summary Report of Issues Identified in the Commission Staff's Examination of Select Credit Rating Agencies." The SEC found an email exchange between two credit rating staffers that revealed that the rating agencies continued to create an "even bigger monster—the CDO market. Let's hope we are all wealthy and retired by the time this house of cards falters."

A thorough story on DBRS and its role in the ABCP fiasco appeared in *The Financial Post* on June 14, 2008, headlined "Credit ratings storm: DBRS faces critics over role in ABCP Fiasco" by Theresa Tedesco and John Greenwood. A report by Investment Industry Regulatory Organization of Canada (IIROC) in October of 2008 on the asset-backed commercial paper (ABCP) fiasco, *Regulatory Study, Review and Recommendations concerning the manufacture and distribution by IIROC member firms of Third-Party Asset-Backed Commercial Paper in Canada*, also examines the role DBRS played.

The record of credit rating agencies in the FMF Capital case is described in two investors' class action lawsuits launched over the matter, by Siskinds LLP in January 2006 in Ontario Superior Court and by Juroviesky & Ricci LLP and Frank, Haron, Weiner & Navarro in the Michigan courts in 2005. Furthermore, on November 8, 2010, BMO Nesbitt Burns made a settlement with the OSC on the FMF Capital matter, which noted, "FMF Capital sold approximately 90% of its loans to five institutional loan purchasers in 2004. [BMO Nesbitt Burns] obtained names of contact persons at each of these institutional loan purchasers from FMF Capital and prepared a list of questions for the institutional loan purchasers. Ultimately, BMONB did not contact or make inquiries of any of the institutional loan purchasers prior to the IPO. In the course of its due diligence, BMONB should have contacted and made inquiries of the institutional loan purchasers prior to the IPO."

The Muddy Waters Research report on Sino-Forest Corp. appeared on June 2, 2011. Muddy Waters is run by Carson Block, who takes short positions on the firms he researches. "As Bernard Madoff reminds us, when an established institution commits fraud, the fraud can become stratospheric in size. Sino-Forest Corp. ('TRE') is such an established institutional fraud, becoming massive due to its early start, luck, and deft navigation," the report's introduction notes. "At nearly seven billion dollars in enterprise value, it will now end."

Egizio Bianchini's role in promoting Bre-X is discussed in a 2002 paper, *A Review of Recent Mining Stock Scams,* by John A. Meech, director of The Centre for Environmental Research in Minerals, Metals and Materials at the University of British Columbia, Department of Mining Engineering. Bianchini's promotion within BMO Capital Markets is mentioned in a September 13, 2011 *Maclean's* article about financial analysts.

"Equity analysts: Still too bullish: After almost a decade of stricter regulation, analysts' earnings forecasts continue to be excessively optimistic," appeared in *McKinsey Quarterly* in April 2010, by Marc Goedhart, Rishi Raj and Abhishek Saxena.

"Do Sell-Side Stock Analysts Exhibit Escalation of Commitment?" was written by John Beshears, Graduate School of Business, Stanford University, and Katherine L. Milkman, The Wharton School, University of Pennsylvania, and published in the *Journal of Economic Behavior & Organization* in March 2011.

Details on the role of Torys LLP and Darren Sukonick and Beth DeMerchant are discussed in the *Report of Investigation by the Special Committee of the Board of Directors of Hollinger International Inc.* The report, led by Richard C. Breeden and submitted to the U.S. Securities and Exchange Commission (SEC), was published on August 30, 2004. Numerous newspaper articles detailed the two lawyers' testimony during the 2007 Conrad Black trial. A good account of Torys LLP's problems as a result of its work on behalf of the Conrad Black case was in *American Lawyer* magazine, August 2007, "Caught in the web: how Conrad Black and the Hollinger case ensnared the Cravath of Canada" by Julie Triedman.

Simon Rosenfeld's crimes were detailed during his trial in Toronto in January and February 2005, presided over by Madam Justice Tamarin Dunnet. His conviction in the Synpro Environmental Services, Inc. case was announced by the SEC on March 14, 2001, in *SEC v. Simon M. Rosenfeld, Terry D. Kochanowski, and John F. Yakimczyk*.

The Stanko Grmovsek and Gil Cornblum cases are detailed in the "Statement of Facts for a Guilty Plea" in the Grmovsek case (Cornblum had committed suicide), the settlement agreement with the OSC in October of 2009 and *SEC v. Stanko J. Grmovsek* complaint. The allegations against former BMO Nesbitt Burns trader Sandy Bortolin were issued by IIROC in a "Notice of Hearing" dated November 2, 2011.

The Mitchell Finkelstein case is detailed in the OSC's amended Statement of Allegations, *In the Matter of Paul Azeff, Korin Bobrow, Mitchell Finkelstein, Howard Jeffrey Miller and Man Kin Cheng (aka Francis Cheng)*, dated November 11, 2010. "Frat brothers and trading tips: The allegations that rocked Bay Street," an article by Paul Waldie, Jacquie McNish and Jeff Gray in *The Globe and Mail* on November 12, 2010, also discusses the alleged scam.

CHAPTER 15

The story of Paul Winkler and Horizon Publications Inc. is told in the Breeden report. The Winkler decision on his constructive dismissal case is *Paul Winkler v. Lower Mainland Publishing Ltd.*, August 13, 2002, by Madam Justice Linda Loo in the Supreme Court of British Columbia. In his memoir *A Matter of Principle* (McClelland & Stewart, 2011), Black contends that he was unaware that Radler's percentage of Horizon was enough to put their shared ownership in excess of 50%, thereby giving them majority stake in competing newspapers; however, not only did Breeden find otherwise, Winkler claims that he sent Black a letter, dated March 21, 2001, explaining his concerns about Hollinger owning competing papers in the same market.

It's Time, the report by the Wise Persons' Committee to Review the Structure of Securities Regulation in Canada, was submitted to the federal Minister of Finance on December 17, 2003.

The figure of one million Canadians losing money to investment fraud came from a study produced by the Innovative Research Group for the Canadian Securities Administrators (CSA) in October of 2007. The CSA is the lobby for Canada's provincial and territorial securities commissions.

"The Global Economic Crime Survey: Economic crime in a downturn" was published by PricewaterhouseCoopers in November 2009.

Regulatory Intensity in the Regulation of Capital Markets: A Preliminary Comparison of Canadian and U.S. Approaches by Howell E. Jackson, was published as a research study for the Task Force to Modernize Securities Legislation in Canada on July 30, 2006.

The research study *Enforcement and its Impact on Cost of Equity and Liquidity of the Market* by Utpal Bhattacharya was published for the Task Force to Modernize Securities Legislation in Canada on May 24, 2006.

For other figures on the OSC's track record see *The Globe and Mail* article "A world of difference on insider trading prosecutions" by Martin Mittelstaedt, March 15, 2011.

Western Standard's investigation of the Alberta Securities Commission (ASC), "The Right Connections" by Andrea Mrozek, was published as a cover story on December 12, 2005.

"Report of the Auditor General on the Alberta Securities Commission's Enforcement System" was produced on October 19, 2005, by Fred J. Dunn, Alberta's Auditor General.

In the matter of Kianosh Rahmani, the IDA permanently banned him from working in the securities industry in a decision made by the disciplinary committee of the IDA's Pacific District Council on August 9, 2004. "This is not a case of mere inadvertence. Nor is it a single incident. We find that there was a reckless attempt to mislead the Association and that, therefore, a permanent bar is warranted," the ruling notes. A BCSC hearing panel overseen by Vice-Chair Brent W. Aitken overturned Rahmani's ban on May 26, 2009.

Remarks made by Michael Watson, head of enforcement for the OSC, appeared in a *Toronto Star* article, "Lawyer defends OSC's record on crime" by Madhavi Acharya-Tom Yew, November 28, 2007.

In the case of IIROC and Mark Allen Dennis, the decision was rendered on June 3, 2011, fining him $1 million for the misappropriation of funds and $32,500 in other fines and costs. He had, however, stolen $1.4 million (and did not defend himself at the IIROC proceedings). But the decision notes, "Counsel for IIROC in the Notice of Hearing calls attention to Rules 20.33 and 20.34 of the Rules of the Investment Dealers Association as giving the authority to punish by fine. They refer to a reprimand, a fine not exceeding the greater of $1,000,000 per contravention and an amount of three times the profit made or the loss avoided by reason of the contravention."

Cooper v. Hobart, [2001] 3 S.C.R. 537, 2001 SCC 79, was issued on November 16, 2001, by the Supreme Court of Canada and said that the regulator in this case "did not owe a duty of care to investors."

Robert Kyle's list of brokers and investment advisers that had not been disciplined can be found on his website at http://investorvoice.ca/IDA/Comset/Comset_index.htm.

In the matter of the IDA and Hugh Damian Bagnell, the decision was made by the Nova Scotia District Council of the Association and was issued on December 12, 2003.

In the matter of the IDA and Bertrand Trudel, the decision was made by the Quebec District Council of the Association on March 23, 2007.

On November 17, 2005, the TSX Venture Exchange ruled that William Nichols was unacceptable to perform investor relations on behalf of any Exchange listed issuer and could not be an employee, agent or consultant, or work on behalf of any Exchange listed issuer company. This decision was overturned by the BCSC, with Douglas Hyndman as chair of the hearing panel, on June 7, 2007 (*William John Nichols and TSX Venture Exchange*). In his information to the TSX about his criminal past, Nichols admitted he had been convicted for first-degree murder in 1976 and had served eighteen years in prison. What he failed to mention was that he fatally shot a police officer after he and three other individuals stole $1,600 from a credit union. During a two-day standoff with police that followed the shooting, three hostages were taken and released. On December 2, 1976, Nichols was convicted of murder and sentenced to life in prison with no parole eligibility for twenty-five years. He later pled guilty to other crimes related to the March 1976 incident, including armed robbery, kidnapping, theft, breaking and entering and mischief. Nichols's criminal record also included convictions for extortion; possession of stolen property; break, enter and theft; possession of narcotics; robbery; causing bodily harm with intent to injure; possession of a weapon; prison breach; forcible confinement; and armed robbery. Nevertheless, the BCSC ruled Nichols should not be banned from providing investors relations.

CHAPTER 16

"Mensch Next Door Charged with Ponzi Scheme" by Nicholas Stein in *The Globe and Mail*, February 14, 2010, describes the Tzvi Erez scandal.

The Fuller Landau Group Inc. was appointed as receiver by the court in the Tzvi Erez case to track down the missing money. Jerry Henechowicz produced a series of reports, with his findings summarized on October 23, 2009, and filed with the Ontario Superior Court of Justice, laying out where the money had gone from Erez's companies, including Erez Graphix Inc. and E Graphix Ltd., which were essentially manifestations of the same printing company.

CIBC's Suspicious Transaction Referral Form and supporting documentation was dated July 6, 2007. FINTRAC's acknowledgement of the form was dated two days later.

The story of William Tencer is laid out in his affidavit in *Glickma Investments Ltd. v. Erez Graphix Inc., E Graphix Limited, Chronos Media*

Inc. and Tzvi Erez. As well, emails between Tencer and Erez were entered as exhibits in this suit.

The case against the Royal Bank of Canada is explained in the motion to institute a class action lawsuit against the bank in *Virginia Nelles vs. Royal Bank of Canada* dated February 5, 2010.

Transcripts of a deposition of Earl Jones by lawyer Neil Stein was made on December 7 and 8, 2009.

Details of the Weizhen Tang Ponzi scheme come from a Statement of Claim in *Aping Co., Ltd. v. Weizhen Tang Corporation; Weizhen Tang & Associates Inc.; Weizhen Tang, Hong Xiao, Wenyi Tang, Jiehua Yu,* dated March 6, 2009, and related exhibits. "The 1% Club" by Nicholas Stein in the November 2010 issue of *Toronto Life* discusses the case.

Afterword

The Sino-Forest Corp. case and the matter of other Chinese companies using Canada's capital markets as a flag of convenience are discussed by David Olive in an August 30, 2011 column in the *Toronto Star,* "A good example of the OSC at its best."

The section on Harry Migirdic is taken from *Markarian v. CIBC World Markets Inc.,* a decision rendered by Quebec Superior Court justice Jean-Pierre Senécal on June 14, 2006.

— ACKNOWLEDGEMENTS —

FIRST AND FOREMOST I would like to thank my amazing wife, Gabrielle Barkany, whose unflagging support and patience, and tolerance of my kvetching over getting this book completed, helped make it all possible. My mother, Lois, my brother, Graham, and my sister, Flora, provided encouragement along the way.

A book like this one is the culmination of the insight, guidance and assistance of many people who played roles big and small — all of whom I am deeply grateful to. My wonderful editor, Ken Alexander, former publisher of *The Walrus*, not only brought the project to Random House Canada but worked diligently to beat the manuscript into a semblance of comprehension. He's a man among men. At Random House, Anne Collins and Craig Pyette have been kind, patient and always a delight to work with. I feel truly blessed to be in their hands.

During my research into the Byzantine world of high finance, Diane Urquhart and her husband, Hugh, stand above everyone else in providing assistance, support and making sense of it all. Without them, this book would not exist. Many former colleagues at the CBC, in particular Evan Solomon, supported my itch to explore the emerging credit crisis and other stories that ended up being part of this book. That list also includes Patsy Pehleman, Michael Kearns, Tony Marchitto, Jeannie Stiglic, Eric Foss, Farid Haerinejad, Carole MacNeil, Nicole Brewster, Joseph Loiero, Harvey Cashore and Gillian Findlay. My friend Gil Shochat, a terrific investigative journalist, was always encouraging with the task at hand. Michael A. Levine offered sage counsel at a critical time. Edward Sapiano, as well as Bilbo Poynter and Alex Roslin at the Canadian Centre for Investigative Reporting, gave much-needed material support and insight. Declan Hill was a true friend and voice of encouragement at the right moment. I also want to thank Ted Mumford, Gail Cohen, David Baines, Jacquie McNish, Jerry Henechowicz, Brent Mudry, Bill Majcher, Wes Voorheis, Larry Elford, Kevin Curran, Joey Davis, Iris Pearce, Daryl Ching, Jim Stanford, Stan Buell, Bud Cramm, Derek Finkle, Carmine Starnino, Dimitri Lascaris, Henry Juroviesky, Joe Groia, Doug Henwood, Jay Naster, Joel Rochon, Utpal Bhattacharya, William Lazonick, John Greenwood, Paul Winkler, Adrian du Plessis, Robert Kyle, Sandra Rubin, Serge Létourneau, Charles Morris, Bruce Marks, Robert Ferchat, Nicholas Stein, Ed Krupa and Jeffrey Kramer, among others. And this book also depended on good friends who offered moral support along the way, in particular Allen Charney and David and Alex Gellman.

BRUCE LIVESEY is an award-winning investigative journalist. His writing has appeared in most major magazines and newspapers in Canada. He also has extensive experience as a television producer, working for the investigative unit of CBC TV's *The National, the fifth estate* and *CBC News Sunday*, as well as outside Canada for a co-production of PBS *Frontline* and *The New York Times*, Al Jazeera English and Al Gore's *Current TV*. He is a co-winner of a Dupont Award, one of the most prestigious U.S. television awards, a Canadian Association of Journalism award, and has been nominated for two Geminis and three National Magazine Awards, winning in 2008. He lives and works in Toronto.